My Pilgrim's Heart

A woman's journey through marriage
and other foreign lands

My Pilgrim's Heart

STEPHANIE DALE

VOYAGER
MOON

First published in Australia in 2009
by Voyager Moon
ABN 60 889 920 117
www.voyagermoon.com

Copyright © Stephanie Dale 2009

Reprinted 2010, 2024

This work is copyright. Apart from any use as permitted under the Copyright Act 1968, no part may be reproduced, copied, scanned, stored in a retrieval system, recorded, or transmitted, in any form or by any means, without the prior written permission of the publisher.

National Library of Australia Cataloguing-in-Publication data:

Dale, Stephanie, 1959–

My pilgrim's heart: a woman's journey through marriage and other foreign lands / Stephanie Dale.

ISBN 9780980704303

1. Dale, Stephanie, 1959–Journey.
2. Voyages and travels.
3. Self-actualization (Psychology).
4. Italy–Description and travel.
5. Turkey–Description and travel.

Cover by Sara Honor, Ignite Art and Design
Typeset by Sunset Digital Pty Ltd, Brisbane, in Fairfield 11.5pt
Printed and bound by IngramSpark
Edited by Jenny Edney, Fine Print Writing and Editing

Acknowledgements

Excerpt from *Rumi's Daughter* by Muriel Maufroy, published by Rider, reprinted by kind permission of The Random House Group Ltd.

Excerpt from *The Gift* by Lewis Hyde, reprinted by kind permission of Lewis Hyde.

Excerpt from *Warrior of the Light: a manual* by Paulo Coelho, 2003, published by HarperCollins.

Excerpt from *The Alchemist* by Paulo Coelho, 1998, published by HarperCollins.

Excerpt from *Nanook's Gift* by Michio Hoshino, 1996, published by Cadence Books.

'Time' poem by Visar Zfuti in *The Condemned Apple*, selected poetry translated by Robert Elsie, © 2005 Robert Elsie, reprinted by kind permission of Green Integer Books.

Lyrics from 'Proud Crowd/Pried Cried' by Ferron, © 1984 Nemesis publishing, reprinted by kind permission of Nemesis Publishing and Ferron Online.

Lyrics from 'You Don't Own Me' by John Madara and David White.

Lyrics from 'Wind Beneath My Wings' by Jeff Silbar and Larry Henley.

With smiling gentle gratitude to Brunette,
for her friendship and encouragement

and Dirk,
who has courage enough to bless this book.

Acknowledgements

I would like to thank my editor, Jenny Edney, for her wellspring of patience, diligence, expertise and goodwill; and Kate Benecke for her exacting eye. Now I know why otherwise proficient writers seem unable to find the words to express their gratitude for their editors.

Thanks also to Sara Honor for her imagination and creative endurance; and Darryl Nixon, Susan Harvey and Jean Irvine for their professionalism and attention to detail.

The Geography

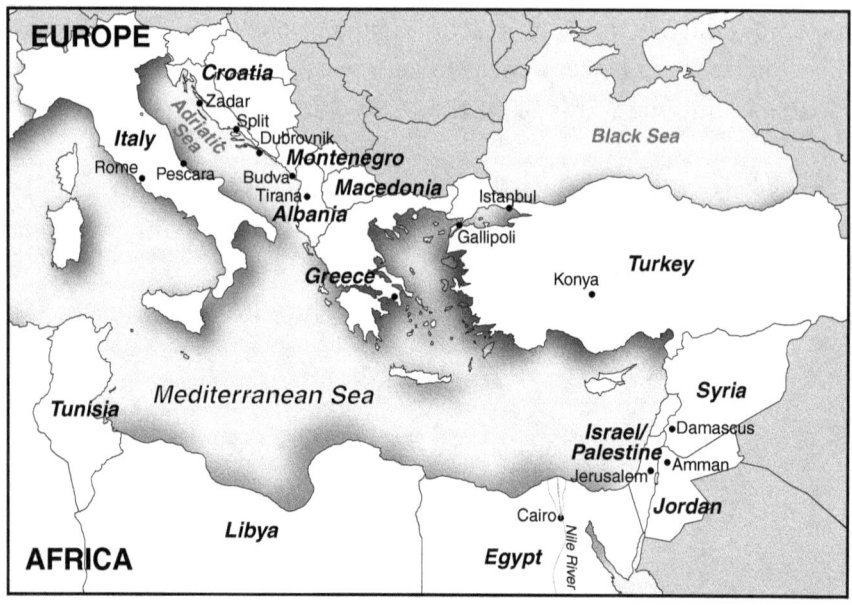

Contents

Mullumbimby	1
Rome	41
Istanbul	225
Jerusalem	293

The Eugenia Street Prayer

I respect myself,
I honour my creativity;
I keep my puppy on a lead,
I see the miracle in others.

Mullumbimby

In May 2007, my son set out on pilgrimage from Canterbury, England, by foot – bound for Jerusalem. By August he had reached Rome. For some time I had felt drawn to join him. *Just for a couple of weeks. Imagine, walking through Italy!* I was honour-bound, however, to a marriage, a young and troubled marriage that was sapping the life from both of us.

My husband and I were planning to drive around Australia. He is Dutch, and had yet to experience the wide brown land west of the sub-tropical paradise that is Byron Bay. I was hopeful the journey would enliven us, would offer us insight, each to the other. I told myself the magnificence of the Australian landscape was a stage upon which we might play out our torments and triumphs; that through shared experience we might *become friends*. At the very least, I reasoned, the trip would give us a modicum of common ground.

At the time, we were living in a rambling old wooden house up Wilsons Creek, outside Mullumbimby. You know the place: verandahs on three sides, bush nudging the backyard, fruit trees as high as the roof. It was the Australia of my childhood and backdrop to the tumble dryer of our marriage. My husband whiled away his days on the verandah, watching the pademelons graze in the soft midday sunshine, a book on his lap, a carpet snake wound around the grape trellis overhead and a steady stream of oolong tea at his elbow. Talk of our journey disturbed him. He was content on the verandah. He did not want to spoil his time at Wilsons Creek planning to be somewhere else. I, meanwhile, began to dream in the night of pilgrimage: of routes woven into intricate rugs, feet treading a dusty road around an ice mountain, weeping with love for pilgrims on the streets of Santiago.

And in the spaces in between, in the corridors and rattly rooms of that old wooden edifice, my husband and I struggled with storms of our own making, the unconscious energies that surface only when they slam into the rocks of someone else's reality. I began to pace, spider in a bottle. The call to walk with my son grew louder. *I am honour-bound, honour-bound, honour-bound to wait this out with my husband.* With each dream I became more restless. *Honour-bound, honour-bound.* Until the truth broke through and there was nothing else to do but answer the call.

Honour-bound.

Honour-bound to meet the challenge of giving truth a seat at our table, as we did on our wedding day.

Honour-bound to answer the call of the soul, each to their own.

*T*here is a feather, black and sleek, on the floor. It pulls me up short. It's in front of my pack, my new pack, the one I bought yesterday and parked pride of place in the corner on the lounge room floor. I kneel on the dusty wooden floorboards and reach for the feather, holding its bleached quill point in one hand and running it scissor-like through the fingers of the other. Crow. My dreaming, if there is such a thing. I take it as a sign, a great universal affirmation for the pilgrimage that is calling me to walk, Rome to Istanbul.

It was the crow who summoned me from solitary existence on my mountain home a few years ago: crow vision snapping me to attention, piercing yellow eyes daring me to claim my life. Then crows along the fenceline as I drove down the mountain, their *caw caw* chorus merry salute to my surrender. For I was bored to tears with myself and the life I had created around me. Given the term of a natural life, I had half a lifetime still to live. I had been directionless since the children left home, nigh on a decade ago. I knew what I could create left to my own devices: *what if I surrender 'I want' to the impulse of what life presents me? What if there is only 'yes'?*

That road led me here, to the backwoods of Mullumbimby, where I wake at first light to sunrays dazzling the greens and tangled browns of the bush outside the window, where I now live with a man I call 'my husband'. I call him this because he is my husband, this stern Dutchman with the dished-out smile.

Every evening I lie in the bath outside on the verandah watching the stars wheel across the night sky. I have become tenderly acquainted with the brightest one, which pierces the warm water and rests in the centre of my chest, so it looks as if it's shining from my heart, beaming its light back to itself. The other day, wandering along the dirt road that runs past our door, I crossed the crumbling cement causeway that bridges the creek and looked into the trees catching the last rays of sunlight colouring the bark. In that tiny moment I experienced a mind-jolting sense of alignment – a clink, clink, clink of understanding bolting into place in my bones. I saw, with a stab of ecstatic awareness, that I cannot be looking at anything but myself. Everywhere I look, anywhere I look, I see only my reflection. It's not possible to see anything *but* my own reflection. There I am as that tree. There I am as that kookaburra. There I am as the road, the creek, the wind. There I am as that chair. There I am as that painting. There I am as my husband. I can see only what I am capable of seeing; beyond that requires commitment and curiosity and then, when the novelty wears off, a willingness to journey into the dark. The law of reflection. I am all that I see. Therefore all I see is illusion. Therefore I am illusion, beaming my light back to myself.

This changes completely the way I receive my husband. When he stands before me at his finger-pointing best, his 'you are' accusations disguised as 'very carefully from the heart' spiritual guidance, delivered from the surefooted high ground of certainty, I am filled with compassion for his earnestness and good intentions, for before me is his arrogant superiority masquerading as … myself! And I am filled with a great and jolly laughter at the hilarity of the image in my mind, that of my husband lecturing himself in the mirror.

We married quickly, my husband and me. A year has not passed since we first met, and we have been married six months. We are not friends; we have little, on a good day, or nothing in common. Everything about me is not him. We sleep alone. We have the house for another month before the owners return to claim it. We are supposed to be driving around Australia, introducing him to his new homeland. But he needs to rest, he says. When I speak of our trip, he tells me to stop projecting into the future. Good wife that I am, I do as he says. I choke on my enthusiasm. And barrelling into the silence comes a siren call. It is the summons to Rome, the one I surrendered to the drive around Australia so that my husband and I might learn to be friends. These past months I have spoken often of my longing to join my son on his pilgrimage from Canterbury to Jerusalem. It was the Rome leg that called me loudest. Just a couple of weeks. A stroll in the countryside. My husband never said a word about it. Never entered into the conversation. Not the one about my longing. Not the one about the huge photograph in the weekend paper of me and my son silhouetted against the dawn at Finis Terre, at the end of our first pilgrimage together two years ago. And not the one about my pilgrim dreams.

I am startled by the sharp poke of crow-call and my attention returns to the feather between my fingers. I stand and place it on the window sill. A shiny black crow shoots from the tree outside and alights onto the grass, eyes yellow-white piercing the glass to meet mine.

For my husband, my pilgrimage has come out of the blue. I guess, occasionally, it is in a man's interests to listen to his wife.

The miracle of flight. Aloft on a cushion of clouds, chasing the sun, I stare into the innocence of a never-ending blue, my thoughts roaming hand in hand with forever. Rome. Istanbul. Me. *Rome!* I squeal to myself and say it again. *Rome!* I think about how long it is since I have spent time with my son, real time, just me-and-him time: only once, I realise, just once in the decade since he left home – and that was the 900-kilometre walk across Spain to Santiago de Compostela. Ben and his then girlfriend, our darling Lily, and me. My son the traveller. My son the roamer, the loner, the world citizen. At twenty-nine he is a kindly stranger to me, the sort one hopes to meet when there is trouble on the road.

I'm can't-sleep excited about our walk. About spending time together. About a marriage on the line. About lives forever changed. I have made a point of not asking Ben which road we'll take to Istanbul. I know already that I do not want to know, that if it was up to me I'd choose the safest trails through the known world: a Discovery Channel journey down the Italian coastline, dining at day's end in noisy restaurants strung with old fishing nets among revellers egged on by accordion players, crossing to Greece on a blue and white ferry and then scurrying quick smart through the unknown (to me) world to Istanbul. Yet I know in my heart that my son will seek the roads less travelled, and that means the Balkans – *landmines, barbarians, darkness*. I shake my head and smile. My hair, yesterday long and blonde, is gone. So too my husband. I miss neither. My eyes pierce the window into the blue outside the plane, the steady roar of the engines lending soundbites to rambling thoughts.

I think of Wilsons Creek, my husband and me sitting at the old laminex table on the verandah in the glorious winter sunshine just before we left, my husband's tea set perched high between us. A recovered alcoholic, it is into tea he pours his liquid obsessions. The white teapot shines with the mystery of one long loved. Precious pot, it sits on a white stand, a tealight candle burning beneath the tray to keep it warm. I didn't know, until I met my husband, that tealight candles were for warming tea. My husband and I venture a conversation. And then he says one of the few truly honest things he's ever said to me: 'I wanted a wife to stand behind me.' I remember thinking, *Yes*, and saying nothing. I remember thinking, *I am behind you*.

I am behind you and I am in front of you. I am above and below you, inside and outside of you. I am a woman, as well as your wife, and I am wherever you put your attention. In this way, I flit in and out of your view. I am omnipresent and multidimensional. I am beyond your control.

And now, I realise, I am calling on him to stand behind me. I hadn't known this would offend him.

'Meet me in Istanbul,' I said. 'I would love you to be there at my journey's end. Or fly to Zagreb and say, "Hello my love, how are you going?" Or walk with me awhile through the mountains of Greece.'

Yet he received not the invitation; rather, he perceived a command, insulting and rude. Perhaps it is the Calvinism of his parents that shapes his world so, or the domestic and sexual subservience to which he grew accustomed as a foreigner, twenty-five years in Thailand. Or perhaps it is the obeisance of the women around the bearded prophet of gloom he calls 'master'. Through these lenses I have deeply offended his righteous sense of place in his house.

Rome. Istanbul. I am a woman on the road and there is only me. As is the way with pilgrimage, it began the moment I committed to going. My life became a hymn to 'yes'. The short walk through Italy became a pilgrimage to Istanbul, *the walk of a thousand incarnations*. I made no 'decision' to go; the only decision would have been not to go. My body hummed with certainty, with the absolute clarity of 'only this'. Nothing else to do but this. I might be risking death, *but to stay is certain death.*

I look out over the darkening world outside the bubble window high in the sky and the big water dreams that filled my nights in the weeks before we left Wilsons Creek flood my mind:

A lake still and dark. *I am walking along a path around the edge of water that is pitch-dark and breathless. It is night and I am wearing a beautiful new dress. Thick scrub blocks my path and without thought I drop headfirst into the deep dark water. Down, down, down I go. And there in a chamber on the sandy bed I meet my children's father.*

An ocean vast and blue. *I am swept away with the running tide – way, way, way out to sea until there is only water. I feel the rise of a little wave and compel myself to ride it, to risk it taking me nowhere because this little wave is all there is. I point my face to a distant shore and the wave picks up. I put my trust in the surging blue water and ride it all the way.*

A harbour grey and dirty. I am sitting on a wooden step that leads into murky water lapping at my bare feet. People unknown sit either side of me, the great ocean liners come and go, sunset flashes orange on a white smokestack across the bay. I feel an irresistible pull into the filthy water, a magnetic force pulling, pulling, pulling me in. I surrender to the force of the water and well-meaning people on either side of me grab my arms to stop me slipping away.

I look down at the Earth below to find the gap between me and the scattered lights of Bangkok closing. The dimness of early evening notwithstanding, I can no longer tell clouds from smog, the purple grey of a coming storm from the purple grey of a deadly haze. I try to make sense of the knowledge my husband is here, right here in Bangkok, the city he calls home. His port in a storm; my stopover for the next flight out. I catch sight of my hair in the plane window, the blonde ends bobbing around my face, and wonder if cutting hair is grounds for divorce. Outside the window the wings rock slightly in the low winds. She holds steady. Landing and taking off are two experiences I never tire of: always I am ready for death. The roar of the engines, the mechanical mastery of mystery, the wonder of the infinitesimal moment the wheels touch, or leave, the ground. Safe passage. Safe landing. Again.

At Suvarnabhumi, Bangkok airport, it can take as long as half an hour to walk from arrivals to baggage. This evening I am a transit passenger – bound for London, then Rome. I wander aimlessly around the cavernous cement hallways. I try to call my husband on the credit card phones, but I cannot make them work. Then again, I have no idea of Thai domestic calling codes. It's a guessing game and it fills the time. I turn my attention to a small café, its fridge a nesting ground for a pod of shiny-skinned coconuts, doffed caps skewered with straws. I sit and sip, elbows on the table, watching the international world go by. We're in a zone, all of us together, everywhere and nowhere. I wonder if it's strange that my husband and I are in the same city. Parallel zones. Same place, different space.

I smile to myself as one of the few fabulously funny things he ever said to me pops to mind. It was another honest thing, in the days following my announcement I will be going to Rome. To walk to Istanbul. *I am going to Rome to walk to Istanbul!* We were sitting in our favourite coffee shop in Lismore, soy chai latte for me, cappuccino for him. I leaned across and scooped a teaspoon of froth from his cup, chocolate sweet, coffee sharp. Spoon poised, I leaned across again and this time looked him right in the eye.

I said, 'I feel honest.'

To which he replied, 'There is a fine line between doing the right thing and the fringe of lunacy.'

I laughed. He smiled. I laughed and laughed. In this moment I was happy. My husband didn't understand me but he was beginning to accept me. After that we had gone to the camping shop: him to stock up on winter clothes, me to purchase a pack. Perfectionist that he is, we spent two hours and hundreds of dollars, my husband trying on every garment in the shop so that he might not only be warm for winter but resonant in his choice of colours. I bought a pack, my 'yes' to the journey ahead. I bought a travel towel. My husband, gadget man that he is, also bought a towel, dark blue to my earthy red.

The pack sits in the lounge room. My husband wanders by. 'I want one!' he exclaims. I laugh. He walks by again and announces, 'I want one.' I laugh again. The third, fourth, fifth and sixth times he does this I grow tired. He is wanting what he does not have and it is a trait in my husband that exhausts me. For I have learned these past months that my husband wants only what he does not have. In this way he creates a world that is ever and always out of his reach. I move the pack to my bedroom and my husband decides he needs boots. Walking boots. Serious walking boots. And a pack. No doubt when I buy my sleeping bag he'll need one of those too. He has a friend organising a trek in Nepal. He thinks he might go. He has friends in Japan he hasn't seen since 1975. He thinks he might visit them. He knows men who might walk around Mt Kailash. He thinks he might join them. I understand his need to take action in the face of his wife's, apparently sudden, defection.

I am saddened, more so than I have been for some time, by my husband's need to hijack anything at all pertaining to me and turn the spotlight on himself. I am also saddened not only that my husband has no true purpose in his life, but by the knowing that I am not able, or willing for that matter, to be that purpose. Mostly, I am saddened that my husband can find the energy to get off the verandah and project into the future when I am not with him, but when I am around his need for ownership of everything material, intellectual, spiritual and emotional, shrinks my world in inverse proportion to the enormity of his fears.

For my husband has built himself a tower and he lives on the 254th floor. The construction of additional floors is underway in response to the outrageousness of my decision to 'abandon' him to his tiny world. I tell him he married me because he is sick to death of his own company up there. I tell him he married me because he is tired of the narcissistic company he keeps. I tell him he married me because he knows I will burn the tower down. I tell him I can't save him when he falls. My husband tells me men fear me, especially those I count among my closest friends. He tells me I am fickle. He tells me I am 'too mental'. No-one, I think, can save us from ourselves. I look into his face and feel the ache in my jaw, the tension in my teeth, the agony of rigidity. I look at my husband's un-smile and in the face of his discontent the lights of my life go on.

The hardest thing I have done in recent times is announce to him I am going to Rome, that with my back against the wall of our marriage there is nothing else to do but yodel from the edge of courage and claim all of myself and all of my life and trust the freefall and fallout will lead our marriage somewhere alive and true.

My husband tells me he is glad I'm going because he will have his freedom. He says, 'You never know what might happen,' which I presume is code for, 'I plan to meet another woman who will please me.'

One morning he sits on the chair in the corner of my room, where I am propped up in bed against the wall, reading. I put down the book and give him my attention. He says he is wondering about my expectations while I am away; he wonders if there is room for him to engage sexually with someone he might meet during this time.

With steady eyes I tell him I am not his keeper. For the rest of the day he whistles along to the spring in his step. He laughs two, perhaps even three times in one day. The tortured expression vanishes from his face. I don't buy into these conversations, for through my husband I am learning about marriage's twin pillars of liberation: discipline and commitment. I am learning that compromise has no place in a healthy marriage, for compromise is death, at least for one and ultimately for both. I am learning to love without condition and, in so doing, free myself from imposing conditions upon others. I am learning about the truth of all of me and thereby allowing the truth of another. I am learning to take responsibility for all that I am and all that I seek. Through marriage I am living my longing and my longing is the path. And none of this is too much to ask of my husband.

My husband reads Siddhartha. This, he says, is who I am.
'Which bit?' I wonder. 'The reckless gambler?'
And then I wonder why he admires Siddhartha and not me?

I am not the first woman stung by the rubber band of reality on her honeymoon; nor the first to experience the cold light of conjugal dawn burning the fairy dust from her eyes; nor even the first to wake to the slow dread of rising panic that *this is the rest of my life!* Our honeymoon was a turning point. Bangkok, actually. The 16th floor of the Marriott, my husband's favourite place in the world. It was there I finally buried my head under pillows white and puffy, desperate for silence in a sea of stories. Old stories. War stories. Nothing stories. My husband spent twenty-five years of his life in this city. The potential of his encyclopaedic bank of tales to tell was terrifying. For six months I had listened to his stories, litanies of miniscule irrelevancies. I could listen no more.

'Darling,' I said, 'shhhhhh. Let's be here. Bangkok Marriott, April 2007. If we see something that prompts a memory and you'd like to share it with me, tell me then.'

I risked the hurt. I risked his pain. Stoic that he is, it danced across his face until he swallowed it. In truth I wanted to scream and strangle him. It started at first light, the moment my eyes popped open in the morning. He didn't look at me while he spoke. He roamed through time and space, one story leading to another to another, spiralling up and down, requiring only the occasional hallelujah-honey nod from me. It was exhausting. It sucked the life out of me. And besides, I needn't have worried. After twenty-five years in this city, my husband had nothing to show me at all, nothing more than the Marriott breakfast bar (downstairs), the Thai restaurant at the Sheraton (up the road) and the Central Department Store (across the road).

One morning I looked at him in horror, tears streaming down my face as I faced a truth too terrible about my new husband. I threw the words at him in despair:

'You are never going to spend a year with me among the reindeer people of the north!'

This was the treasure of my dream chest, nurtured for as long as I could remember, bottom-of-the-harbour deep, Everest of my spirit-world; a dream so obvious to me I may as well have been wearing antlers on my head. Who wouldn't want to roam the Earth with the nomadic people of the reindeer? My husband blinked as he came to terms with this new insight into the gulf of longing between himself and his wife.

'No,' he finally said, sobered by the ridiculous.

The things we don't speak.

In Bangkok, our power struggles crystalised with the air-conditioning wars. My husband liked everything just so. Exactly to his liking. He was genuinely perplexed by my desire to feel the tropical air on my skin. Cars. Hotels. Home. Wherever we were in the world, he'd have twenty-six degrees if you please. Or don't please. Driving together was a nightmare because he wouldn't allow the windows down. I get car sick. I need fresh air. More than this, I am Australian – we drive with the windows down, our elbows out, the wind on our faces and our spirits brushing the land. I took to sitting outside on the deck of the Marriott business centre, not coincidentally also 16th floor. I closed my eyes and the warm wind blew, telling tales of the city far below.

Our greatest arguments were reserved for his 'teacher', the mesmerist who lived across the valley from our first home in the hills of Byron Bay. Master and disciple, they were conspiracy theorists both; and like all clever conspiracists neither stood for questioning, especially regarding such trivialities as source and contradiction.

My husband truly believed that anyone who did not follow the master was an inferior being. Hence we could not converse, for my husband sought only reverence for his intelligence and mastery. We didn't speak, but for a while there we fought like hell. Or at least I did. His conversations were a trap and I fell into those traps time and time again. There was only one response to his seminal rantings and that was agreement; anything less was treason, a personal assault, an offence punishable with his standard tactical response: taking his toys and the fast track elevator home to the 254th floor. And if I was out of line contradicting my husband, I was out of the ballpark questioning the master.

The closest I came to leaving my marriage was one morning after we'd returned from our honeymoon, waltzing out the door heading for the markets, when the shit hit the fan about nothing much at all. As we hugged and I apologised for my fury he said, 'Actually it excites me.' It was a turned-to-stone moment, the kind where the world turns and the blood runs cold and nothing will be as it was. My husband's anger is rarely expressed, even less acknowledged. Unable to access and experience his own anger, he had co-opted me. I was the vehicle for his release. I left the house, stricken by the capacity of human beings to annihilate and destroy what they love in defence of their desperation not to be seen, and awed by the power of the unconscious.

I slurp the last of the coconut water from its shell, my mother's disapproval replacing my husband's as the voice in my head. I smile and shake the voices away. These past weeks have been a shocker. If anyone had been peeking through our windows they would have seen nothing much happening at all, just an old man sitting on a verandah drinking tea and a middle-aged woman rattling around in an old house. Yet those days at Wilsons Creek were consumed by internal journeys and wars that ripped our fragile truces apart.

A million miles away, in Bangkok's newest airport, my thoughts run like children through the house, seeking light among the shadows: *I am in someone else's house filled with someone else's old and dusty things, yet there we are in the kitchen, there we are in 'my' room, the lightest room in the house, and there we are in the lounge room, dark but for the light of the fire, taut and tense, a psalm of contradiction as we laze back on the old brown leather chairs.*

My husband has a beautiful face. It is a face of simple lines. When he smiles he could be the man I spent my life looking for. He doesn't smile very often. He laughs even less.

In reality I have been living with a man who wants sex or a fight. For months the tiresome undercurrent of our discontent has been sex. Simple really. He wants it. And as with anyone who 'wants' anything, what he gets is never enough. It's like ice-cream. Or chocolate. Or shopping. As for me, I am so completely and utterly over sex that I don't care if I never experience it again for the rest of my life! Don't even talk to me about it, because for reasons that are exhaustingly inexplicable to me we failed over and over and over to even have the conversation. I am tired, tired, tired of its static in my brain, tired of the psychic pressure and the unexpressed disappointments. Tired of being wanted from. Tired of being colonised. Tired of denial. And sick to bloody death of my husband's response in lieu of the conversation: 'I'm just a simple farmer's dick.'

Sex, said the Indian philosopher Krishnamurti, is a brutal word.

The bile rises in my belly as I remember the last of our days together, a week in which we made love two days running. It was beautiful, honest, each time an act of freedom and love. Day three he wants more; I need to rest, to rejuvenate. I need time to fill the well. So he steps on my toes, commanding me to dance, and soon his bitter words reduce our lovemaking to a dusty songsheet trampled beneath the dancers' feet. A couple of days later I made love to please the general, offering him the gift of my body from the secret world of my antiquity. I do not mean to be poetic. I had been exploring new ways to meet him in his need without breaking promises to myself about the sexual availability of my body and spirit.

I push the coconut across the table, the silent laughter of contempt whistling through my lips as I recall our discordant dance. The day I made love to please the general, my face, to him, was a celebration of sweetness and softness. He did not see me or my silent despair, nor did he connect with me; he saw only himself in the mirror. The last time we made love he scoffed at my fakeness, expressing disgust for my softness and smile. Again, he was seeing only himself.

The day I made love to please the general, I made him lunch afterwards. He followed me around the kitchen, seeking more, more, more of my softness; he followed me around knowing something was awry, agitated because he hadn't had enough. Our lovemaking had been demanding and hungry, even though we'd met between the bedsheets in a spirit of fun. The general had not seen a woman for some time, at least a few days, and it took, oh, about ten minutes for him to feel not-complete. I walked around the kitchen observing my inner world, a world that a few weeks ago was a riot of dismay and distress but was now, unburdened by the overload of an overwhelmed woman, a new and welcome way of being that was so far unnamed. I had accepted that I did not have the language to speak to my husband about the myriad prisms of light and dark we had projected onto our globe of sexual expression, and I was not prepared to cause him any more pain in our efforts to understand each other.

I push the shiny aluminium chair away from the table and wander back through the echoing hallways of Suvarnabhumi Airport, this time looking for a clock. I am so tired of feeling alone in my marriage. Tired of my husband's contempt when I am vulnerable. Tired of commands to be and do and please. Tired of accusations that I am withholding sex. Tired of a man who lies about his feelings. Tired of sex being the answer to *everything*. Tired of trivialities. Tired of ignorance and inaccessibility. Tired of the appeaser seeking to be appeased. Tired of his unwillingness to admit hurt. Exhausted that after all this time we still can't have a conversation. And, most of all, tired of the law of reflection. Because if this is all of me, then I am also tired, so very tired, of the self-loathing. I wonder that he can reflect all this, *all this*, but not the best of me. *Why not the best of me?*

I find the departure gate.

It is time to fly.

I settle in for the longest leg of the journey, face pressed to the window. I watch the men on the ground readying the plane for takeoff. In all my flying days, I have never seen them look up at those of us seated in straight lines behind the bubble windows. Rome! Istanbul! I laugh. My marriage is such a nightmare that walking to Istanbul feels like a stroll in the park. I don't even know where Istanbul is! Well, not really. Nor Rome for that matter. As for what lies between Rome and Istanbul – *I have no idea.* With a decent run of blue spots, I'll beat just about anyone hands-down at Trivial Pursuit – blue for geography. No shortage of data in my brain, just an odd incongruence in its practical application. Before leaving Mullumbimby I borrowed every book in the library about the old civilisations of Europe. My interest coincided with the high school project that week, so there were only seven. Seven books that threw up the old words like a child throwing sand in the wind: Byzantium. Constantinople. Pompeii. Persia. Alexander the Great. *Alexander the bloody Great!* Bloody hell, Gallipoli! Backgammon! Ottoman. Istanbul. East meets West. A city on two continents. Goosebumps for buildings I'd never heard of.

Heart and mind, I embraced the road ahead. My body began to hum. *The walk of a thousand incarnations.* Rome, Istanbul. Just what, exactly, *is* in between?

More words played in my heart: crusades, conquerors, queens, explorers, storytellers, empires. Grazing the pages of simple books, I sank through layers of my own being, senses slowly opening to the dust of tide and time. I received the old stories, not so much the words as the vibration, the resonance of ancient peoples flowing backwards and forwards in time, the inside-out of all that is.

My husband worried my family would think he drove me away.

'They know who I am,' I said.

And then I added, 'I was born for this.'

It is an extraordinary feeling, the risking of all there is for truth, all the while knowing that this truth is nothing more than the intangibility of 'my' being. *The longing is the path.* All of me was surrendered to the road. No longer skirting the edge of my life,

I was over the edge. For the first time in my life I was seeking nothing. I was – and am – beyond the boundaries of my own existence. This was the moment I had lived for since the summons of the crow called me from my mountain home. I was offering my life to freedom, freedom for freedom's sake. And in so doing, I was fulfilling my greatest longing – *that I not die wondering*. Consequently my world, the world I had created at Wilsons Creek, was fading from reality, releasing me and, involuntarily, my husband. In walking to Istanbul I was putting all that I love and all that I am on the line. And I became excruciatingly aware that *I do not choose death, death chooses me* and this gave me courage – that and the noble words of Walter Scott: *One crowded hour of glorious life is worth an age without a name.*

In my husband's world, no-one walks from Rome to Jerusalem. In my world, my sister accompanied a handful of human beings and camels across a desert, Alice Springs to Broome. In my world, my son and I put one foot in front of the other up over the Pyrenees to Santiago de Compostela, traversing Spain's northern interior through cities and villages, farms and forests; crossing the *meseta* in the blazing hot sun and mountains in the wind and icy rain, and walking all night beneath the great arcing wheel of the Milky Way.

Pilgrimage is the art of ancient travel, a subpoena from the heart that defies all common sense. It is a meeting, at once terrestrial and supernal, between the body and the Earth, the heart and God. The pilgrim is not unlike a comet, burning off all that is futile and unnecessary until what is left is the essential, unmalleable core. The pilgrim walks the Earth, walks the wheel, walks the turning seasons, surrendering all of who she is and all she thinks she knows and all she thinks she wants to the road and the weather – the sun, rain, wind and snow – experiencing humanity in our onward-ever-onward glory. As it is. As we are.

Pilgrimage is where the romance of the road meets reality, boots to the bitumen. Rome to Istanbul, the walk of a thousand incarnations, however alluring, would be an entirely different undertaking to El Camino, the mystical road to Santiago. This time, for starters, we would be unsupported – no *refugios* (pilgrim hostels); no steady ant-stream of pilgrims sharing the journey; no yellow arrows to keep us on the path. However well-worn this route through the ages, Ben and I would be making it up as we went along, Rome to Istanbul.

Night after night as I lay in bed at Wilsons Creek, staring out the windows into the blackness of the night forest, the irrational did its damnedest to terrorise my confidence in the road ahead. Two words became the hooligans of my heart: *Kosovo. Landmines.* They were Bonnie and Clyde to my Texas backcountry. Even though I continued to entertain fantasies about walking through Italy, deep in my bones I knew Ben would choose the Balkans. I wanted the romance of the road. He hankered for the know-you're-alive unknown.

The Balkans. Jeez, truth be told I don't even know where the Balkans are, let alone *what* they are. You want an opinion on Kosovo, Serbia, Bosnia? As dinner party conversation, I am relatively well-informed. Not because I am relatively well-informed but because I can parrot information articulately and confidently, especially if I've read the day's newspapers; although it's always a bit embarrassing in the presence of someone who is genuinely well informed. Fortunately that's not often.

Kosovo. Landmines. I wish the thought police would lock up the hooligans. Over and over in the dark I replayed a war scene from an old Australian television series called 'The Sullivans'. Tom Sullivan and his mate were making their way across open fields, bayonets ready, when his mate trod on a landmine ... and froze. I have never, ever forgotten the click as his foot went down and the agony of the ensuing, what was it – ten? twenty? – minutes of excruciating television as the lives of two young men sank into the quicksand of hopelessness, knowing one of them was about to die. *That scene.* A young man with his foot on a landmine, knowing he would live only as long as he kept his leg planted steady on the pin. Click. That terrible click. I hadn't thought of it in years. And now, lying in bed at Wilsons Creek, sunshine slashing the crumpled white sheets, I heard that click over and over. It played so loud I swear I could hear it outside my head. Over and over. I saw in my mind the horror of two young men trapped in one long torturous moment. Click. Me. Ben. Click.

Before I left my mountain home, often when I closed my eyes I saw an image of myself standing at a station, suitcase beside me on the platform, waiting for my train. Now I am on that train, racing out of control through the night, leaving that which I have sought for so long – a husband – to walk God knows how far through God knows what war-ravaged countries and this looks like heaven compared to the unbearability of staying at Wilsons Creek with the face of my discontent. I feel attached to life, to my life, certain that I will die if I go walking, knowing that if I stay I will die anyway, suffocating in a hidden pocket of fear; sheltering, not living. If I stay at Wilsons Creek ... my lips bite down on the words of condition: *if, stop, don't, won't, can't, should, shouldn't, if, if, if, if, if, if, if.*

As the plane taxis to the runway, a small rain drizzling Bangkok's steamy tarmac, I think of Moira Kelly, an Australian woman I met years ago while working as a reporter on the Gold Coast; courageous Moira, whose philosophy of life was an illuminated version of the famous Aussie 'fair go'. If the children of Kosovo couldn't escape the war that landmined their limbs for lack of something as mindlessly simple as a legal document, then neither would Moira. While the Western world flew out, Moira flew in.

During those last weeks at Wilsons Creek, fear was the inner soundtrack to my packing and planning as my chattering mind did its stealthy best to sabotage my certainty. There was no question of giving voice to the movies in my head, other than an occasional shared 'joke' with my daughter when we needed to release the pressure on our hearts. Otherwise, she and I did not speak the same thoughts and I revealed the deadly inner chaos to no-one.

The plane takes a breath before the engines roar down the runway and we soar into the night. I wonder what it's like to have a plastic leg. Or one arm. Or no arms.

I settle back in my seat, the tiny plane pillow tucked into the space between my neck and shoulders. I smile at the stars outside the window, looking for the moon. Not so long ago I pledged myself to another journey. A different journey. A marriage. A journey with a man. Yet it was as if our wedding day was the beginning of the end. Six weeks after our honeymoon my husband went to Thailand for a month. He had to go. For my sake, one of us had to go. Somewhere. Anywhere. Away. I needed, desperately needed, time out to recover. I was fighting for air, drowning in my willingness to please a man.

His absence gave me time enough to find a footing, time enough to get my head above water, time enough to wade to shore and collapse on the sand, and time enough to recover from my exhaustion and recreate the same illusion that sank me in the first place.

I took to sleeping by the fire while he was away. And it was there, as I stared into the flames one dark-moon night in the house we shared before Wilsons Creek, the door of the fireplace open (something my husband did not allow), the raw heat warming my skin, it was there that I made a vow: I will not add to my husband's pain, his wounds. If it comes to a choice between what I want and him, I will choose him. I will give myself wholly to my marriage. I will learn selflessness. I will give my marriage, and my husband, everything I have. That means my love, my wellbeing, my fullness, my life, my integrity. This, I believed, that long lonely night by the fire, this would be my road to freedom. Life's paradox, my road. My husband and I were in agreement that marriage would be our spiritual pathway. There were patterns in my relationships that did not serve me, and the common ground in all of these relationships was me. All I had to do was get out of the way, out of my own way and out of his way, and surrender myself to my marriage. As far as I could tell the whole world managed to do what I had failed to do. If they could do it, then surely I could too. And this raised a question that played like poison on my mind: *what do they know that I do not?*

That night I dreamed of a dam, bridged by a long, flat cement pathway. *The path has no railings. I dive deep, down, down, down into the mud and return with a pearl that contains a belief I have value only for sex.*

My husband returned on the new moon. I met him at the airport in my best dress, black and white, and presented him with a rose, blood red. In the days that followed I took responsibility for all of our collisions and rearranged myself accordingly. When I buckled under my husband's complaint, I found the complainer in my own heart. When I tired of his wanting, I went in search of the wanter within. When he spoke I listened. When he failed to listen I let my voice drop away mid-stream and reminded myself that I did not need to be seen. And when I became distressed by his sexual hunger, I sought out the sexual zealot in myself, the angry one, the corrupt one, the terrorist on the inside. I became confused. Is he demanding sex or is it me, demanding that he demand?

I dreamed of a fast-flowing river, wide and brown. *I am riding the rushing water on my belly, headfirst. The river splits around a small treed island up ahead. There are bumpy rocks and rapids to the right and a clear run down the left. I hope to avoid the rapids. Beyond the island I see a great expanse of water, a bay, and I worry for a moment about sharks. Then I surrender to the knowing that whatever is there I must meet. For I am in the river and I am in the flow and where it leads me is choiceless.*

By the time the moon was full, I was emotionally battered, bruised and exhausted, as if I had crawled on my knees through a desert. Marriage had become my pilgrimage and I had crossed the burning sands. Worn and weary as I was, I felt as if I'd been handed the keys to the next kingdom. And then, early one morning as we sipped tea in bed, I unwittingly tripped the hair trigger of our lives by daring to explore the concept of limitless vision through the eyes of a media baron, one Rupert Murdoch, and the volcano slowly boiling inside me erupted with the force and fury of a woman denied. Out on the verandah I lanced the boil of my complicity. I howled with rage. I screamed my throat raw. I tore at my hair. My husband worried what the neighbours would think. There were none within cooee of the house, so they were the least of my concerns. Besides, the house was sold. We were planning to drive around Australia. We were moving in the meantime to Wilsons Creek.

I close my eyes and listen to the muffled roar of the jets. The screen map in front of me tells me we are 30,000 feet above India, flying over the mountainous northern borders of that vast and chaotic nation. I wonder if the people way below can see us passing in the night. I wonder if guerilla rockets can fly this high?

My thoughts return to one bright morning at Wilsons Creek where, sprawled face to the sky on the warm wooden floorboards of the verandah, I lay awash in the winter sunshine and the most extraordinary sense that the house was receiving me. I remember wondering, *How much can I let go and still be received?*

All the way, said the house. *All the way, my darling; I will hold you.*

I had been holding myself so tightly, so taut and rigid around my Dutch husband, that I wept as I surrendered to the house at Wilsons

Creek. The fresh wind of the Australia I grew up in stirred in my bones. And as the house received me, courage blossomed in my heart. The house said, *You are who you are and that is wonderful and perfect.*

The house at Wilsons Creek became my guide. Enthusiasm replaced tension and resistance in my body. My creativity, which had been in hibernation for the past year, began to surge. For my husband, dark clouds rolled in over the verandah at Wilsons Creek. For me, the lights of my life went on. My vision sharpened. I surrendered my need for outcome in my marriage. I no longer needed to 'know'. I turned my attention away from the wasteland world of 'what if' to focus on 'what is'. I became present in my body. I showed up in my own life. My tail dropped beneath my skirts. I left muddy footprints on the floor. In the absence of music, for my husband cannot abide music, I attuned to my own responses, catching reactive fears and angers before they took hold in my body. I felt alive and full, rich and abundant, because when there is only this moment, this is all there is. I did not waste energy on distant futures, on wishing. Everything I needed was right there in the house at Wilsons Creek, right here in the body of a woman blessed.

It was at this time I dreamed of an ice mountain, hovering white, calling to me as I was on my way somewhere else. It was more than a dream, for I was not the watcher. Rather, I *felt* the loose stones beneath my bare feet as I walked the dusty road; I *met* the women and girls of the mountain tribes, heart to heart. I woke alive to the voice within.

This was the last of the three pilgrim dreams, a trilogy whose first two instalments had me weeping on the streets of Santiago and tracing routes woven into intricate rugs. This was the point at which I could no longer ignore the call to Rome.

A week later I found the crow feather by the pack on the lounge room floor. And after that I woke morning after morning to a pair of crows landing on the ragged branch of the tree outside my bedroom window, calling A-A-A-A before one would swoop to the ground and pace, wading knee-deep through the dewy grass outside my door.

Soon after, on the night of the full moon, I dreamed an angel dream. *My children's grandmothers – my mother and the woman who would be my mother-in-law had I married her son – stand together chatting on a suburban street corner. I am shimmering, my presence in my body only just; I have great white feathered wings and I wonder if they'll notice. They smile when they see me. They don't see my wings, although my mother says, 'Look at Steph, look at her shining.' I come to the road and wonder if I can fly across. I stretch my wings, feeling their fluid weight. I fly, softly, across the road. Then I am in bed, semiconscious – in waking time I hear an animal cough outside my bedroom, in my dream I hear the children coming, my darling grandchildren, Krystle and Dylan, and I realise Krys is sobbing. 'Who has upset her so?' I wonder. I realise I cannot help her; I am dead. I think, 'She is probably crying for me.' And I am at peace with the knowing that this world is a dream and death is nought but transformation and her journey and Dylan's journey are what they are and that love is all there is.*

Just before we moved to Wilsons Creek, my husband and I found a counsellor with whom we shared the agony of our existence. One day, as I sat with him in the tiny office in the garden of his home, his attention was diverted to the window.

'I've never seen that bird before,' he said.

I turned to look. There was a crow behind the glass.

'She's here for me,' I said.

The counsellor paid no attention.

'My Jungian wasp moment,' I added softly, as I smiled awkwardly at yet another man deaf to the mystery. Or to women. Now I wonder if there's a difference?

My husband does not understand the call to Rome. How do I explain to him that I am not a domestic animal? That I am the wolf who comes to the door for a good meal and a seat by the fire, who stays awhile for the company and who always, always returns to the forest when she hears the call of the wild. *The call of the wild. The call of deepest, darkest, truest Self. The call to Love on Earth.*

Love is not 'being good' and it is especially not being a 'good wife'. And oh my, oh my, I have done all I can to be a 'good wife'. A Good Wife. A Thankful Wife. A wife who stays. A wife who celebrates her tether. A wife who does not upset her husband. A woman thankful that someone wanted to marry her. And, blessed gratitude of gratitudes, a woman thankful for a man who would support her.

Can you imagine? Mother and grandmother, a near half-century old, and for the first time since I cried in the cradle a man was supporting me. I cannot begin to describe the enormity of accepting such a gift. The profound sense of rightness that a man with such resources would offer to share them unconditionally with a woman. That as a woman I no longer have to work to shore up my own survival. That as a woman I am free to live a creative life, supported – *supported by my husband*.

Yet the price! The price was too much to bear. The price was that he exacted no price. And this caused a tension in me that first drowned me and then hung me out to dry. I am not sure whether this was because we were incapable of having the conversation about what we were each offering the other, and the expectations we held in our hearts for a return, or whether there was, in truth, no price. I know that only once in our year together did he come close to expressing his confusion about our 'exchange', unwritten and unspoken as it was. And that was the one night I failed to make him dinner, the longest night at Wilsons Creek. And this brought me dangerously close to the core of my suspicions: that he was buying my domestic and sexual availability.

Touch me because you care to touch me, not because I owe you touch – or anything else – in return.

When we first met, my opening line to my prospective husband, right at the beginning our relationship, was that I would not make him dinner from any sense of obligation or duress or duty. Believing that any right-thinking man would seek such service only as a gift – and as an act of self-preservation – I assured him every meal he received from me would be an offering, an act of love.

Food was easier than sex, over which I tied myself in knots in my efforts to deliver without obligation. For if a man is married and a man is supporting his wife, for what other reason would he attend to such an arrangement if not for the sexual availability of his wife?

Obligation became my Mount Vesuvius. I bowed to his needs in gratitude. I bowed to his needs because I was his wife. I bowed to his needs because I wanted his approval. I bowed for all the reasons women through the ages have bowed, and still bow, to men. And I bowed to experience what it was like to bow to a husband. And in the absence of conversation, my dispirited guessing game fertilised the garden of my contempt for him and, more so, for myself.

Our last night in Wilsons Creek was the night before my husband flew to Bangkok. He flew out on the eve of the anniversary of our first meeting; I flew out the day after. This date once hung like gossamer between the open palms of our hands. It sat now whole and heavy between our clenched fists, worlds apart. We were bound by nothing more or less powerful than the gold bands on our ring fingers.

Our last night in Wilsons Creek we slept together, apart. For the longest time I lay staring at the ceiling in the dark, wondering: *How did I go to war with a man who wanted only love?*

The plane eventually outruns the dawn and touches down at Heathrow, the early morning mists streaked pink with England's milky sunlight. Lily, now my son's ex-girlfriend and a London-based Heathrow habitué, has organised a taxi to greet me. The transition between Australian dollars and British pounds is one of modern life's more jittery experiences, one best kept brief and to the point. However, having just spent a sleepless thirty-two hours travelling from one side of the world to the other, twenty-two of them in the air, the next step is a no-brainer: I can stumble blind with my baggage through the busiest airport on Earth into London's public transport system or I can ignore the pounding in my inner brain urging me to do my sums and fork out forty quid for an angel with a cardboard sign bearing my name who will sweep me away and deposit me at the door of Lily's little flat.

Lily lives above a Chinese herbalist in Goodge Street – *Goodge Street!* Always I say it twice. Goodge Street. London-quaint. *Old world*. Butchers, bakers and candlestick makers. Lily is holidaying in Ibiza and won't be home until tomorrow. Lily, bright and beautiful, is perpetually holidaying, exploring Europe as if its tribe of nations were suburbs of Sydney. Ben is *somewhere*, I am never certain where Ben is; he will show up when he is good and ready, which – now he's older – is mostly sooner rather than later.

Baggage on the footpath, I pop into the herbalist's to borrow the phone to ring Luis, the Spanish student who lives in the flat underneath Lily. Luis has the key. Four flights of stairs later (praise Luis) I am in the door and on the bed. Home – or the closest I'll come to home for some time.

I lie on Lily's big bed in her tiny room and gently close my eyes. Exhaustion rumbles through the morning light and hits me where it hurts – smack in my resolve. *What am I thinking! Walking to Istanbul!* Memories stark and bold and true of the endlessness and agony of El Camino pour into that gaping hole in my resolve: worn out and weary; aching, wretched feet; limping spirits; *horrible* food. I am thirty years vegetarian. Wheat swells me up and puts me to sleep. Peasant

Europe is wheat and meat Nirvana. I am Byron Bay spoilt, organic and fresh and available on demand. I let sleep carry me into the street noises outside the window. London is on its way to work.

I wake hungry, ready for lunch. Strange light fringes the room, a darkish glow. I kneel on the pillow and peel open the blinds. Reality check. The darkish is night and the glow is the streetlight piercing the papery white blinds. I have slept all day. London is on its way home. I wander around the flat. The fridge yields cheese and fresh dates. I find the teas and brew a chamomile. I sit cross-legged on the navy blue futon folded into a lounge and orientate while munching and sipping.

Somewhat restored, I wonder when Ben will come. He has been in Morocco, taking a break from his pilgrimage while he waits for me to arrive. Time with my son. I am nervous as well as excited, in an unacknowledged way. At times we rattle each other, Ben and I, and at others we are too careful. Other than the walk to Santiago, 900 kilometres in the company of his mother *and* his girlfriend, Ben and I catch up only when he is in Australia – a few days a year, on a good year. There is no time to fathom or fix, so we skirt each other. We are polite. We like each other. There is a good deal of respect and even admiration. But we do not know each other, this worldly son and his impassioned mother.

Compellingly, I am walking my marriage from Rome to Istanbul. More subtly, I have the strongest sense I am completing a karmic cycle with my son. It is the strangest notion, completing a karmic cycle. Neither the language nor the concept is mine. They are the words and ideas of a different realm and another generation. Yet they are what I am left with when the tides of marital confusion recede from my heart: completing a karmic cycle with the boy who asked only that he be allowed through when his teenage mother buckled under the weight of public shame and sought an abortion to restore her life and her self-confidence. *'Just let me through,'* he seemed to say, as I lay in a white gown beneath the anaesthetist's dozy mask. *'We'll be okay.'*

I have four stand-out photographs of Ben and me. In the first, he is six weeks old and I am newly nineteen, my white-gold hair shining and curly as cheek to cheek we look out at the world together. In the second, he is three years old and we are walking strong and steady in gumboots and winter jackets, hand in hand across the barren hills of a Canberra winter landscape. The third was taken ten years later, on the steps of our home in Lismore, leaning into each other with sun-browned arms stretched across each other's shoulders. In the fourth, taken when he was twenty, we stand on a windblown hilltop overlooking a beach, soaking wet and holding up the fruits of our fishing expedition. In all of them, Ben and I look out at the world together. Confident. Sure of ourselves. Independent. Side by side. This is the boy I let through. *This is the boy who knew we'd be okay.* And now we are walking the mystery.

As I sip the last of the chamomile tea, I wonder about the vastness of each and every one of the six billion people with whom I share this Earth – *the enormity of us!* I cannot accept that I am alone in being swept along by the undercurrents of my life. And if what goes on inside me goes on six billion–fold then there's a pandemic of illusion out there in holy rhythm with its counterweight, disillusion – and there is nothing else to do but help each other through. To put 'me' ahead of anybody is to destroy us all. There is nothing else to do but help. Perhaps this is all there is to love? *Perhaps this is Love.*

I think of sport. I am Australian. We like to play and there was a time before we played only to win. My husband hates sport. Hates everything about it. Even if, as I like to point out, his favourite movie is a golf film, 'Bagger Vance'. Games teach us focus, motivation, discipline, coordination, teamwork and love, yes even love. (It's a golf film.) Yet there is a point where the joy of winning becomes lust for destruction; where in the absence of love there is aggression and violence, a need to destroy 'the other'. It's a fine line and a wide field and for a moment I wonder if marriage is simply sport dressed in drag.

I have a lovely sport story to tell about my husband, about the compulsory backyard cricket match on his introductory antipodean Christmas Day, when he stood in the shade of a gum tree bemused and sipping tea as his wife belted balls into the fence for six. At one point a ball rolled along the ground and stopped right at his feet. Any self-respecting Aussie would have picked it up and pelted it at the stumps. At the very least they would have thrown it, however awkwardly, to the bowler. Not my husband. He did what I have never, ever seen anyone in my country do. He glanced, unresponsive and undisturbed, at the ball at his feet, while the batsmen (men, women, children and feminists, we're all batsmen) ran and ran and ran with glee. He made no effort to pick up the ball. Put another way, there is *not one cell* in his body coded to respond to a ball that comes his way. I love this story because I love surprises. I tell him he has just failed John Howard's Australian citizenship test.

I blink to the present. Night has settled in for the long haul and London's late shift is coming to life. I go back to sleep in Lily's bed and wake in the deep end of night thinking about the law of reflection: if I accept that others have a message for me, it is not necessarily what I see or hear that is the message – *it may also be my response to the message.*

I have drowned in several seas of responses to my husband and my marriage. If I have learned nothing else I have learned there is a world of difference between what I see and my responses to what I see. These days I bide my time and bite my tongue when propelled to pronouncement about others, or myself in relation to others. Because of course I am right! Hammer and anvil I have constructed reality to my own specifications. *I can't not be right!* I am bored with 'right', for when I am right the moment is over, preserved in stone, rigid and impossible to dance. Life is much more interesting if I put on a new dress and make an entrance into a world beyond the arrogance of right, where myriad possibilities of right tango with potential and promise. Right tempered with kindness, for instance. Right laced with mercy, for example. For nothing is right if it is unkind. And there is no truth without mercy. Kindness, truth and mercy. Perhaps this is the holy trinity of Grace.

Morning comes and I wake slowly, content to be alone in Lily's little flat. I love her décor, sleek and simple and modern, a less than chaotic expression of a dynamic young woman with a thousand pairs of shoes begging for homes and pleading to stay together. I am filled with love for her. We, my daughter and I, are very pleased to have her in the family. My son, too, though for reasons of his own. I split the blinds and peek through to Goodge Street. Traffic. Londoners in t-shirts clinging to a faded summer.

Easing gently into the day with a hot lemon and ginger tea, I browse Lily's books. Wall-to-wall Paulo Coelho. I reach for one and let it fall open in my hands: *Transparent in actions; secretive in plans.*

It's the answer to yesterday's question: does a commitment to truth mean I have to disclose everything? Honesty is a compulsion with me. I can't help it. You ask, you get. If I were to pick a fairytale character who best sums up my personality it would be the child in 'The Emperor's New Clothes'. It took me years and years to learn that *the people don't want to know.* And even longer to truly understand that they would point their fingers not at the emperor, but at me. The best I have been able to muster with maturity is a modicum of diplomacy.

It took marriage to reveal my inner, invisible war with obligation. I struggle with it like a kitten in a sack thrown into the drowning pond. *I am not obliged to tell anyone anything.* There are women who know this whose lives go underground; and women who know this whose lives are metagalactic universes of bitterness; and women who refuse to know this, whose bodies are dams of denial as they unwittingly and resentfully live everyone else's lives but their own. These are the ones with little voices. Paulo delivers me the key: *Explore everything in the privacy of my own heart. And stand accountable for my actions.*

Lily is big on Osho too, part of a new, less spiritually dependent generation ripe for the freshly marketed teachings of the great Bagwan. I return Paulo to his place on the shelf and reach for Osho. The book opens at a well-marked page and I am netted by a quote from one of the Rothschild patriarchs: *Keep jumping. In this way you will see the sun of opportunity as it is rising, rather than as it is passing already risen.*

I bounce once in gratitude and delight and put the book back. I cannot read while London is calling. The British Museum is around the corner. I pull on my jeans and a jumper, clean my teeth and brush my hair, grab the keys and fly down the steps. London! Before pulling the door shut I'm back up the stairs for a jacket. My fabulous white jacket with the Eskimo hood, which has sat at the back of a more temperate wardrobe for all of the two years since I bought it in Norway. Arctic memento making its street debut; souvenir for the soul. My jacket and I walk into the street crowd, lemmings against the tide of Londoners whooshing along streets with iconic names. Bloomsbury. Oxford. Past buses marked not for their tourism value but for their geography. Trafalgar Square. Mayfair. Into the museum for a stroll among the booty of the ancients. No wonder their descendants want it back. I wander through Rome. Crane my neck at Greece. Stop in my tracks for the outstanding grace and power of Egypt, the beauty and felicity of statues and stonework the triumph of civilisations past.

I amble home, kicking up the first leaves of autumn rather than grinding them into the damp footpath. I smile up at the chimney pots. Heart-warm for a country woman I hum a merry tune. *Chim chim-in-ey, chim chim cher-ee*. I'm not alone in my amazement that an Australian, one Helen Lyndon Goff, wrote 'Mary Poppins', and when I see the red chimneypots of London I am looking, ever and always, through the eyes of the daughter of a Queensland cane farmer (or bank clerk, depending upon your historical source).

Lily bowls in and we bowl straight out again, my shout, to our favourite Lebanese restaurant on the corner of Tottenham Court Road. As usual, we order too much and stuff ourselves witless.

Ben blows in with the afternoon wind from Morocco and we play with the mail-order parcels awaiting him at Lily's. My movie camera! His new microphone! We laugh. Neither of us is a filmmaker. And that's about to change.

I peel open my pack. Ben reminds me that no matter how lightly I think I've packed, I'll be sending stuff home. I get ruthless. One change of clothes. Seven pairs of undies. Three pairs of socks. Tent. Blow up mattress. Sleeping bag. Pocket knife. Headlamp. Water bladder. Notebook. Camera gear. Toothbrush. Mobile phone. Charger. Betadine. Hat. Crappy plastic travel backgammon. Boots. A token pack of Compeed for blisters. Experience is as experience does – I walked 900 kilometres across Spain in boots of the same brand and model that I'm about to set off in from Rome; my feet will ache, this I know, but I will be safe from blisters.

Late in the evening I fold out the navy blue futon and lie in bed while Ben finishes packing. He asks what my husband thinks of the walk.

'Is he excited for you?'

My heart sinks, but not too far.

'We haven't discussed it,' I say.

We laugh, but not too much.

I'm sad about the absence of shared enthusiasm between my husband and me, not just for my walk but for anything at all. *How on earth,* I wonder, *did this man and I ever think, much less believe, we had what it took to get married?*

Eventually Ben and I get around to the conversation I've been waiting for but have been unwilling to initiate: the road to Istanbul. I have two scenarios running way down there in my subconscious mind and our proposed route is to be neither: not up over the top of Italy and down through the Balkans; nor south through Italy's heart via iconic ruins and across the water to Greece. Ours will be the most straightforward path, unsurprisingly, given that Ben has walked several thousand kilometres already from Canterbury and is immune to detours for such frivolities as the romance of the ancients. So much for Pompeii.

Our road to Istanbul will take us due east from Rome, straight over Italy's mountainous spine and across the Adriatic by ferry to Croatia (Ben's concession to common sense), down the coast through Montenegro and Albania before turning east and cutting through the mountains of Macedonia to Istanbul.

There, in Lily's tiny flat in London, the pins on all my landmines are pulled at once. I remind myself that I have no rules about my pilgrimage, that I don't have to walk every step of the way. Yet in truth I am thankful for my son's leadership, for throwing me into a bear-pit of strangers and stereotypes. And besides, I tell myself, if the going gets too tough I can always return to Italy and hang out in Pompeii.

I close my eyes and plunge into an internal freefall, plummeting through darkness and terror into the unknown. This journey will take me beyond 'the West' and I am stunned by the security I feel, unacknowledged until this moment, about being in the West, even when I am in the East, which these days is geared to the West. As the blackness and blindness of a fearful gloom whistle by in my head, the romance of the journey hits the ice-cold shock of reality and a voice, small and strong and even a little bit excited, tells me it'll do me good to step into the dark ages, to experience countries not long emerged from the shadows of war and, perhaps, even hatred. Wanting and fear pulse ferociously in my veins. Eyes still closed I take a deep breath and dedicate my pilgrimage to life, to meeting 'the other' and to meeting the best of me.

We wake to the day before we leave for Rome. Or I do, lying in the early morning light waiting for Ben and Lily to stir. My pack rests silhouette-fancy against the wall, like Santa's sack bulging with goodies on Christmas morning. I resolve to ask my husband for his message for me, for clearly there must be a reason for us being together and I'm tired of shooting the messenger. And, naturally, tired of being shot at. I resolve to ask him this because I have a message for him. I will tell him, 'You confuse love with wanting and truth with fear.'

My legs pound the bed in excitement. *I am going to Rome. I'm walking the old roads. I'm going to Istanbul!* I am breathless with anticipation.

I feel for my husband. Driving around Australia was more than a way of making friends: it would have created shared memories and experiences, a detour from the worn-out trails of the first fifty-six years of his life, a long overdue resurfacing of Memory Lane. Indeed, I had an agenda, and agendas – even when exposed to the light – are rarely truthful. Because we forget we are an infinitesimal speck in the wheel of time and it is impossible for us to know the trails and trials and purposes of the whole story; and besides, agendas are always, always fuelled by fear. More than making friends, more than wanting to *show* him his adopted homeland, I wanted to sit with him in the red dirt of the west beneath the gum trees, lie on the warm sands of the north and listen to the ocean beneath a wheeling night sky, drive with the windows down and the music blaring, blowing with the wind. Yes, I had an agenda and it was to unfasten the zip lock on my husband's life and breathe love and warmth and spontaneity into his soul.

I saw the starkness and sadness of my hidden agenda when, obediently, I stopped projecting into the future and the pilgrimage train came barrelling into my station. In reality, my obligation was not to the rigidity of my husband and mythical futures carefully constructed to save us from ourselves, but to the truth of my own life: and that is nothing more or less than Rome and the road to Istanbul.

My skin tingles. My heart beats a little faster. The doorway of my life stands wide open to the footsteps of the ancients. And here I am, blinking into the light, stone-blind and ignorant.

I recall a song I used to belt out nearly twenty years ago, its poetry working on my heart as I drove the mountain tracks of New Zealand:

> *I won't ask the purpose of all of my footsteps*
> *and I won't let my eyelids cast down,*
> *I'm looking for something outside of forgiveness,*
> *You might call it the jewel in the crown.*

And now I understand. I'm looking for something outside of forgiveness; yes, more than this, I seek the jewel in the crown.

I get up and clatter around the kitchen, hoping to disturb Ben. I bang the saucepan on the stove and boil up fresh ginger root, rattling the dishes as I look for the lemon squeezer. I rustle around in the cupboards for clean mugs. My mind mingles with the days before we left Wilsons Creek and settles on an evening in the brown leather armchairs when I asked my husband what he liked about me. He thought about it and said, 'Your bum,' to which I added silently, 'My hair.' He then went on to identify a few things he appreciated which, sadly, were things I do for him.

There are three things I would love, require, need from a man to whom I dedicate my life and, in thinking this, I cringe from the poisonous words of condition. How then to express my longing for friendship, enthusiasm and interest in my marriage without condition? Perhaps in their non-negotiability, perhaps by not insisting on them or fighting for them. *Perhaps by living them myself.*

The banging around the kitchen yields results. Ben surfaces and Lily, who treats sleep like a lazy Sunday lover, moans about morning. I dive into the shower and duck out onto the street for hot croissants from the bakery across the road. Crumbs fly as we stuff them with cheese and onion for toasting in the oven. We've a busy day ahead.

Ben and I leave Lily to wrap herself in the arms of sleep while we hoof blind around the neighbourhood sorting out international SIM cards and finding last minute gear, such as waterproof bags for the camera equipment.

About a dozen blocks from home we see the pièce de résistance, the travel backgammon set I've been looking for all my life. It is blue leather with red and white points and it rolls up around a board-length pouch containing the pieces and dice. It is perfect. It is soft. It is strong. It is not too small and not too big. It is fifty pounds. Fifty bloody pounds! Pounds are fine if you earn pounds. They are impossible if you earn Australian dollars. Fifty pounds for a backgammon set. Fifty pounds is one hundred and twenty Aussie dollars. Fifty pounds is a day's pay for workers in my nation. My husband would have a stroke.

I peel myself away from the window. We find the camping shop. My eyes assess waterproof bags while the blue leather backgammon board wrestles with my heart. Backgammon is our game. Ben is unbeatable and I taught him to play. Before that I was unbeatable and his father taught me to play, each of us in turn out-mastering the master. I'd found a tiny tinny board in a toyshop in the days before leaving Wilsons Creek. In the absence of any other, it would do. I loathed it. I wanted its crappy plastic to shatter. I want, want, wanted a lovely board on which to roll the dice and summon the old energy to gleefully and brilliantly slay my son.

On the way back to Goodge Street desire won out. My husband would, in his words, 'suffer a minor contraction', but in truth he would happily allow me the board if it made my heart sing – and my bosom was heaving with operatic crescendo for the blue leather roll-up board. What price love?

Our shopping for the journey complete, souls surging with the blast of carte blanche we purchased with the blue leather board, we chat and laugh our way back to Lily's. An air of bemusement sets in as we create chaos in the little flat, sorting and packing ready for tomorrow. I long for the innocence and romance of the inexperienced as I eliminate my clothing down to a handful of garments. The aesthetic mind mounts impressive cases for pretty choices, but the rational mind, weathered by the road to Santiago, wins out every time. There will be only one change of clothes for the next three months. And although I am excited about the *idea* of walking to Istanbul, I am also apprehensive. Physically I am up and down, alive with the moment one minute, tired and heavy the next. I zip up the pack and stand it once more against the wall.

Ben packs and repacks while I lie on the navy blue futon and gaze at the ceiling, scrutinising my marriage and justifying my relationship to it. I think of the man I was with before my husband. By then, I was so exhausted by relationships that I was determined to make that one work. *This is it*, I said to myself. And a not-very-small voice inside said, *This one and one more*. And even knowing this was the truth, the heart of my mind cried, *NO!* and set about hammering this mournful attempt at loving partnership into the shape I desired, until sheer fatigue scuttled my efforts and I could hammer no more.

Then I met my husband. And we married. And I truly believed 'this is it' because the not-very-small voice had told me so. And I puffed up the pillows of my life, put my feet up on the lounge and settled in for the end of the relationship road. And indeed it was! And is! Though not in the way I believed or understood or thought I understood. Yes I am at the end of the road – this road. There is more. Much more than this. And I may journey on with my husband or I may not. Either way, I am embarked on a new road. The freedom road. The truthful road. The beyond obligation and condition road. I am walking into the rising sun, heart point-blank with the light of a new dawn.

And into the amplitude of the moment barrels a belly blow of recognition. Oh! The grip my husband has on his life is a mirror image of the lifeless grip I have on my own. Ow! Here it is! And here! And there! Currents of horror and loss shoot through my body. I watch and release the tired energies, giving thanks and thanks again to the irreproachable hands of destiny that delivered this man to me. For if I am honest, I can see I wanted a husband who would open up my life for me and this he has done. And I wanted a man who would be all that I longed to be but was not, thus enabling me to taste the fruits of my longing beyond my own efforts. I see! I see!

I roll off the lounge to answer the phone. It is my husband. His voice is seductive and I'm tired of being lulled into puerile security. I offer him polite lassitude. I offer him forbearance. I offer him the sobriety of one who has given away too much and is unapologetically hoarding what's left. I hang up, my spirit drained. I despair that I am not enlivened by my husband's presence and wonder how I might allow his force of obligation to wash over and through me, renewing rather than annihilating me. This is not a matter of trying. It is a matter of being myself. My heart sinks. I already know he does not like who I am. Yet he genuinely cares for me, and I for him. I mourn for friendship in my marriage; my husband mourns for sex. I vow to rewrite this dynamic, to no longer be available for mutual entrapment. I take off the beautiful silver Celtic knot he gave me as a parting gift. I know he would love me to walk with it, but I cannot. I will walk with just one piece of jewellery and that is my wedding ring.

Night closes in. We bed down. In the silent heart of stillness, I open my eyes to the darkness and see the pack leaning up against the wall. I smile with the contentedness of a child who knows she's loved and the anticipation of a woman on an inbound outbound journey. Apprehension leaves my body and, wraith-like, drifts from the room. I roll over, and when I finally sleep I dream I am on a big red London bus. *It drives up a winding mountain road through the bush and we come to a lightly flooded causeway. I offer to check it out and leap off the bus, wading through the rushing water. I turn around and the bus is gone! And there is a great body of water, like an estuary, between where I stand and the place I left the bus. I am perplexed. I am puzzled. And through the confusion I slowly let go the need to get back on the bus.*

Rome

Rome! I am in Rome!!! I am in a gorgeous city that is warm and friendly and pulsing with the ages. I cannot remember ever being more pleased to be anywhere. Perhaps that is freedom's colossal high, truth's freewheeling zenith. Nowhere else to be but here. And it is my good fortune that 'here' is Rome. Getting here took the best part of the day, most of it in slow-mo through security at Gatwick – until the announcement of our flight's imminent departure compelled us to jump the queue and sprint a mini-marathon to Gate 105. Puffing and laughing in our seats at the back of the plane, I remind Ben of his furious vow never to fly with me again, after I made him hurry to beat the crowd through immigration on a flight home from New Zealand half his lifetime ago. As it turned out, that was our last flight together, until now. We laugh so hard with the memory our eyes fill with tears. In an act of culinary desperation we stuff our faces with Toblerone for breakfast, taking turns to stare out the window, snow-struck by the white mountains far below.

Rome! Fiumicino Airport might have been forgetful had I not lost 250 Australian dollars to a wheeler-dealer at the exchange counter. The ride in from the airport might have been forgetful had I not insisted on taking the train (robbing Peter to pay Paul for the backgammon board) only to end up having to get a taxi to our room near the Vatican anyway. The taxi drops us into the traffic on the outside of the vast cobbled plain that stretches to the Vatican steps. From there we lug our packs up the hill on the Vatican's western flank, to the same apartment where Ben stayed when he walked in from Canterbury six weeks ago.

We dump the bags on our beds, grab the cameras and head straight out for lunch at the little deli on the corner, sitting in a basement at the foot of a small set of narrow wooden stairs, at a table with a red chequered cloth and a mound of white bread. And there the journey begins. We order wine. I order vegetarian antipasto, which comes, eventually, loaded with chunky cured meats. Ben orders spaghetti bolognaise and I can't believe he's come all this way for a spag-bol. We practise filming as we wait. We film the elderly waiter as he goes up and down the stairs, bringing food for all the guests but us. We raise our glasses and film a toast for the road ahead. We interview each other for the camera and laugh at our self-consciousness and our Australian-ness, stark against the ease of the Romans. *The Romans!*

We spend the afternoon walking around the streets, laughing in the heat of the day about the burning in our shoulder blades from the daypacks, knowing that it's going to get one hell of a lot worse. We return to our room and collapse on the beds, rolling about laughing as we kick off our shoes with tell-tale groans because our feet are hot and tired and the walk hasn't even begun. And we breathe in the simple pleasure of our small apartment, because come Saturday, September 22, two days from now, when day equals night and the sun turns on its heels for its southbound run, even the simplest of comforts – a clean bed, or any bed; a hearty meal, or any meal – will no longer be ours for the asking. For me, the madness is about to begin. For Ben, the madness is about to begin again. It is a privilege to be sharing this walk with my son. He has a grace and ease about him that is uncommon in our world. The first leg of his journey was a quintessential rollercoaster ride of challenge and fun, filling him with the lightness of being that comes to those who meet life as it presents itself. His is a steady eye and an open heart. This is the gift of the road.

Late in the afternoon, we decide to experiment with night filming at the *Fontana di Trevi*, the city's famous Trevi Fountain. We ask around for the bus and board with the workday crowds, oblivious to systemic demands that we buy a ticket first, shrugging with the nonchalance of the stranger who doesn't know and shouldering the free ride. We roll off the bus into the crowded evening, following our senses with the grace of tumbleweeds into the breezy, fluid night.

As far as I know, the only picture I have ever seen of the Trevi Fountain is in the opening credits of an American sitcom I liked to watch as a kid, 'To Rome With Love'. I was captivated by the notion that children could have a dead mother and I'd watch the kids on that show like a tiger in the grass, wired for proof of the impossible. In the opening, the children are sitting on the edge of the fountain. In my memory of the opening, the fountain is big and round and white and dramatic and there's a busy road running around it. So I'm somewhat surprised to find the *Fontana di Trevi* is: a) neither big nor round; b) doesn't have a road in sight; and c) packed with tourists jostling in the dark for viewing space. Of course, that was before I knew that the building behind it, the *Palazzo Poli*, is, depending on who you ask and what you read, considered part of the fountain.

Here in the company of Neptune rising, sea horses galloping and the berobed virgin who found the source of the gushing water in the first place; in the presence of stone waves, tritons and chariots; among tourists crushed alive with the night and locals fishing coins from the water with long magnetic poles; in the heart of a city that hasn't missed a beat for three millennia, my world stills and I tilt my head to the night, listening ham-radio curious for the ones who walked this way before. Before me. Before you. Before.

I look to the night sky and come face to face with the colours of antiquity: a gold half moon, crisp and poised on its tip, egged on by an audacious indigo sky. Longing rises within me like sap to the warm sun, and I glimpse the obsessive fervour of the artisans, the crazed desire that commanded them to reproduce the ethereal, to give it form, to make it solid, to arrest God and celebrate their genius – or go mad in the trying. Face to the heavens, I smile at the enormity of the challenge before them: *to find that blue on Earth!*

We wander home, munching our way through a handful of Baci chocolates, shortcutting through the backstreets and plazas of the eternal city, happily lost among ruins that keep surprising us from the shadows, iconic stone beasts and statues, massive buildings and pillars and … bloody hell, it's the Pantheon! We look at each other blankly, knowing we're in the presence of something important. What's the Pantheon? I'm sorry I haven't read 'I, Claudius'. We stick our new-world noses in the door and, startlingly alone, bounce our ignorance around the walls of the cavernous stone chamber. Ben shoots some impressive footage inside and out before we wander on into the night.

We meet the main road, east of the river, just in time to be accosted by the ring-roar-racket of a parade caterwauling its way through the traffic. A brass band cruising the night, afloat on a float, Radio Radicale with a message for the world: 'No Vatican. No Taliban.' *No Vatican. No Taliban.* Sounds like a fair trade to me. I take a good long look at the people around me. Put a gladiator helmet on their heads, winged with gold, and nothing has changed! They are the same people as those who have gone before. Same hair, same beards, same noses, same foreheads. Same sky, same dirt. Same heart. Just one long steady stream of humanity, generation after generation giving birth to each other, passing on the city, passing it on, passing it on.

The current civilisation in my country is just over 200 years old. I savour the liberation of the new world – and sense the mourning that comes with it for the loss of the old ways, favourable and terrible or both, depending upon your place in the endless chain.

I get a stitch in my side as we make our way back up the hill west of the Vatican. I cannot remember a time when I have been as blob-unfit as I am at the moment. I guess that's about to change.

Morning comes and with it the familiarity of waking with my son sound asleep in a narrow bed in another corner of the house. Ben never wakes willingly, unless of course there's an extraordinary imperative. There was a time when that did not include catching planes or, further back in time, going to school. I, to his bemusement and, depending on the circumstances, frustration, wake with the sun, shamelessly alive and enthralled with the morning no matter how much sleep I've had in the night. Needless to say, I have never missed a plane.

I am so pleased to be in the same room as my son, wrapped in my sleeping bag, content to lie alone with morning teasing me through cracks of light in the blind. Church bells shatter the silence. They ring their immodest dominion over land and life, reminding me I am once again in Christian lands. I would have thought, had I thought about it at all, that the Vatican would have beautiful bells. Musical bells. Hallelujah bells. *Clang-bonngggg thud, clang-bonnggg thud.* The Vatican does not have bells: it has saucepans donged with wooden clubs.

I am a long, long way from my husband (speaking of saucepans). I hold up my left hand and twirl the diamonds of my wedding ring around to the outside of my finger. There are three things I travel with that are gifts from my husband: my wedding ring, a pashmina of wool so soft it sits like angels on my shoulders, and a beautiful black and gold pen. I also have a photograph he took in our last days at Wilsons Creek. It captures a bee hovering face-on to the camera above a flower shaded yellow-gold. I cut it into a circle and it travels in my passport, my prayer for my husband's creative potential. I gaze at the ring, still astonished by its presence in my life. In the weeks leading up to our wedding I dreamed often of the number nine. In choosing the ring I could have had seven diamonds or nine and I went with the dreams. Much later I googled nine. Nine for completion, which I understand to mean nine for the consummation of my life's journey. Nine for my relationship with the universal presence some call God. Nine for the courage to stay true to my path. The ring may have entered my life via marriage, but it stands for all of me.

I survey the shining stones and, momentarily free from emotion, consider my husband. I am ready to rewrite my story of our time together. This is my prayer for the road. *Because it is only a story. And it's only my story. And because it's my story I can tell it any way I want.* I drop my hand to the bed, bored now. I roll up pieces of scrap paper and, reaching for a rubber band from the bedside table, fire them across the room at Ben. He stirs. He groans, no doubt with the joy of having his mother in the room.

'Rome!' I announce to the deadweight in the blue sleeping bag in the far corner. 'Let's go!'

We kick off the morning with a visit to the venerable Don Bruno Vercessi, the Vatican's head beaver for pilgrims. It's not often these days the affable Don has cause to bless a pilgrim fresh in from Canterbury; rarer still he gets to bless one on his or her way to Jerusalem. Getting through Don Bruno's door is a feat in itself: first past the blue and orange Swiss guards who stand watch at the wrought iron gates on the Vatican's west wing, who as far as we are concerned take themselves far too seriously considering the white lizard collars and jester outfits; and then past the officials inside the gate, who insist we hand over our passports. It takes a while to get in but Ben is not a man for 'no' and besides, he has a longstanding date with Don Bruno. Ben, I learn in the months to come, is a man who likes his stamps and he wasn't leaving Rome without his pilgrim passport validated with a blessing from the good Don.

We sit in Don Bruno's office among wooden desks and shelves and carpets worn with the timely needs of bureaucrats, administrators and scholars of the ages. Through these rooms and corridors I begin to get a sense of the passage of time. Don Bruno takes us on a tour of the Vatican, down into the stone underbelly of the Catholic nation, through the backwoods and byways of the world's smallest sovereign territory along marble floors all the colours of the Earth, to a small private chapel dedicated to Mary, mother of Jesus. Here I impress Ben with my recitation of 'The Lord's Prayer', in unison with Don Bruno (the things we don't know about our mothers). Don Bruno blesses our journey ahead and then invites us to reflect upon an important turning point in Jesus's life. I'm startled when he asks which moment we have chosen, because I am thinking of the other Mary, Jesus's wife.

'Mary,' I say, content to let him suppose I am speaking of the mother and touched when he honours me as a mother walking with her son.

Don Bruno leads us out of the small chapel, describing in holy litany the stories in the walls along the way. We follow in single file to the Vatican bookshop, where Don Bruno traverses a wall of Bibles before selecting a fat blue one, which he presents to Ben. He blesses us with the touch of St Peter and farewells us with the smile of the gentle. Ben grins as we tumble into the sunlight. He had wanted to read a Bible along the road from Canterbury to Rome and hadn't made the effort to find one. Now one has found him.

'And now all I need,' he says, 'is a Koran to read on the way to Jerusalem.'

Like all good pilgrims, we decide we may as well visit Michelangelo's famous *Cappella Sistina*, the Sistine Chapel, while we're here at the Vatican. *Michelangelo, Sistine Chapel, Vatican City.* They're all just words to me, daughter of a new world and incorrigible product of a modern, secular education system. We wander past the local *polizia* gang lurking in the shadows of the concourse, a dozen police officers in uniform hanging over the open doors of their cars, chatting on mobile phones, cigarettes dangling from the corners of their mouths. Then up a couple of stairs, through a gap in the circular sweep of pillars and onto the cobbled stones of the concourse that sweeps the front steps of the Vatican. It is as if we stand ankle deep on the edge of a great pond teeming with the amoebic life of all the world.

I wish again, for the ten thousandth time in my life, that I was Marco Polo: the miracle of reaching distant lands that not only you have never been to, not only you have never heard of, but that you have never, ever seen, not even in a picture; the marvel of standing in the hub of far-flung crossroads, beacons for either commercial or spiritual compulsions, filled with the robes and headdresses and beards and shoes and songs and prayers and voices of not only different, but *unimagined* times and places ... well, the Vatican concourse wasn't quite like that. Nonetheless, the parade of monks and nuns enswathed in long, flowing fancy-dress was a treat. I had no idea we still dressed like this! Myriad combinations of rippling blacks, whites, greys and blues, lined with crimsons and gold, frame faces all the colours and shapes of the world, to-ing and fro-ing across the concourse with purpose and importance. Every nation has its Friar Tuck.

For two hours and a good half kilometre we queue to glimpse the *Cappella Sistina*, snaking around the old stone walls of the Vatican in the heat of the day, filming the idling good-natured crowd and having fun with making fools of ourselves as we practise speaking to the cameras. It is so good to be travelling in the company of laughter.

Inside the doors, the queue only thickens. Shuffling through the corridors leading to the great chapel is a pilgrimage in itself, past walls creased with gigantic tapestries and frilled with chalky-white statues, an endless artistic celebration of the masculine; through the castle grounds of Narnia's Ice Queen ... oops ... I mean the impressive papal collection of stone people and animals. I wonder when and under whose instructions small cement leaves were placed over certain parts of the male anatomy. (Surely the Ice Queen wouldn't have bothered.) We cross floors lined with mosaic centaurs and circular dioramas containing barnyards of mythical marble creatures. Funny, the men in the paintings high on the walls don't wear leaves. Oh, of course! They're not at eye level.

Philistines that we are (there's another of those words – I look around me: *who are the Philistines?*), the thrill of being in such a passionate and manly parade wears off. Soon we are bored and in danger of missing the celebrated *cappella* altogether.

Now why did I think it was a thousand feet high and the really famous bit was an angel? Ben has me on film twirling a tiny circle inside the chapel scoffing under my breath with antipodean insolence: *'Is that it?'* The downside of ignorance. The upside is that cities like Rome hold wonderful surprises, such as the colour of the sky above the Trevi Fountain at night – behold the blue of Michelangelo's ceiling!

If we'd walked straight in off the street to see the Sistine Chapel we might have been blown away. By the time we get there all we want to do is go and eat.

We grab cheese and salami rolls and coffees, my salute to the road ahead: I will learn to eat what I am given. I am tired of my head-trips about food, or anything else for that matter, of being so certain about what I do and do not do. The great gift of pilgrimage, and the vexation, is that you get to shake hands with your own myths: the ideas, concepts and musts that shape and limit our lives. I have been telling myself since I was twenty-nine years old that I don't drink coffee because I won't sleep for days. It was true then – what if it's not true now? As for meat, becoming vegetarian was not an ideological exercise for me. While others of my generation struggled with their commitment to a gentler new world I had no trouble at all – I never liked meat. I overheard the word 'vegetarian' when I was eighteen years old, sheltering from a tropical storm beneath an awning on the streets of Darwin, and it was a hallelujah moment for me. I had the reason that had eluded me all my life for not eating what was on my plate: *'I am a vegetarian.'*

Give or take the occasional fish, I haven't eaten meat in the thirty years since. And having walked the road to Santiago on a near starvation diet I like to think I'm cured of holding fast to proclivities. Preserved meats are the easiest place for me to start, probably because if I close my eyes they don't taste like meat. We eat on the stone steps with the pigeons in the shade of the tall white pillars, watching the milling Vatican crowds. I throw away only half the meat, which Ben delightedly scoops from the paper wrapper and crams into his own sandwich. As I look around it occurs to me that we are all guests of each other in this world, everyone visiting everybody else.

By midafternoon we are sitting on a stone seat in the heart of ancient Rome, in the company of the old and the new, the crumbling and restored. It seems wherever we go in Rome we queue for two hours to get fifteen minutes worth of wonder. At least that's the reality for those of us with two days to see the city and a terminal case of cultural illiteracy. The Colosseum, gap-toothed and hungry for time, is no exception. Tourists crawl all over the broken grey amphitheatre, ears to the stone for the battle cries of the gladiators, the screams of the martyrs, the cheers of spectators excited and repulsed – the upper classes and the hoi polloi whose sandalled feet climbed these steps and whose linen-draped arses sat on these seats.

Old stories settle in my bones. *They really did throw Christians to the lions.* And new stories. *Thousands of wild animals, 9,000 if you're one for numbers, all the beasts of Africa if you're one for details, lambs to the slaughter, or, to be precise, elephants, rhinoceroses and giraffes, sacrificed for the glory of Caput Mundi, the capital of the world.* And that was just at the opening.

I try to imagine how they got them to Rome for such theatre, startling and cruel and even funny in a prodigiously ridiculous way – unless of course you happened to be the entertainment. The world turns. *How the world turns.* The Christians have claimed the Colosseum as a sacred site, venerating the blood of their own spilled on the sand. More interesting to me, the iconic relic is today a rallying cry for the international campaign against the death penalty. Whenever anyone anywhere in the world gets their death sentence commuted, the night lights at the Colosseum change from white to gold.

Two thousand years of the best and the worst of us. Not either/or, but all at once.

We wander on, down the steps, across the road and through a relatively humble archway. Living, breathing antiquity, colonised by cats. We sit awhile in the shade beneath a gnarly old tree. A black kitten stalks insects between blades of grass on a bright green knoll. The sun blares through the columns of the ancient city, daring us to naysay the great ones who built the old walls. We are surrounded by people on pilgrimage to the monuments of their ancestors, pillars and arches and towering facades standing tall and true, words and images carved into stone. I wonder if they are *graven*? They are Roman.

Of course they are. I am breathless. I didn't know places like this existed. I wonder, daughter of a new world, who among us has not descended from the Roman Empire? I wonder, if I sit here long enough, will I hear the whispers of the ancient ones? I lament that I do not have days and days to lie on the earth at the feet of the great columns. Days and days to be still. And listen.

It is past midnight by the time we get home. We've been out doing what the Romans do best at such hours – drinking wine and eating pizza. And now we prepare to walk into the dawn for the next one hundred days. I am being poetic. We have no idea how long the walk to Istanbul will take. I would like to sleep but I am wide-eyed and keen with the morning's coffee. Ben dives into his sleeping bag. I swear my son can sleep anywhere, anytime. It's been that way since he was a child. In his teens, his sleeping bag tendered the kind of companionship others might expect from a faithful dog. He took it everywhere. We act normal, as if tomorrow will be like any other day, wide open grins and bursts of uproarious laughter giving the game away. September 22. Vernal equinox. A Saturday unlike any other. I bed down and do my best to settle.

I think of the Vatican, just down the road, imposing and cold by day, a stunningly majestic apparition bobbing about in the sky by night. This particular night it is backlit by the silver-gold half moon. If you're going to proclaim yourself God's spokesman for all time, then by night it's a hard act to follow. I can only imagine what the medieval ones might have given for that lighting. I edge into restless sleep to the tune of a t-shirt I saw this afternoon outside the Sistine Chapel. It is the perfect pilgrim shirt. In three words it sums up the road ahead:

Free and Dirty.

I wake in the pre-dawn light and listen to the waking city. Even though we plan to leave early, Ben is holding tight to sleep and I am content to have the stillness of morning to myself. I call to presence the two human beings who are, to me at this time, angels here on Earth. They are my Guiding Light and my Steadying Hand.

It is the Steadying Hand who gave me the seeds of the creed I wrote for the road, so named for its salutation to the time we spent together, The Eugenia Street Prayer:

> *I respect myself,*
> *I honour my creativity;*
> *I keep my puppy on a lead,*
> *I see the miracle in others.*

There is nothing else I need to know and the third line, which I presume pertains to the ego, always makes me laugh. The Steadying Hand is the counsellor from whom my husband and I sought assistance when we lived at Wilsons Creek, the therapist my husband wished to befriend and whom I was happy to fence off at professional distance. I don't need his friendship. I need what he represents, and that is the sparkle-and-shine intelligence of a steadying hand when all of who I am and all of what I know abandons me blind and blameless to the unknowable edge of my own chosen, and momentarily limited, consciousness. Just before I left Australia I dreamed of him, lying along a dead log that was damming a wide brown river. The log was his love and I felt sad that he was giving his love to a dead place. I would have wanted more for him. This is the man to whom we entrusted our marriage and, ignoring that, saved my sanity. It was he who taught me about the wave of inertia when I was at the peak of my distress about certain qualities I shared with my husband, personal traits I thought I'd left behind me on the mountain that seemed to pop up again and again, Chucky-like, in my marriage:

'How did this happen?' I sobbed one day, as I sat on the couch in the little office in his garden.

'I wanted a man who would show me what I don't know, who would be all that I needed myself to be, who would show me the way.'

'The wave of inertia,' he said, tapping the tissue box on the small coffee table beside us, so it slid along the polished wood towards me.

'The point at which it leaves my hand and keeps travelling by itself, that's the wave of inertia,' he explained.

'How do I stop it?' I asked through my tears.

'You can't,' he said. *'It has to peter out.'*

'What do I do?' I asked.

'You wait. You make no decisions until it runs its course.'

'How do I make sure I don't set new waves in motion? More than that – how do I set in motion waves of what I do want?'

'You don't,' he said quietly, *'because that is magic and magic stretches space and time and this will only extend the distance between you and the one calling you home.'*

I blinked. *Me and the one calling me home.* In my way, I had practised magic all my life. Creating. Manifesting. Controlling. In that one moment my tears dried up and my emotional life stabilised. The Steadying Hand had opened a doorway I hadn't even *suspected* existed. The appearance of the wave of inertia gave merit and motion to ill-considered 'needs' I'd put into play a long time ago.

In the days and weeks that followed, I began working on shortening the distance between me and the end of time, calling in all of my wishes and wants and intents, reining in to the present as much of myself as I could find. Senses tuned, I saw through this lens that everything I desire is right here, inside me. From this place I am empowered to rewrite the past and I have no need for a future. For perhaps the first time in my life I was really listening. I was receiving. At the end of a tiresome and terrible tether, I was allowing myself to be shown the way. The way home. And so I became the light calling me home. Past, present, future – all here, now. And I saw, eyes-wide-open, how from this place it is possible to recreate the past and in so doing rewrite the future. And this is how I understood the cataclysmic power of stories.

My Guiding Light has a name. She is Illumina. She is the one with whom I sat on Monday nights, before she attracted a crowd; the one who taught me to connect to the Great Central Sun and Moon, out there in the indescribable world of light and imagination; the gentle one who 'read my energy body' and gave me insight into the timeless war between the masculine and the feminine *within*, and its this-worldly mirror, the incomprehensible theatre of marriage and relationship. Hers is the realm of the heart and her message, only love. Illumina works with women and she works with men. Once I heard a woman ask her what it was like to work with the men. She replied: 'They're just like us.' *Fancy that, just like us.*

I stretch into the morning, feeling into my body. My mind and belly are a little woozy from the wine we drank at midnight. I do a body rollcall. Feet sweet. Shoulders relaxed. Heart raring to go! I make ready to walk into a hundred sunrises. We haven't been able to find a map to the scale we need, but we know we're heading to Pescara, due east on Italy's Adriatic seaboard, and from there we will catch a ferry to Split, on Croatia's central coast. East to Pescara. East to Istanbul! *East to Byzantium.* East to the East. Besides, we looked it up online and have a vague idea of how to get out of Rome. Memories of Don Bruno's blessing tingle the top of my head and trickle through my body. I holler into the morning: 'Yeeeeeeehaaaaaaa!'

'Hey Ben,' I say, lest he missed the wake-up call. 'Let's go!'

We rise. We pack. We load up and we take a good long look at each other and smile. Let the journey begin, we seem to say. Let the journey begin. We roll down the hill to God's Castle where, still running high on yesterday's brew, my biggest decision is whether or not to have another coffee. With a good 2,000 kilometres to walk on four hours sleep, naturally I lean towards the affirmative. We buy cheese and salami rolls at the deli across the road and return to the Vatican concourse, propping ourselves up against a small fountain. We sit on the cobblestones, unfurl the new backgammon board between us, and eat as we roll the dice for the inaugural backgammon challenge. We film ourselves against the backdrop of the papal palace, speaking our dream-prayers for the road to the camera. For Ben, it is a journey continued, the minor matter of 5,000 kilometres between him and Jerusalem. For me, it is a new chapter in my life begun, the walk of a thousand incarnations, the minor matter of a showdown with myself that I hope will clear the path for the rest of my life.

Let the pilgrimage begin!

With Ben high on the first backgammon victory, his by a throw of the dice, we heft our heavy packs onto our backs, raise our eyes to the light of our first sunrise (romantically speaking, because in truth the morning is long gone) and turn our backs on the Vatican. Walking east with the high sun as our guide, we lumber along the *Via della Conciliazione*, a wide and busy avenue running down to the river, the *Fiume Tevere*. Much later I learn it is the Tiber River. *Imagine that, the Tiber River.*

Riverside, we circle the towering *Castel Sant'Angelo* with the delight of children of a new world discovering the ruins of an old one – and much later learn it is the tomb of the Roman emperor Hadrian, built in 138. Hadrian! 138 AD! I glance around for his wall.

We cross the river on the now-pedestrian *Ponte Sant'Angelo*, beneath statues of angelic saints that for nigh on two millennia have welcomed pilgrims into Rome. We wander along the Tiber, buildings and bridges keeping time, hearts alive to sumptuous architecture and illustrious monuments and the epic faultlines of ages past. We count seven bridges and arbitrarily turn right. The presence of the ancient ones gives way to the architectural priorities of the city's 21st-century inhabitants: modern streets peppered with old, very sensible and oddly beautiful water fountains, repose for travellers long gone – the crusaders, merchants and pilgrims who must once have made common procession to and from the heartbeat of the empire, rather than two lone pilgrims, lost and abandoned by their native tongue, out of step with their time and generation.

We wander around the backstreets of suburban Rome, now and then asking for directions to Tivoli, the first major town on the road to Pescara and the most straightforward road to Istanbul. Over and over again people point us in the opposite direction, to the bus *stazione*. My communication skills are reduced to a word and three gestures: 'Tivoli?' followed by a shrug, raised eyebrows and a swivelling finger pointing in several directions at once. Ben, for whom pidgin English is lingua franca, does not ask directions. At first I think this is one of those frustrating manly things. I am soon to learn it is sound philosophy, tried and true. It is easier to wander about lost for a couple of hours than to scurry back and forwards chasing dud leads from people who have: a) no idea what you are saying, and b) no comprehension of what you are doing.

Eventually we collapse into the corner of a dark, narrow bar for coffee and delicious toasted ham and cheese sandwiches. To our kiss-kiss-kiss-his-feet delight the barman speaks English. He tells us we need Tiburtina Road, which actually is not news to us. Having failed to write it down when we looked it up online, we'd just forgotten its name. The news that we are entirely on the wrong side of town causes us to laugh so hard we can barely hold our seats. As the tears roll down our faces, we roll out the backgammon. When Ben was at high school, the backgammon board sat perennially on the corner of the kitchen table. Either one of us would signal the first challenge of the day with the rattle of the dice on the wooden board. Summoned to the game, we'd drop whatever we were doing and take our seats at the table. It took him years to beat me and, even now, I hold to the illusion his victories are rare. It drives him crazy, my refusal to accept he is the superior player. So, sanctimoniously, I am happy to hand him the second challenge of the walk.

Refreshed and happy, we load up again and head for Tiburtina Road. Despite events of the past two hours, Ben's pilgrim's nose is finely tuned. He leads us up over a small, incredibly steep hill. By way of distraction from the heat in my feet and the weight on my back, I tell myself it is one of the seven famous hills of Rome. We stagger past the homes of the city's modern day middle classes, along weathered stone avenues lined with twisted trees, when Ben spies a Mac shop and is inspired to drop off his computer for disk repairs. He says he'll catch the train back in a few days time to pick it up. Even though I think he's being ambitious, I hold my tongue and wait on the footpath, literally, sprawled against my pack outside the chemist shop on the busy street, giving my feet a breather while I stare into the bubbling water of a fancy fountain splotched with black and streaked with slime in the middle of the bustling intersection.

Spirits bright, we roll on, steady now in our rhythm, on and onto Tiburtina Road. The clean streets of affluence give way to the heat and fumes of trains and traffic and lots and lots of rubbish. By midafternoon, we are pilgrim-small beneath the giant cement free-ways funnelling traffic in and out of the great city. It is one thing to imagine walking from Rome to Istanbul, the romance of the ages beneath our feet. It is another altogether to stand on the edge of those grey cement overpasses and their exit ramps, navigating safe passage through a hustling maze of speedways. I cannot believe I am attempting this. I feel stupid and dangerous. Ben, with 2,000 pilgrim kilometres under his boots, simply walks on. I take a deep breath, seeking clarity rather than confusion, and follow. The veils of confusion lift and I see the way forward.

Eventually, we stop for a rest in the dusty shade of an island beneath one of the overpasses. Ben sprawls out flat on his back with his feet up on his pack. I take off my shoes and socks, glad for the breeze from the whoosh of traffic either side of us. A crowded bus goes by. The look on the face of a young man in a window seat when he sees Ben is priceless. I wince as his neck swivels so fast it seems to snap. Then he sees me. And we laugh. We laugh out loud at the incongruity of the moment. And we laugh with delight. Love in the eyes of a stranger.

It is nigh on dinnertime, Australian, not Roman, when I declare that we have done enough for one day. I am tired, but not exhausted. My feet are in good shape and my shoulders have coped admirably. Ben is happy to call it a day and we agree to stop at the first hotel we find. And there it is, about a kilometre down the road, right where the freeway levels out on the edge of Tiburtina. *Fancy that, Tiburtina Road goes to Tiburtina.* We reach the hotel. We climb the stairs. The innkeeper takes one look at us and pronounces his hotel 'full', despite the jangling of a hundred room keys behind him. It takes a minute for me to digest this, as I was certain we were home. *Home!* We leave, spirits undampened, thinking Motel Industrial is a strange name for a hotel anyway.

Down the road, on the other side of the highway, is another hotel. This one's friendly – but also full. We find it hard to believe. Why would anyone want a hotel out here?

We down packs at the café next door and Ben buys his first beer for the road. I'm content with the bowl of pistachios we order in lieu of anything else in the place resembling food. Taped to the glass door of the café is a small sign advertising a bed and breakfast with sweet white and yellow rooms, beckoning us to *come, come, come*. The café is empty but for a young man with shiny long black hair and three mobile phones. He is perched on a stool feeding a poker machine in the far corner of the room. He has enough English to tell us the B&B is in the back streets, about 500 metres back the way we came.

Now, Lesson 1 of the road to Santiago was *Keep Moving Forward*. As is the way with us humans, lessons have a habit of becoming rules and so, rather than turn around and walk back aways, we happily agree to keep moving forward ... and spend the next two hours staggering through an industrial corridor that looks like any other industrial wasteland in any other city in the world on a Saturday evening – car yards, paint warehouses, abandoned buildings, lots of wire fencing, weeds with pretty flowers. *Thank God for weeds with pretty flowers!* Nowhere to pitch a tent. Nowhere to grab a bite. Nowhere.

Trailing along after Ben, I wonder about Lesson 1 of the road and recall how cheerfully that little B&B had called to me from the glass door of the café – *come, come, come* – and how I thought I knew better. I overrode instinct because I had *expectations*. I *expected* to find another hotel just up the road, for example. Expectations based on nothing more substantial than 'I want'. Indeed, these past couple of hours I had expected a lot of things that were not mine to expect. I had expected food in the café. I had expected a simple road out of Rome, even if it was busy. I had expected cafés in the industrial area. I had expected bloody hotels!

Just as I make peace with my error of judgement, a small church comes into view. Hallelujah! A church! Church means church steps and, in the absence of anything else resembling a bed, they'll do me and my screaming shoulders and aching feet just fine. Ben thinks I'm joking. Not about sleeping on church steps, but about sleeping on *those* church steps. I fail to notice that the steps are six inches wide, sloping and crumbling. Besides, there is an eight-foot wire fence around them. All I see is a bed.

And then hallelujah again. A (relatively) modern church spire rising from the shadows of tall green trees signals hope. We stumble across the road and around the corner, through the gates and up the stone path. Ben knocks at the door at the side of the church, seeking the assistance of the good Father. I just want to hide in the shed out the back and wait until he locks us in. The good Father does not come to the door. He bellows at us to come back after Mass. I notice a small bar adjoining the churchyard. It has white plastic chairs that look to me like feather beds. I hobble over, peel off my pack and lay it on one chair, gingerly lowering myself into another. I ignore the barman. There is nothing he can do for me and I am not remotely interested in anything he has to say that might contain such words as 'can't' or 'closing'. The church bells ring for Mass and the old ones appear from nowhere, shuffling up the path to the church. I take off my shoes and lay weary feet to rest on a third chair, wincing and stretching my neck, which is frozen from the weight of the pack, staring semiconscious at the clear blue sky above. Moans and groans keep the barman at a distance while I scrutinise the day's lessons: Lesson 1 on the road to Santiago – *Keep Moving Forward*; Lesson 1 on the road to Istanbul – *Never Make Rules*.

I hatch my plan. I will hide out at the back of the church and wait till after Mass, when we will emerge from the darkness to pitch our tents in the church grounds. Ben rocks up with a determined smile, perhaps because he knows I am serious about hiding in the church grounds. The barman must have read my mind, because he tells Ben about a motel up the road. It seems in our delirium we walked right past it. Ben goes to check it out while on behalf of my piercingly painful shoulders and agonisingly world-weary feet, I make a vow: I dedicate my walk to harmonising effort and ease.

My body slowly returns to life. I wiggle my toes. I hear the birds. I sit up straight in my chair. I think of the laughter I shared with strangers during the day. The man on the bus. The barber outside his shop who took one look at me and then the pack and, unlike just about everyone else in Christendom, knew exactly what we were doing. He looked into my eyes and we laughed. We laughed and laughed with the hilarity of foolishness shared and witnessed. I think of the many hostile looks we received throughout the day from those for whom we are nothing more than untrustworthy strangers. I think of Ben's stated purpose for his journey: to make a documentary that illustrates no matter where he goes, anywhere in the world, regardless of religion or politics or culture, he will be met with love and kindness. On a white chair in a café beside a church on the outskirts of Rome, at the end of day one of the walk of a thousand incarnations, I think, *Yes, he's right, we will be met by love and kindness everywhere we go – just not by everyone*. I reckon though, with a little bit of effort and a lot of love in my own heart, the hostile ones will be up for a smile.

Mirror mirror on the wall …

Ben returns with a skip in his step, inordinately pleased with himself because the motel is full but they found a cupboard for us to sleep in anyway. Loathsomely, I return my darling feet to their shoes and the pack to my shoulders. We bid the barman farewell, stagger around the corner and collapse onto narrow beds in our little room. We stink! And there is no hot water. All I want is a bucket of hot water to soak my feet. We opt for dinner in lieu of showers, surprised to find ourselves eating fabulous plates of pasta and salad right across the road from the old church steps that, in different times, might indeed have been our bed for the night. And with no thought at all for tomorrow, we lay our weary bodies down to rest. Free and dirty.

We wake late in our fabulously overpriced little hotel with its deliciously affordable pasta. *Funny how last night I didn't give expense a thought.* I wake with a sore hip, stiff legs and burning shoulders. And it's okay. I'm okay. Thanks to yesterday's excelsior effort we are only fifteen kilometres from Tivoli and I promise my feet that will be far enough for me today. Ben stirs and rolls over. I tell him I need better socks. We laugh so hard our bellies ache with the notion that all my pilgrimage woes will be fixed *if only I had better socks*. And we laugh about last night's agony, delicately stretching, testing our feet and bones and muscles for signs of life.

By midmorning, which in Italy is the equivalent of Aussie lunchtime, we are on the road, fuelled by typical *Italiani* breakfasts of coffee and pastries. We walk along busy, busy roads in the sunshine, all day. Tivoli, today's Nirvana, glares at us from high atop a distant mountain, all day – although for most of the day, thanks to ageing eyesight, I think the township is just an interesting rock formation. We walk with our cameras at the ready, in my case holding it by the stick of its perpetually affixed monopod. I'm surprised to find that walking along the roadside isn't entirely unpleasurable, despite the cars and trucks and buses barrelling towards us with the urgency of Time and Destination. It's fascinating, watching all these people, all of us including us, thinking we're going somewhere.

It takes surprisingly little time for the leg muscles to warm up. Senses long dormant kick to life and I settle into the rhythm of the road. In no time at all pain gives way to a warm breeze on my skin and thoughts give way to a clear blue sky. For every thousand cars someone toots us; for every two hundred cyclists we get a wave; for every fifty shopkeepers there's a smile and sometimes even a hearty laugh for a pair of crazy pilgrims, packs like tortoiseshells on their backs causing them to lean forward into their day, walking along the edge of a road that hasn't seen a pedestrian since weeds and rubbish choked the crops from the roadside.

We take our first break in the middle of a busy traffic island, seeking shade beneath a bulbous palm. I peel the pack from my back, almost welcoming the familiar stab of dagger-sharp pain between my shoulder blades, grateful for its ecstatic release. Life very quickly has been reduced to the simple things: food, bed, shade, smiles, feet. I laugh out loud at the three words that come to mind: painful, delirious, entertaining. This is the pilgrim's journey and it is madness, pure and simple. We lie flat on our backs on the grass, heads resting on packs. We film each other in this incongruous place, resting on a traffic island in the middle of a major traffic artery on the fringe of one of the world's great cities.

We walk on. And on. Into the ceaseless traffic. We walk all day beneath a pounding sun and the sweat pours off. I'm not sure if it's the smog or the quality of the atmosphere, but if this was an Australian sun we'd have been fried and smouldering remains of our former selves, small mounds of cinders and soot to be obliterated by the next downpour.

Shade is tantalisingly close, just on the other side of the road, but the only thing worse than having to walk in the sun is having the traffic come at us from behind. Now and then, I give my mind a break from the steady stream of metal bearing down on my flesh and step over the steel traffic barrier, trading the bitumen for a bumpy narrow strip of sodden weeds and rubbish, rolling the seeds of the wild fennel between my fingers as I walk.

By late afternoon Tivoli declares her hand as the interesting rock formation – and reality dawns that we will be climbing that sheer hill that has not budged from our horizon, neither closer nor further, all day. We stop for pizza. It is Sunday. We learn that Italy is closed on Sundays. Except, on this little strip, for the local pizza bar. We do our pilgrim thing. Find a table. Down packs. Down cameras.

Order food. Collapse on chairs. Take off our shoes. Act normal. Eat. Drink. Play backgammon. Refreshed, we hit the road, soon parting company with the traffic to take the vertical narrow winding trail straight up the mountain. There are still cars, but they are in single file and there are breaks in the flow. Now and then, the distance between me and the cars on the bends drives me over the guardrail to shortcut through the olive groves. The heat is relentless. A siren wails and wails from the top of the hill and I fantasise that it is coming for us. About a kilometre from town I have had enough. I am so hot I am cooking. I tell Ben I'm not here to kill myself. I announce that I am hitchhiking the rest of the way. There is a driveway on the next bend in the mountain road. He sits on his pack in the shade of an old fig tree, rotting fruit at his feet, grinning from ear to ear as he watches his mother stick out her thumb. He starts to cackle.

'How long since you've hitched?' he asks.

I start to laugh too. It is too long. High school long. Five minutes and no takers and I've cooled down enough to make the final run to the top.

From the edge of Tivoli the whole world is at our feet. Literally. This is a town so high you could fall off. By the time we reach the town plaza, we realise we have walked in the back way. And what a surprise is here to greet us! Tivoli is humming with Italians streaming through narrow medieval streets lined with performers and a young man whose three big dogs sit mournfully in the shade, noses to the begging bowl. The crackle of microphones intermittently splits the evening, a sound check from behind the wall of a fantastic castle promising live entertainment later in the night.

We find a room across the road. A great room. A roomy room. A room with soap to do some washing. A room with hot water and windows that open onto the plaza. *I am in Italy!* We wander through the streets, filming crowds and fountains and jugglers and clowns. And we reward ourselves with a fabulous meal, 21st-century vegetarian cuisine in a medieval restaurant. We order wine and toast day two of the walk of a thousand incarnations. We close the evening sitting peacefully in the shadows of the great grey castle walls, on the cold and crumbling stable ruins, listening to music by the light of the near-full moon.

We wake early in our wonderful room below the castle to excessive traffic and people noises. How on earth, we wonder, does such a tiny town high on a hill so far from the *autostrada* get so loud and so busy so early in the morning? Ben, having walked from Italy's north into Rome, is especially puzzled.

'Italians don't get up this early,' he says. 'And if they do, they go to the bars for their coffee.'

In which case Tivoli is frenetically un-Italian.

A cool breeze blows through the shutters, drying the washing, and we're pleased to meet a cloudy day. I lie in bed and do a rollcall: big blister under the ball of one foot (thank God for the Compeed) and a very sore little toe (nothing a bandaid won't fix). My legs aren't quite as sore and my shoulders not as stiff. In two days I'm already feeling a lot stronger and I'm sitting up a lot straighter.

We have breakfast on the other side of the castle, coffee and pastries. Ben, whose Italian is pretty good for a rambling stranger, asks the innkeeper how to say 'breakfast' in Italian.

'Cappuccino,' he says.

We all laugh. I cannot keep my eyes from the castle walls. I wonder how the medieval ones ever had time to get a castle built before an invading army came to snatch it away. And I wonder when and why and how the castle passed from being pivotal to village life to being 'the past'. The axis of time. Yesterday. Today. Yesterday. Today. Where is the tipping point?

We are surprised how big Tivoli is on the other side of the castle. We load up with cheese, bread and chocolate for the road and by midafternoon, having taken advantage of the offerings of a good-sized town, including finding a decent map of the mountains, we are on the road. We forget to look at the map and take the long way out of Tivoli. Eventually, fancy stone villas and city walls give way to trees and fields and *supermercatos* in the middle of nowhere, relatively speaking that is. 'Nowhere' in Europe is a very different land to 'nowhere' in Australia.

As we walk along the back roads I ponder the wisdom of choosing country roads over the *autostrada*. At least on the *autostrada* there would be room for us. On this particular back road, our path is a narrow strip of bitumen between the white-painted line on the edge of the road and a cement retaining wall dripping with blackberry snags. By 'narrow strip' I mean anywhere between six and eighteen inches. Where new bitumen has been laid our path widens to three or four feet. Ironically, this is not good news: cars cut corners on the wider sections. Our little path is like a parallel zone, as if we've wandered into an Otherworld, unseen and unacknowledged by those loud metal machines bearing down upon us. We stop by the roadside amid the brambles and rubbish for a rest. My shoulders scream and my feet ache.

'Does it get any better?' I ask Ben.

'I assure you,' he says, 'it gets better. It doesn't stop hurting, but it gets better.'

We crack up laughing. We share chocolate. I am loving being on the road again. I wonder what it is about choosing such agony that releases the spirit. I lie back on my pack with my face to the sky. Like turning a dial, I tune in and the white noise of pain clears. Life is crystal clear and broadcasting all around me: the tiny black berries high on the tree above, the soft whistles of the songbirds, the slow yellow of the turning leaves. Moving on is a lot like getting out of the water when you're surfing – there's no right time to do it. We load up. We walk on.

Ben's rhythm puts him a couple of hundred metres ahead. I enjoy the solitude; the presence of the wild fennel, yarrow, pennyroyal and mint sprouting along the roadside is like keeping company with old friends.

We make it to San Cosimato and neither of us is willing to scale the steep steps straight up the hill into the town proper to scout for a bed and food. We walk on. We take a break for bread and cheese and chocolate among the shattered glass and graffitied walls of a roadside bus shelter. Night is falling. We walk on, winding around the narrow road overlooking a small river below.

We come to a rather closed looking restaurant. We ask for pasta and happily they feed us. We ask for a hotel. They shake their heads. We ask for a camping ground. They shrug. We ask for *'tente'*. More shrugs. Our fingers make the shapes of church steeples. *'Tente,'* we say. They shrug again. Delirium takes a sharp, silent left-hand turn. I don't know what our faces look like but they're enough for the owners to take pity on the pilgrims and offer us their verandah for the night, tiled and clean.

We pitch our tents in the dark beneath the full-bellied moon. Both of us have new tents. Neither of us has put them up before. We have no idea how they work and neither tent stands without ropes. A half hour of madness ensues, until we each tie one end of our tent to the legs of a wrought iron table and on the other end I post my sentinels for the night, a pot of rosemary and a money plant. We return to the restaurant, which is around the corner of the same verandah, and order wine. I write while Ben reads Don Bruno's bible. We roll out the backgammon. Ben asks how I feel.

'Very tired. Very sore. Better than yesterday,' I say.

Pilgrim humour being what it is we roll around laughing.

'That about sums up every day,' says Ben.

The family who owns the restaurant gathers for photographs with us. They are as delirious about our presence on their verandah as we are. We film them. Our common language is the language of joy. I give the mother the only prize I have, a small handful of Baci chocolates. We hold hands as she receives them.

It's not long before I leave Ben to his carafe of wine and the company of two young women who have rolled in with the night. I lie down in my tent. The body remembers. I have walked the road to Santiago de Compostela and there is nothing novel about this pilgrimage as it lives in my body. What is novel is a land of no hotels or rooms or camping grounds; just the earthen-tiled verandah of strangers kind enough to meet the needs of those they don't understand, linguistically or otherwise. I close my eyes. *Tired. Sore. Better than yesterday.*

We wake before the songbirds and pack our tents in the new light of dawn. Given the cold, hard tiles and the dogs baying all night beneath the big moon, I am surprised I slept at all. Further still, I am surprised to find it is easier to get going this morning than previous mornings, when I've felt as stiff as a bandy-legged cement gnome getting out of bed.

We are on the road well before sunrise, reflectors strapped to our arms and headlamps flashing, mixing it with the workday commuters. We reckon we can make Arsoli by lunchtime.

I identify four kinds of people on the road: those who don't see us; those who do and wish they hadn't; those who see us with the air of the curious, the confused or the hostile; and those who recognise us. The latter toot. They wave. They laugh and smile. A tractor driver takes his hands off the wheel and claps with glee. Fellow pilgrims sharing the journey, each in their own way.

The first rays of sunshine touch the mountains. It is a glorious morning and a beautiful time to be on the road. The sun flashes silver on the silver birch. Roosters crow from distant hilltops. We turn a corner and morning streams up the valley.

The traffic is ceaseless. It's an odd situation for the quick-reflexed like myself. Laden with seventeen kilograms, I haven't a hope in heaven of getting out of the way of anything quickly. I am, therefore, learning the art of thoughtful response to life and (imminent) death. I walk out on the road where they can see me, for example. In this way, I'm in a position to take a slow step sideways while the wheeled ones make an effort to drive around me. Trucks, however, get a different thoughtful response altogether. In their case I press as closely as possible to the retaining wall and pray they appreciate my thoughtfulness. Right-hand curves and left-hand curves are a toss-up. Right-hand curves run the risk of cars taking them too fast and slamming into me and the wall. Left-hand curves carry the novelty of making me invisible right up until the split second before they see me. Ben, meanwhile, with several thousand pilgrim miles up his sleeve, walks on with pilgrim's purpose. They see him, he sees them. Each to their own path. Life on the road. Literally.

Every now and then there is a break in the traffic and the stillness of the mountains is breathtaking. I look up into the wooded forests on the distant hillsides and if there's not boar in them now, there surely was once. A lifetime ago, for three years, I was a hunter in the wild places of New Zealand. I raise my eyes to the clear-morning mountain light and my heart quickens, remembering what it was to follow the tracks of the wild boar through the beauty of the forest underbelly.

Soon we begin to climb again. Uh-oh. Straight up. Steep. Hot. Exhausting. No breakfast. The few bites of last night's leftover pizza don't count. Ben makes Arsoli jokes, about the shapes of their pasta and the joys of eating *Arsoli marinara*. I'm too stuffed to laugh.

It is too early in the pilgrimage for me to detach sheer physical agony from the mental torture of resistance. I stagger into Arsoli, emotional anguish fusing with physical distress. Arsoli is another of those towns it would be easy to fall off. I wouldn't want to raise a baby up here.

We reach the top and collapse in the corner of another bar. This one doesn't sell toasted ham and cheese sandwiches. It sells pastries. And Powerade, which is fast becoming my drink of choice as I rapidly lose interest in pasta, pizza and pastries.

We retire to the small square overlooking forever. I take off my shoes to inspect my feet. Fortunately for me, the blister on my little toe bursts as I take off its bandaid, sparing me the decision about whether or not to pop it. My little toe is so sore, so blistered, so agonisingly red raw. Sadness descends like sudden fog and my spirits tumble off the heights of Arsoli. Unlike Ben, I am not committed to walking all the way. I'm here for the ride, to share this leg of his journey. I'm happy to partake of some of the agony and lots of the fun. I'm not here to torture myself. I am also sick to bloody death of pasta, pizza and pastries. I decide to take the train to Avezzano and meet Ben there tomorrow. Or the day after.

We climb out of town, surprised to discover Arsoli is on the side of a hill, not the top, and part company at the train station. It isn't easy, because this next leg of the walk will take Ben through deserted forest roads. No traffic. Pilgrim heaven on Earth.

I sit in the deserted railway station feeling somewhat like the station itself – not quite abandoned. Loneliness pulls into the station. It's been a wonderful week. London. Rome. Pilgrimage begun. A cat all the shades of yellow-beige sits with me, looking into my eyes. I am grateful for the company. I don't want to be where I am. I don't want to feel what I feel. I am overwhelmed with longing for 'other' (anywhere but here) and 'the other' (someone to save me from myself). My husband texts me with the news that he has found an MSG-free restaurant in Bangkok. Tears roll slowly down my cheeks. I wonder how it is I so consistently end up alone.

I'm sorry not to be walking on. I have done the hardest thing in the world for a pilgrim – stop. Yet also I seek a break from walking with someone who is stronger and fitter and bigger and whose rhythm is not mine. Ben and I have walked well together. He has stopped whenever I need to and he has taken responsibility for leading us through the mountains. But I seek more. I seek to share the romance of the mountains. All in all, I am feeling very sorry for myself when who should come galloping by but my Steadying Hand, in the form of line three of the Eugenia Street Prayer: *I keep my puppy on a lead.* I smile and surrender, reining in my emotions and sitting tall on the concrete bench. Time and space and all that I am condense into this moment. And *voila!* In canters my Guiding Light with her gentle reminder: *I am the love of my life.*

How about that? I am the love of my life. This thought softens me, every time. It brings me home, every time. It gives me courage. Energy pours into my body, rising with the evening tide. My spirits lift. Loneliness begone! Let the journey continue.

I dry my tears and giggle when I notice the long, dry weeds growing on the railway tracks nearest the platform – they still have their seeds on. Surely this means there is no train running on the line?

A train pulls in on the second set of tracks, heading back the way we've come, towards Rome. At least there are trains. I am confused by the red and white sign on the first track, warning travellers not to cross the tracks. It has a picture of a man with one leg, just in case we don't get the message. There is no timetable and there are no staff at the station, which is boarded up. As if to make the point, a young black cat swaggers eloquently down one rusty, unused track. I wonder if I'll be spending the night in Arsoli.

Cats. Me. Tracks. Weeds. I film myself to fill the time, singing Michelle Shocked for the camera: *I'm waiting for a station just like, some people wait for a train ch chhhh, ch chhhh.* I film the cats. I film the weeds.

And then a bunch of boys turns up, good-natured rowdy teenagers who ignore me completely. And what do you know! A train pulls in on the second line. And without a glance at the red and white sign, which is neither rusty nor old, they bundle across the first line, me in their wake, and we all climb aboard for Avezzano.

Within the hour I'm flat on my back between cool white sheets, across the road from the railway station in a dark and poky room at the back of the Avezzano Hotel, pondering the fine line between receiving what's on offer and asking for more, guilt's triumph both. Guilty for asking and guilty for wanting more; guilty for accepting the least of what's on offer. For neither is in the flow. Neither values and respects myself. And neither sees the miracle in others. There is more to life than receiving what's on offer *or* asking for more. *I'm looking for something outside of forgiveness, you might call it the jewel in the crown.*

I relish the clean white sheets, pleased (with myself) and content (to be in Avezzano). Feet wrapped tenderly in clean socks, arms folded behind my head, I stare at the white stucco ceiling and take stock of my life: I have parted company with my constant companion of the past year (however problematic our time together), I have no home, I have left the orbit of my daughter and darling grandchildren. I'm on the other side of the world in a foreign country where few people speak my language. It's almost impossible to find a good meal and I have agonisingly painful feet. I surrender to rest.

I wake hankering for daylight in the dark and poky room. I ease my feet to the floor and do a now familiar stand-stumble as they adjust to the weight of my body, in this case obligingly taking me to the bathroom. Whether I stop for a breather by the roadside or a good night's sleep, it takes about ten minutes for my feet to begin working again, as if the bones have to separate nub by nub and the muscles have to stretch, fibre by fibre. It is *agonising*. And that's without the *tour de force* of blisters. Blisters are pilgrims' blight. Open wounds, yellow and red; torn flesh, pink and white; liquid tears, opaque and transparent. My feet – heels, toes and balls – are painted yellow-brown with Betadine to prevent infection. In praise of Betadine. And plastered with thick white wads of Compeed. In praise of Compeed. And wrapped in clean fat socks. In praise of clean fat socks.

I push the socks in between my two biggest toes and slide my feet into the thongs that were almost left behind and are now integral to my podiatry arsenal. As any pilgrim will tell you, feet are the bedrock and the warranty of a pilgrimage. No feet, no walk. Agonising feet, agonising walk. And yet and yet, I am amazed, constantly, surprisingly, godsendingly amazed, at how quickly the pain disappears when purpose takes the reins.

I limp into Avezzano proper and spend the day wandering around in my socks and thongs. Everywhere I walk, in a great loop from the train station to the old castle to the nearly-as-old church and back to the hotel, dusty hills that are ochre by day and slate-grey in my mind ring the town. Avezzano is corralled by mountains. High mountains. I-hope-Ben-doesn't-have-to-walk-over-those-mountains mountains. At lunchtime I sit on the wide steps of the church in the plaza and sun my blisters. I'm surprised by how quiet it is. Then I notice stallholders curled up sound asleep on benches and realise that Italians too have their siesta. The town is deserted and the shops are closed. A cool breeze blows in, crossing the square with the faint chill of coming winter. Clouds roll in from the west. Dark clouds. It's cold when they steal the sun, which now shines only occasionally through swabs of blue. I wonder how Ben's doing out in the forest. My spirit would love to be out there with him; my body knows there is nowhere else to be but right here in Avezzano, feet tucked up safe and warm between clean white sheets.

I tune into the soundtrack in my mind, the one that has been playing non-stop every step of the way since I left Rome. It is a hit parade of marital arias: 'Obligation', 'Justification', 'Sex', 'Money', 'Obligation Reprise'.

'Obligation' is playing at the moment. Over the years I have asked people how they manage to be married. Without exception their answer is compromise. *Compromise!* Until now, my longing for love never stretched that far. Compromise is readily confused with give and take. It is easy to give up what doesn't matter and not so easy to accept what does. Give and take is the healthy trade of human relationship. Compromise is the demand we give up what matters most, the sacrifice of our hearts' desires. And now, having stood at the altar of sacred union and vowed to honour and be honoured as a sovereign being, I have learned that compromise is the acceptable and petty face of a volcanic behemoth that is, in reality, obligation; snow to the simmering mountain. Sitting on stone steps in the heart of Italy's mountainous spine I look to the blackening sky and shudder, shaking the unwelcome barnacle from my shoulders. Obligation, like its snowy shroud compromise, is death. The only reason we could possibly have for choosing compromise, says my tumbling mind, is that we need others to be obligated to us. Obligation to them is the price we pay.

I wonder why we need to obligate others, why we insist that people owe us? Perhaps we fear their freedom and therefore willingly sacrifice our own.

Why would we fear freedom? Of course! Because then others are beyond our control!

I create a formula for compromise: *If I don't do x, then she won't do y; if I do x for you, then you must do y for me.*

And obligation: *If I don't do y, then he can't do x.*

The first drops of rain drip slowly from the sky. As they fall I pray to the mountains surrounding me that I will never again ask, 'But what about me?' when the ones I claim to love announce their commitment to fulfilling their call to life. For if I must ask, 'What will *I* do?' then clearly I am standing with one foot in the grave of compromise – and my opportunity to embrace the life I was born to live has just arrived, unannounced, at my door.

I stand and hobble across the square, hoping to beat the rain to the Avezzano Hotel, justification weighing heavy in my heart. How else can I explain my absence from my marriage? My unwifely behaviour? My inability to live the life another imagines for me? I pop by the internet café to revel in line two of the Eugenia Street Prayer and honour my creativity by writing the blog Ben and I have been posting on his website.

On sundown I hobble back into town, three blocks south and one to the west. *I am in Italy.* Like the Spanish, the Italians come to life when the sun goes down. I find the plaza and a gigantic slice of takeaway pizza and sit on a stone step among families alive to their own existence – the old ones sitting on benches in spirited conversation, kids riding bikes and kicking balls, the little ones vrooming toy cars around the fountain, teenagers laughing and grandfathers pushing prams – all of us held in place by that posse of dark mountains just begging for snow.

In Italy I have noticed that men hold the babies. From Rome to Avezzano, it is the men, old and young, who hold the little ones. And how they hold them! Firm and steady in strong arms, gazing adoringly into *this is my birthright* eyes. As a woman not well-fathered,

I am warmed by the arms of the fathers and touched by the birthright eyes of the babies; and so pleased, so very, very pleased, for the little ones and the old ones, for theirs is the generational reward of everlasting love.

I am sitting on the side of the plaza furthest from the church, the flat circular fountain between the families and me. I'm surprised to see a relatively new church in the plaza of such an old town. Later, much later, I google 'Avezzano' and learn three things: 1. somewhere between 12,000 and 30,000 people were killed here a near century ago when an earthquake shook the land; 2. the town was flattened again in the Second World War (either of which explains the state of the castle); and 3. the town stands on what was once the biggest lake in central Italy, Lake Fucino, a troublesome water body with no natural drainage and, therefore, an affection for flooding and malaria. None of this is visible to a 21st-century stranger with hobbled feet, sitting on a stone step in the plaza in the threatening rain.

I ring Ben. His says his phone is about to die. He is fifteen kilometres away. We reckon that'll put him at the train station at lunchtime tomorrow.

I wander home, a little more surefooted than I was this morning. Tucked up in bed, I'm unsurprised to discover 'Obligation' is still playing in my mind, this time to the tune of 'Entrapment': *If I don't do as he or she wants then s/he won't love me and if s/he doesn't love me then s/he will leave – abandon – me.*

Obligation, then, is fear of abandonment! So this is why we are available for co-option to the deadly scripts of others.

Like an opera that rolls one fabulous melody into another, so too the tracks in my mind. 'Obligation' has become the chorus, 'Sex' the next verse. My husband is thinking of reversing his vasectomy because he believes it is the reason our sex life deteriorated, his latest euphemism for me 'withholding' sex. Interestingly, now he's brought it to my attention, I think he's right about the timing. Only I think our sex life deteriorated because he got greedy when he no longer had to pull out before ejaculation. Now, all he has to think about are his own orgasmic heights. Sex. I am ragged from thinking about sex. Dealing with sex. Trying to please someone with sex while the drums of my discontent threaten war, if not with him then with myself.

In the vacuum of Avezzano, warm and snug in the dark and poky room, I switch to the present, brooding over the current state of my social life. I pledge to give my attention to those who are giving me theirs, thus not wanting what I do not have. This is the gift of Avezzano, a community engaged amongst themselves, with no time for outsiders. Their attention is on each other, on what and who they know. I get gut-honest. *I suffer the contempt that comes with familiarity, perhaps even a dose of whoever wants to know me isn't worth knowing. Why would they choose me? Even I want more than me!* I think of the affection the Italians share. Even the old men walk arm in arm. Australian men have come a long way in my lifetime. We play soccer. Our cricketers hug and kiss with exuberance. But men walking along the street arm in arm? Old men? We haven't come that far. Then I am slugged sideways by another stream of thought altogether: *the only reason my husband thinks he can demand sex is because I am available to be demanded from.*

I wake slowly, taking my time to surface. Breakfast doesn't call. Neither does lunch. I am choked on a diet of wheat and sugar. *Italia's* pasta-pizza-pastry merry-go-round has me bloated and vagued-out. My ankles are disappearing. I'm no-good-reason tired. Even the yoghurt is riddled with sugar.

The thought of Ben blowing into town is enough to get me going. Last night was cold, much colder than the night before. I wander into the street, geared up for rain. Dark clouds have set in. It starts to pour. I walk down to the *farmacia* to stock up on Compeed and then back up past the hotel to the park outside the railway station.

The rain eases off and there I sit, waiting for Ben, on a bench beside the ugliest fountain on Earth. The park is long and narrow, laced with cement pathways that separate the fountain from the trees. It is a fountain of block-harsh grey cement decorated with the trappings of men at work, ladders and a huge rusty chain leaking from holes in the blocks. There are only men in the park. They're not threatening, but they are curious about me. Daughter of a new world, I am used to sitting where I please and I haven't yet noticed that Italian women rarely take up public space beyond their designated time and place, such as the square on sundown. I see Ben across the road and let out an Aussie bush call, 'cooooo-ee', which echoes from the benches around the park through the mouths of men ripe for a good laugh.

'What's that!' are his first words.

He means the fountain. We hug and head straight for the dark and poky room. He has a shower and we roll out onto the street again, across the road to catch a train back to Rome to pick up his computer. Pilgrim's timing is with us and we have only ten minutes to wait.

As we rattle our way back the way we've come, a journey that will take us less than two hours on the train, Ben fills me in on the highlights of his adventure.

'Arsoli,' he says, 'lived up to its name.'

After leaving me at the station, he walked for two hours – only to end up in Arsoli. We laugh. I'm glad I caught the train to Avezzano.

'I did a big circle! There were little roads everywhere and I completely lost my sense of direction. I ended up taking a track all the way up this bloody great hill to a dead end and after three hours I could see Arsoli just across the valley. I could throw rocks at Arsoli.

'The day was well and truly fading by the time I worked out where I was. I walked back the way I came, all the way back to the main road. Psychologically, this was really painful. I made it back to a little town called Camerata Nuova and walked in circles looking for the right road. And then this little black cat runs out and starts pawing and purring and head-butting my ankles. I've got it on camera! I followed it down a really steep hill and it led me to a dirt track, which turned out to be the road I was looking for!

'When I finally got off the main road into the mountains this car pulls up. A bloke sticks his head out the window and wants to know where I'm staying the night. I said 'camping' and he says 'jump in'. Considering it was almost dark I was happy to go back to town and have a warm bed for the night. His name was Emilio. He made a great dinner: cheeses and breads and salamis that we washed down with his dad's homemade wine. He drives the school bus in the mornings, so you'll be pleased to know I got an early start the next day.

'In no time the road turned into a dry riverbed and I followed it up through a gorge into a valley, climbing all day. I didn't see anyone the whole way up – had the whole day to myself. The valley opened up to big plains with wild horses and cattle grazing. My map wasn't corresponding at all to what I could see and it wasn't long before I was completely lost, but it was a beautiful place to be. I came across a little shepherd's hut where I stopped for a rest, and while I rummaged through my bag the cows came up and surrounded me! The head cow with her big horns stood centimetres away, waiting expectantly. It was slightly disconcerting. Then I tossed a coin to work out which track to take.'

Ben turned to me then, looking quizzically into my face.

'Why don't I have a compass?' he said. 'I'm 2,000 kilometres into this journey and I still don't have a compass.'

He grinned and returned to his story.

'I was buggered by the time I got back into civilisation. None of the restaurants were open in this little town called Cappidicia, so I was forced to have a couple of beers for calories. The next town was only two kilometres down the road, so I tried my luck for food there – and got a great big plate of spaghetti and a half litre of wine for seven euros! Bargain!

'I set off into the darkness for the last six kilometres, which didn't faze me, thanks to the wine. It was looking like rain so I thought I'd try my luck at the parish, but the first house on the edge of town was a bar. I couldn't resist. A couple of glasses of wine later and Franco, the bar owner, offers to let me camp out the back. So there was nothing else to do but wait for the bar to close … and just as everything was winding up a young couple heard what I was doing and decided I could stay in their mountain chalet for the night. It was gorgeous. Heaven. I had the whole place to myself.

'I went back to Franco's bar for breakfast and found out he was the local bocce champion. So we went next door to the boules court and he gave me a few lessons. And then I had a wonderful walk down the mountain to Cappistrello. Awesome views. But if I was going to get to Avezzano to meet you by lunchtime there wasn't much time for rest. This also meant I had to take the highway, which was about seven kilometres shorter than the smaller roads. The only obstacle was a kilometre-long tunnel, just before Avezzano. It had a small footpath, so I figured I'd be safe – but I wasn't counting on it having no bloody ventilation!

'About halfway through the oxygen was really thin and the exhaust fumes were getting thick. I looked around for fans and was shocked to discover there weren't any. I was having visions of myself dropping dead from fumes. I was really starting to wonder if it was physically possible to get to the other side.'

I laughed.

'Yeah,' I said. 'They'd probably think you were a pile of rubbish.'

We laughed.

'And now,' he says, 'I'm buggered.'

And with that he does what Ben can always do: he curls up and goes to sleep. I settle back in my window seat, content to rattle and roll my way to Rome, watching for familiar roads and rest-stops, retracing the way we've come from the comfort of a carriage. I glance at the roadside width, because glancing is all that is possible at this speed, and wonder about my sanity in walking such a fine line.

Rome is an adventure. It is raining. I am still in my socks and thongs. We jump off the train at God-knows-where and discover ourselves to be … God-knows-where. I allow Ben's pilgrim's nose to take the lead. Personally, I would have headed in the opposite direction and, as it turns out, dug us deeper into God-knows-where. We walk and find ourselves on the fringe of civilisation and the probable direction of the computer. We have no idea where we are going, other than to the Apple shop on *Via Flaminia*, near a bubbling fountain splotched with slime in the middle of an intersection outside a chemist shop. Aha! A bus stop. We decide taking the bus is a good idea. It takes us up Tiburtina Road. Our old stomping ground! There is the train station where I went to the loo inside a big silver-metal monster that had me locked inside, like pissing in a safe with the locks on the outside. There is the overpass we rested beneath. The bus comes to the end of its line and we jump aboard another bus, riding until we figure we've come far enough. At least we are in the thick of peak-hour traffic, six lanes wide. We decide to flag a taxi. No taxis. We walk on until we finally ask directions and discover we are heading entirely in the wrong direction. The person we ask is kind enough to print us a Google map. We begin to get a grip on where we are going. We run for a bus. Ben jumps on and it closes its doors. I run harder and bang on the back doors. The driver lets me in. Ben and I laugh with the freedom of those with no dignity to uphold.

We roll on. We get off the bus at a random stop and *voila*! I don't know how we do it but we are right across the road from the computer shop. Phew, I think. Mission accomplished.

'Great,' says Ben, his baby tucked under his arm, 'now let's go get some more hard drive.'

I blink and try to make sense of this. The shop where he left his computer is only a warranty repair. He wants to go to the Apple Store for 'more hard drive'. He wants to cross Rome in the pouring rain through peak-hour traffic to another God-knows-where to find a shop we don't even know will be open when we get there. Very well. And so our mission begins all over again.

Bizarrely, our quest takes us down the same street we were lost in on Saturday, trying to find our way out of Rome. We know where we are! There is the bar where we ate toasted ham and cheese sandwiches while we recovered our direction. I ponder the number of times in my life I have been lost only to find that within days I return to a place I might never have found had I not been lost there in the first place. The bus terminates at an ancient aquaduct running at cross purposes to the traffic. We swap the bus for a tram, holding tight with the commuters as we rattle and ring our way up the centre of the busy street. Dripping wet and hungry, we sit in the shop while the Apple is brought up to speed. The woman behind the counter recognises more than a fellow traveller: she recognises a woman on the road. She offers me the toilet. She brings me a drink of water.

Then we backtrack, but not the way we came – we couldn't do that if we tried! This time we take the sardine subway and then the lemming subway until, on the outskirts of the city, we finally track down the train to Avezzano. It is 7.30 pm. The next train isn't until 8.30 pm. We are hungry. Very hungry. So hungry I do something I haven't done since I was fourteen years old and the first McDonald's came to Canberra. I walk boldly, and worse, unapologetically, to the counter and order a burger. Bacon and cheese is the best I can do. I'm not so hungry I can go the pattie. Not yet. Not today. It is what you might call a grateful-for-small-mercies moment: at least it's not pasta, pizza or pastry. Ben, for whom I spent not a single cent in his childhood on McDonald's, is so gobsmackingly astonished he films the moment. The first bite. The mother redeemed.

We rattle and roll and laugh our way back to Avezzano, pulling into the hotel around 10 pm. We are exhausted. As for tomorrow, to walk on or rest over, we agree to see how the morning greets us.

Okay, I confess. These past two days resting in Avezzano, recovering my aching feet, weary shoulders and tumbling spirits, I've thought often about lingering escapes … maybe I should get the train to Istanbul … or fly to Bilbao to visit much-loved friends … or rest awhile in Koh Samui at the health resort in which my husband owns shares … Then this morning I wake rejuvenated! Ready to pack! Feet primed for the road.

We spend the morning organising ourselves – posting blogs on the internet, fuelling bellies with a long and lazy *Italiani* lunch and loading up with supplies from the local supermarket. By four o'clock we hoist up our packs and we're on the road out of Avezzano, but not before taking a photo of the ugliest fountain on Earth.

We make great time. There is room in my boots for my feet! I can finally take a deep breath with the pack on my back. With wings on our feet we follow the signs to Pescara, breaking free from the stone suburbs of Avezzano into dry, golden farmlands freckled with dark green trees. A wild sky snatches at the mountain tops; swarthy greys dashing the fairest of bright blues as the clouds outrun each other, the splendour of late afternoon lit silver by the setting sun behind us. We walk along the edge of the road, now and then cutting onto what might loosely be called a bike track running parallel to the steady stream of evening traffic. We manage twelve kilometres without stopping and, sitting on our packs for a breather, peeling mandarins and eating chocolate, we agree to take the first bed on offer. Any bed will do. A few kilometres on and we photograph a signpost that has us kicking up our heels – Pescara 100 km, Avezzano 16 km. I forget that what might take us an hour or so in the car is a good four or five days' walk.

Soon after, we down packs for dinner at a huge seafood restaurant on the outskirts of *Italiani* nowhere. We are the first diners in and I am learning already that those I truly love on the road are those who welcome us as we are – our packs, our weariness, our travelling clothes. And so it is this evening. The hostess, a gorgeous smile of a woman of middle age, her bouffed hair and pressed linen the antithesis of us, invites us to take a seat, nods pleasantly when Ben asks if he can charge his computer on the wall socket and details cheerfully for us the merry virtues of her *pasta marinara*. I risk overriding doubts about her limited English and go the *frutti di mare*, 'fruits of the sea'.

While we wait, we ask about the nearest hotel. She shakes her head. She says it is forty-five kilometres away. I find this absurd. We can return to Avezanno but of course that is out of the question. We ask for *'comping'*. She shakes her head. Nope. No hotels. No camping grounds. We are in the middle of civilisation, give or take the sweep of a ploughed field or two, where there is clientele enough for a restaurant the size of a barn but no accommodation within cooee. Clearly, tonight will be my first night 'wild camping', which is pilgrim talk for 'make your own bed'. I digest this information over *frutti di mare* that manifests as a bowl of bland spaghetti spiked with a dozen black mussels in their shells. This I receive with the limited grace of a plummeting mood. Ben is deeply impressed with his *marinara* and offers a helping hand with the mussels.

Wild camping. This is the romance of the road bit hard. I adore the idea of bedding down in the fields, sleeping on the earth beneath a starry sky; I do not enjoy the idea of finding my bed in the dark. I adore the idea of being a pilgrim on the road, making her bed where she wills; I do not enjoy the absence of control over where and how I will sleep. I do not speak my imperilled heart and swallow my fear, not of the darkness but of what might be in it (murderers and dog shit). I 'act normal'. I don't fool Ben, who doesn't speak to me of my vulnerability but writes about it for all the world to read on his next blog. I hate that he can see me. Worse, I hate that he tells the world.

Headlamps flashing, we walk into the night, into the headlights of the diminishing evening traffic. The whoosh of a car passing from behind, overtaking another at top speed, barrels me to my senses. It is one thing to walk into traffic on the edge of the road in the pitch dark of a late moon night. It is another to have one rocket past from behind, sucking the air from my ears. There is a big ditch at the edge of the road. I can walk no further away from the traffic than I am already. At least, I rationalise, I wouldn't know what hit me.

It's not long before we find a side road and Ben's pilgrim's nose leads us down a muddy crossroad. There, behind a row of thin trees on a small raised bank in the far corner of a paddock overgrown with a sparse crop of weeds, we find our bed for the night. We scramble around, trying to be quiet. We have no idea where we are or what's around us. We unfurl our tents on the rough clodded dirt, not minding the stones, and say goodnight. I roll up my ultra-light soft fleece jacket for a pillow. Anticipating the cold, I zip up the sleeping bag. I snuggle down. I listen to the night, when ... Pong! What's that smell? Yuk! It seems to be coming from the floor of the tent. I turn over. In it pours with the evening breeze through the gauze in the tent. Have I camped on a pile of shit? I toss and turn, trying to find respite from the smell. The soft munch, munch, munch of an animal shaves my ear. I put my head out the door to check it out. Nothing. I raise my nose to the breeze, delighted to find the waning moon, a great wobbly ball in the sky, spreading so much light over the land it may as well be daylight. I watch. I sniff. Nothing. I zip up and lie down. The smell comes again. Have we camped on a sewerage pond? The ground didn't seem that muddy. Perhaps it's fertiliser on the field? Uh-oh ... will it burn a hole in the tent? What about my lungs? I take to breathing through the down of the sleeping bag. Are there cows in the paddock? I hope it's not a bull! Or goats. And why is my mobile phone lighting up every five minutes with the eerie green glow of technology possessed? And so it goes for most of the night. At least I'm warm.

I wake with the birds, well before sunlight, surprised I slept at all through the smell. I sing a good morning song to Ben and he growls that I can't tell morning from moonlight. He makes a bid for 6.30 am and kindly I give him until 6.45, when the warmth of the sun gives momentum to the morning. We lie in bed and chat awhile through the walls of our tents, laughing about a smell he didn't notice and animals he didn't hear, and then rise to find there's a stagnant black pond beside my tent near-buried by a tangle of weeds. We agree it's suspect number one for the smell. We also discover we've camped in the wave zone of a gigantic meccano-set power pole, one of a string shuttling electricity across the mountains. This explains the goblin glow in the phone. That just leaves the grazing animals, which Ben puts down to his mother's skittish imagination.

Within the hour, a couple of sesame bars in our bellies, we're on our way, walking into a glorious sunrise as we climb out of the valley beneath a clear blue sky. Counting on breakfast and a back way through the mountains, we take a side road to Collarmele, pleased to leave the traffic behind us. The morning's walk is a pleasure of magnificent views stretching valley-long to a distant gap in the mountains. Three kilometres later we walk confidently into a neat little village whose gun-barrel empty streets belie its productivity. The usual bar, coloured plastic strings in the doorway unsuccessfully keeping out the flies, offers up coffees and strange red orange juices that neither of us wants but the barman clearly thinks we need. I ask for cheese in my croissant and he shakes his head. Not because he doesn't have any, necessarily, but because he doesn't understand a word we say. We wrack our brains for *Italiani* for cheese – we figure the Spanish *'queso'* can't be far off but we are incredibly wrong. We moo. We milk with our hands. We do not get cheese. I am hungry for protein of the non-brawn variety, but it seems he has only jam. I try for butter with my jam. More shrugs and plenty of laughter. But he does get 'warm' and so do I, a limp croissant with strawberry jam warmed in the toaster.

We fuel up and walk on, past the children being dropped off for school, past the old men standing around, past the little church with its clean new walls and straight up a ribbon of empty bitumen into the mountains!

We catch up to a local woman out for a morning stroll. She keeps company with us awhile, curious about the turtleback strangers. For the zillionth time I am impressed with Ben's ability to converse with people with whom he shares no common language. And I begin to understand the loss of his own tongue, his limited and simplistic vocabulary that gives me *this-is-my-son?* frowns. He is ten years on the road. He speaks Japanese and a smattering of Russian, thanks to three years in Japan selling second-hand cars to Russians. He speaks pidgin Spanish and pidgin English and pidgin just-about-anything-at-all except Norwegian, despite two long summers there driving trucks and putting up big top tents during the arctic festival season, round-the-clock work that enables him to spend the rest of his time pleasing himself ... surfing Costa Rica ... World Cup soccer in Germany ... New Year in New York ... on pilgrimage from Canterbury to Jerusalem. And here on the edge of a small settlement in the heart of *Italia*'s mountain region he makes fine conversation with a plump *Italiani* matron with a love of fresh air. She eventually falls behind and Ben and I are left to ourselves. Just us and the stark come-snow mountains. Just us and the shifting gears of a cyclist who whistles by on his morning run.

We climb high. It's a gorgeous day! I make suggestions to Ben about filming. He is curt. This upsets me. We boil with our own stories. He films me fuming, which infuriates me! I refuse to perform. I am lines one and three of the Eugenia Street Prayer in motion – I respect myself and my puppy is nicely at heel. Later, I'm pleased to see the footage shows only a woman walking a mountain road, face and eyes steady as she looks into the camera. I'm pleased not because he doesn't get the drama he's looking for, but because I am at last becoming skilled at not betraying my feelings. My father had a problem with what he called my 'silent insubordination', my contempt for him writ wild on my pretty teenaged face and only amplified by his fists.

I find out later from Ben's blog that he is challenged by having company on his walk. He doesn't say it, but I suspect the fact the company is his mother heightens the load – firstly because there's the small matter of *a certain tone*; secondly, the minor matter of morning brightness; and finally, I come with the added responsibility of 'looking out for mother'. I like that he describes himself as a 'dickhead' in his blog, because if there's one thing that makes me more nervous than anything else, it is the rumbling roar of judgement in my veins accompanied by its drum, the fear of exposure. *Exposure of what? Anything at all of my inner world that might be used against me.* I also like that he writes: 'It's lucky we have a strong relationship and after a few serious words we are once again laughing and enjoying each other's company.' Self-loathing makes way for validation. It will be another year before I consistently cease to seek that validation from another:

I am the love of my life.

Mountains everywhere sing the same song. They might differ in shades of tone or pitch, but like good folk songs that circle round and back again, everyone everywhere thinks them their own. We climb on, stopping regularly to gaze at the valley below, where sunshine strikes gold the clipped fields of autumn and even the giant cement *autostrada* looks as if it's tiptoeing through the morning. We turn our backs on the now-blue valley and spend hours meandering through the hills, winding on and on into the rolling yellow mountains, stark and brittle, shapely and strong. We have the road to ourselves, sharing it occasionally with gung-ho contenders for Italy's world championship motorcycle Grand Prix. Sheep the colour of the earth swarm the face of a distant mountain. Dogs with purpose let us pass in peace. The soft wind brings to us the secrets of the golden valleys. We walk and we rest, basking in sunshine and stillness found only in the mountains. We reach the summit and laugh till we cry when we see the town we've been counting on for lunch. Forca Caruso is a battered sign and a crumbling barn.

Having climbed all morning, we are now on the downward run. I have blisters from walking flat, blisters from walking up, blisters on my bandaids and bandaids on my blisters. Now I can complete my prized collection with a series of blisters from walking downhill. We wander deeper into the mountains, which peel back like a hall of mirrors. Only the occasional tinkle of a sheep bell or the yap of a distant dog interrupt the steady rhythm of our feet on the road. All we can hear are our own footsteps. We stop for the last of our mandarins and chocolate on a prickly patch of grassy hillside and Ben makes use of the downtime to practise hooking up his camera to his computer. It is an incongruent sight: all that technology, so little civilisation.

We walk on. The mountains now are bare-topped, brown and grey, picked clean by snowmelt. On their lower reaches, where we are, they're covered in hardy snowgrasses and scattered weeds sowing the last of their seeds before the snows come, making ready for the far-off spring. About the same time as the clouds begin to gather above, we see our destination below, the old yellow church tower of Goriano

Sicoli rising square above white walls and red roofs. And at the same time as the rain begins to fall from the clouds, my feet cave in. Like naughty children in the back seat of a car on a family holiday, they begin to fight among themselves, to scream and make life hell on wheels. We scramble into rain ponchos, which give us all the finesse of wicked goblins with hunchbacks – a suspicion confirmed by the faces in the intermittent cars zigzagging past us, up and down the mountain, to and from Goriano Sicoli. Ben is delighted with the rain because he gets to use the new waterproof casing he bought for his camera. He ducks into an abandoned cement pipe and rigs it up while I take advantage of gravity's steady pull and walk on. My feet howl. The rain pours. Goriano Sicoli proves elusive. Around this corner. Around this corner. This one. This one. Down, down, down, as if all surrounding civilisation has slipped down the mountain into a basin they named Goriano Sicoli. In the end there is nothing else to do but burrow cold wet hands into damp pockets and pretend for all the world as if I am on a merry wander in the mountains. The burning in my shoulders from the pack becomes the sun warming my back and instead of paying attention to the naughty children in my shoes, I concentrate on the minutiae of the wet mountain road: a tiny white flower, a squashed cigarette butt, the road surface lit up like Google maps by night.

We limp into town. Okay, so Ben doesn't limp. He springs, all the while buoying my spirits with the good news that he knows how I feel. I collapse on the nearest bench, at the street end of a pathway fairytale-steep leading up to the church. The locals stare and don't smile, even when I practise line four of the Eugenia Street Prayer and see the miracle in others. I think it's the wicked goblin thing. Ben scales the stairs, knight to the tower princess (it's that kind of town), and returns with no news. We are seeking a parish bed and the good Father isn't home. We do the hand signal thing with local children brave enough to speak to us and they point us down the road to a bed and breakfast hostel, the only accommodation in town.

It's not open. It's not open and she says we can stay … she says we can stay but she wishes we wouldn't … she wishes we wouldn't but we do because she made the offer. She made the offer and we've walked a good thirty kilometres all day in the heat and the driving rain and it's nearly dark and it's still raining and we haven't eaten and there's nowhere else to stay and I can't walk another step. She shows us a room. I collapse on the bed. We ask about the restaurant. That's not open either and there's nowhere else in town to eat. Her husband sticks his head in the door. Oh heaven, he speaks Australian-accented English. I think he feels sorry for me, sprawled bewildered, wet and filthy on the clean white bed staring into the face of his wife's pleasant hostility, because he offers to make us sandwiches. We accept gratefully, although I suffer a silent and very ungracious who-wants-a-bloody-fuckin'-white-bread-sandwich-for-dinner moment. We love him. I love his Australian-ness. His easiness. He's a 'no worries' man and his is the *Italiani* voice of home. They give us separate rooms and leave us in peace, but not before his wife takes one last potshot about using only one bed in each room. I love her too. She doesn't want us but she has received what came her way this night. *I love her.* I love her but we don't hold out for the breakfast end of 'bed and breakfast'.

I untie wet laces and take off my boots, peel off my socks and in wincing agony pare back the Compeed from tender flesh. I lie back on the pillows and wriggle darling pink toes in the fresh air. My heels are a horseshoe of red and white blisters. Strips of bleached skin dangle from my toes and the balls of my feet. And my little toe, my left little toe, is so swollen and so red that I can barely see a toenail. Our sandwiches arrive. And not because I'm starving hungry and not because there's nothing else to eat in all the world and not because I'm exhausted and dinner has come to me – those sandwiches, I have to say, are the best sandwiches I have *ever* eaten in all my born days: fresh white Italian bread in big crusty chunks, real ham, real cheese and juicy red tomato. Tomato! Can I believe it? Fresh food! I devour. I shower. I lay my precious feet between clean white sheets and kiss them goodnight, content that all will be well in the morning.

I wake easy and snuggle down into the dawn. It's a chilly little bed and I kept warm by getting dressed in the night. Through the window I watch the sun rise over Goriano Sicoli, fluffy pinks and oranges lighting the sky behind the church tower on the hill. Ben, inordinately pleased with himself, sticks his head in the door, dressed and packed and ready to roll. He is pleased on two fronts – firstly, that he is up and I am still in bed; and secondly, he spent last night working out how to get the video footage onto his computer. He sits on my bed and we lose a good hour laughing till we cry as we review our filmmaking efforts. Our host, her spirits brightened, comes good with breakfast: coffee and croissants to start the day. We leave the hostel in good spirits, filming the husband before we leave. It turns out he was a bus driver in Adelaide. He is in Goriano Sicoli because it is his wife's town. He tells us that Goriano Sicoli has a famous round cake. He waves hello to all his friends in Australia. It is classic Borat cinema.

We roam through town, stopping at the local bar before heading into the mountains. We figure it's best to eat while we can; much as I appreciated the goodwill that came with the morning croissants, chocolate croissant in a plastic wrapper isn't so appealing to me that I ate it. Not so Ben, for whom food is food in any clothing. We wade through the posse of locals on the footpath, which in this instance includes a woman (!), through the plastic threads dripping from the doorway and into the morning gloom of the only bar in town. No food. This is a town with no food. And the only bar sells coffee, booze and lollies. I throw down a handful of Baci chocolates and a bottle of Gatorade and we hit the road. We have a ball filming Goriano Sicoli on our way out: gloriously pagan stonework inscribing the dark, the light and the celestial on cobbled pavements; intriguing churches with doorways barred against the delight of curious strangers; narrow alleys that are home to ancient pathways, steps and doorways; a 300-year-old fountain, the *Fontana Pubblica*, and the sanctuary of Saint Gemma the Virgin, whose heroic virginity was the gem of Christ – whatever that means. We leave the Gorianesi to their round cake and their virgin and climb out of town.

It is a steep climb. Not as sheer as the roads into Tivoli and Arsoli, but up, up, up all the way, nonetheless. On a clear day like this one, getting going in our own good time means we're on the road beneath a risen sun. I pant. I sweat. My feet ache. *Tired, sore, better than yesterday*. Within the hour we're atop the mountain looking out over another magnificent view, changing valleys like shuffling cards. Our destination is Raiano, one of the myriad settlements way down there in a valley so long and wide I can't tell blue from green.

I tiptoe down the other side, feet screaming. It's a long, long hike down a newly laid ribbon of bitumen with curves like a Scalextric set. The mountainside is alive with the wildfire of autumn. Lower down, Raiano's olive groves have claimed the land. I am busting for a wee. *Busting.* In the end I have no choice but to dump my pack on the roadside and duck sideways onto the precipitous mountainside, hoping I can stay steady on my feet on the slippery dirt and that the faces in the cars will look politely the other way.

We stroll into town at lunchtime, our minds on breakfast. We down packs in a little park outside the first place we see, a *gelataria*, where there are benches and sunshine and somewhere for Ben, with his eye on the ice-cream, to ask directions for the nearest *pizzeria*. He has a fine chat with the bloke behind the bar. Turns out the *gelataria* is next door and, anyway, it's closed. He leaves the bar and then swivels on his heels to walk straight back in. I watch from the park across the road, amusement turning to bemusement. The barman doesn't sell pizza but he has some for his own lunch. When he realises we have walked from Goriano Sicoli he's happy to share. It's a pilgrim moment. Ben calls me in. We collapse in the corner of the bar, plug our cameras into the walls and stuff ourselves on his pizza. An officious woman walks in and declares the place closed in fifteen minutes. Without understanding a word she says, we get her drift. We look at each other, shell-shocked, and an awful truth dawns, one that explains the absence of food anywhere and everywhere.

'It's Sunday!' I announce.

As if this is news. Which it is, to us.

We load up, deciding to try our food luck down the road at Vittarito, before finding somewhere to camp in the mountains this side of Popoli. I am thinking of catching the train from Popoli to Pescara, to give me a day to take Ben's advice and trade my fabbo hiking boots for Gore-Tex runners, his pilgrim footwear of choice.

The walk into Vittarito is sublime, winding pad, pad, pad down the narrowest of mountain roads with edges sheering into the river below, the fruits of fertile lands shining green from the valley.

Vittarito too is a town Sunday-sweet: 300-year-old locals sitting around staring benignly at unlikely strangers, and walls so old I don't understand what's holding them up. Ben spies a couple of blokes loading what looks like wine into a storehouse. He asks if he can buy a bottle. The old man nods, crosses the road and enters a small door in a wall that is no higher than his tiny self. He returns with a bottle of rosé, magnificently named 'Oppulentus'. He gives it to Ben and shoos him on, unwilling to accept payment. As Ben receives the gift, the other man, I guess the old man's son, grabs it and checks the label. He wants to know what the old man is giving away. He hands it back to Ben with a grunt and we are on our way again, wandering through a medieval town hunting for food.

An old woman points us down a narrow road to the *pasticcerio*, a fabulously fancy bakery, and there we meet Nino, our second *Italiani* Aussie in one day! Nino follows us around his bright and roomy establishment as we order pizzas and lemonade, regaling us with tales of Melbourne in the 1960s. He may well have been a stationmaster in Melbourne a good half-century ago, but he's a bloody good baker now. Like the host husband in Goriano Sicoli, whose name we didn't catch, Nino has the easy linguistic gait of Australians. He shows us his wallet stitched with a furry leather kangaroo and smiles for the camera saying, 'Hi to my friends in Australia.' We leave Nino's as the sun sighs, on the lookout for the first suitable camping place we can find.

About a kilometre out of town, in the corner of a field of dry-gold stalks laid flat by the harvesters, we pitch our tents. We sit on clodded dirt and watch the last of the sunshine slide up the west-facing mountains, turning dusty browns and pinks to hazy living pinks and purples. The shadow of a castle turret clambers out of a distant hillside, clawing at my attention, shape-shifting with the light into a cluster of rocks. It's wonderful to feel the closing of the day, the evening breeze picking up, a pair of eagles joyriding in the heavens high above. Darkness descends and we sit on the earth among the twinkling stars, sharing a bottle of Vittarito's best. Oppulentus takes the two of us all our tug-of-war strength to open. We talk politics with the urgency of Italians and the laughter of pilgrims at ease beneath a rising moon. We toast our beautiful life.

We wake in the golden field from a night that was dirt-cold. I'm sorry now I bought a three-quarter self-inflating mattress, unwittingly sacrificing warmth for weight, because I'm sleeping with my feet on the pack to stay warm. We rise with merry spirits, keen to be on the road before the farmer comes by, packing tents wet with dew.

It's a gorgeous walk into Popoli and only three kilometres to breakfast, the narrow road from Vittarito drawing us closer and closer towards that crumbling castle ruin high above the town, lit sharp now by the morning sunshine. We walk along the roadside where the slasher's just been through, the breeze trailing the breath of wild herbs.

We hit Popoli on its industrial fringe, navigating trucks and trains on the backtracks leading us to town. We find fabulous coffee and yesterday's pastries, always yesterday's pastries, and finally I am compelled to pay serious attention to the toilets in this country. *Italia*, fabled for her roads and waterways and marvels of human comfort, has consistently produced the most terrible toilets. They are high, so high I feel like Alice dangling her legs from the Queen's throne, all the while trying to get my balance. As for the toilet seat, if there is one, it doesn't fit. It wobbles, startling warm skin with ice-cold porcelain and prolonging an already uncomfortable latrine experience. As we leave the café I catch sight of myself in the shop window. No wonder people are staring. We look wild! A little untamed. A little unchained.

We wander into Popoli's civic centre and find an internet café. As seems to be the case, ever and always, we are there until suddenly we are not. Siesta creeps up on us again and we are thrown onto the street while civilisation closes down for the afternoon.

We find a bar to grab some lunch. All this one sells is ''am-burger'.

'Sure,' I say, thinking at least I'll get salad in a toasted roll.

We set up our computers and the bar comes good with wireless. Our burgers come. Fatty meat patties all alone in a cold roll. No sign of colour anywhere. I look closely at the pattie. There is no way I am that hungry. Ben gets the meat and I get the roll. Just as we settle into our computers, online and connected with a wider world, the bar closes. We bundle ourselves up and out onto the tables at the front and, joy of joys, we can still get internet. I'm soon bored and decide to trade Ben and the road for Pescara and the train. It's a toss-up, because physically I'm feeling good – the pack is lightening up and my feet are doing okay; yet, and yet, it will be a good opportunity for the blisters to heal before we cross into Croatia, and really, truth be told, I won't be sorry to miss out on a walk through endless traffic streaming in and out of a big city.

Pilgrims' timing is with me again and I wait just fifteen minutes for the train, puzzled still by the red and white signs at yet another small railway station, bold letters and a picture of a man with a missing leg warning us not to cross the tracks – and then the train pulls in and there's no way over to the platform but across the line.

The train is sweet. I choose a pretty turquoise couch and settle in for a stunning ride out of the valley, the mountains nudging both sides of the train. The old road, the *autostrada* and the train tracks crisscross each other through the narrow corridor, irregular as child's plaiting. The conductor comes by and I hold out money to buy a ticket, knowing that I probably should have bought one at the station and lacking the patience to navigate a machine that refuses to speak my language. I figured I'd just buy my way out of it. He is a burly man. I smile. I hold out my money, a twenty euro note. He shakes his head, gruff and cranky. I hold out more money, this time a fifty.

'Biglietto,' I say. 'Biglietto.'

The fabulous thing about travelling in non-English speaking lands is that it's so easy to please yourself. I am off the hook. There are no rules to obey unless it pleases me because there are no clues available through the usual channels of bureaucratic communication. The stout conductor smiles and says sternly, 'Pescara, Pescara,' and I nod. See how easy it is? I will buy my ticket in Pescara. It is not so easy for a boy of about fourteen who also does not have a ticket. He is distressed. The girl with him is concerned. They reason with the conductor in Italian. I do not know their explanation, the downside of my ignorance. They are thrown off at the next station. Teenagers are between lifelines, post-parents and pre-independent financial resources, and I'm sorry I don't act quickly by giving them the money.

The train pulls into a busy city station. The conductor is the only person I know in town, so pack hoisted high I wander up the platform to ask where the city centre is. He thinks I am there to buy my ticket, which was to be my next task. He waves me away with one of those smiles for a welcome stranger and I wonder why such helpfulness does not extend to his own. I don't push my luck by asking directions, turning instead to follow the flow of *Italiani* humanity into a giant carpark filled with buses and cars.

I cross the bitumen wilderness and head down a mall, ducking into the nearest hotel, a Best Western. The man at the desk welcomes me, pack and all. But I am unwilling to pay his price. He tells me about a cheaper option down the lane across the mall.

I check it out and, at fifty euros a night, it'll do just fine. I get the key and I'm shocked to find myself in a corner shoebox, freshly painted a confident steely blue. I shower for the first time in three days, skylarking with the glorious sensation of water cascading on skin, cleansing me inside and out. I am in wash-my-hair heaven. I empty the pack, air my sleeping bag over a chair, dry the tent on the small patch of floor, and hang freshly washed undies and shirts over the enclosed balcony railings. It is a pocket balcony, a serenade balcony, the kind from which ladies might once have watched a parade or carefully dropped a white lace hanky.

It is midafternoon. In my country, the day would be closing. In Italy, it hasn't yet begun. Comfy now in my socks and thongs, I skip down two flights of stairs, out the doors and into the square. I'm drawn to the end of the street, towards a hazy blue, towards emptiness. At mall's end I stop short, breathless and teary. It is the ocean! The Adriatic Sea! Of course Pescara, being so named, was always going to be on the water – I had no idea the city centre would open out onto the sea! I reel with the sense of what it might be for mountain people to see the ocean for the first time. The Adriatic no less. I think the last time I had anything to do with the Adriatic Sea was colouring in a map in fifth grade. And here it is to greet me in Pescara, unexpected and unannounced.

I sit on one of the smooth whitestone benches that surround a strange fountain, whose saving grace is that it is not hideous, and watch evening come, the powder blues and pinks of a watercolour sky turning dark, until there is nothing at all above: no moon, no sun, no clouds, no stars; just the strange blue hue of evening sheer. This is a landmark evening. I have crossed Italy. I have walked through her mountainous heart and I am now sitting on the edge of the Adriatic Sea, conjuring ghosts of sirens and conquerors. I stare through rows of vaporous white umbrella stalks planted in the sand, shade for tourists of the summer past, watching for the shadows of ancient ships on the sea. I decide to have a fabulous dinner. To eat long and slow. To eat after eight, the way the Italians do.

I leave the Adriatic shore and wander around the mall, filling time until the restaurant I have chosen opens its doors. I order *gnocchi* in *gorgonzola* sauce. I order salad. It comes with fresh-baked bread drenched in chilli oil. I watch an Italian soap opera on the big screen above as I eat, just the pictures, no sound. I presume it is Italian. It is about a middle-aged man, an immigrant, and an Italian woman who move in together, each with two children, a girl and a boy. Her children are typically Italian, his Muslim. The kids are at war with each other's righteousness; the parents get along with loving and being in love, while all the children are appalled at their parents' obvious affection for each other. Anyway, that's my story of the charade I see played out before me. My attention shifts. I watch Italians dining together. I'm full. My food is fabulous and very rich and, even so, I decide to have the one thing for which I have yearned since arriving in Italy yet am always too full to order by the time I get around to it – *tiramisu*! It is not possible to come all the way to Italy and not have *tiramisu*. I order. The *tiramisu* is strange. It is not my idea of *tiramisu*. It is delicious.

I wander home past the old ones hanging out in the square. I sit among them awhile and conclude that it ought to be compulsory for elderly Australians to meet at night in city squares. More than this, it ought to be compulsory for all of us to sit awhile together in the evening and make peace with our day.

I wake to Pescara's ocean light slicing through cracks in the white shutters, the lingering presence of the Adriatic calling me to the sea. *Adriatica*. I wander down to the seaside, this morning cold-green and flat, and wriggle my toes into the sand, white and cold. I raise my eyes to a thin blue line marking deeper waters on the horizon, above which there is only blue. *The sky is blue*. It is a simple blue, true blue, the blue of childhood summers.

I look out over Adriatica and wonder about a city that rises and falls and rises again with the tides of time and man. I ponder what it is to be descended from the risen and the fallen. This is a city sacked hard and often over the centuries by myriad exotic namesakes, most recently by the exceedingly un-exotic British during the Second World War.

Consequently, Pescara is a city built all at once, its buildings uniform and functional and pleasing to neither heart nor eye. I wonder about the towns we have passed through, about the people of Popoli, the old ones who would have been children when the British, being the most recent of the invaders, dropped a bomb on the town hall the day the women and children were queuing for their bread. I wonder about forgiveness; about the human capacity for moving on, and not moving on, and who moves on and why and who and what wins accordingly in the end. *Spoils of war.*

I wonder about the small towns through which we have passed, the ones whose homes are the same colour as the earth and in varying stages of returning to source. I wonder about the merchants and the crusaders who have left no trace of their passing, their footsteps erased by time, at least to the ignorant such as myself.

I sit on a whitestone bench in the cavernous yawn between Pescara's cityscape and the sea, gazing over a solitude of sand leading to the shore, watching the water for shadows of gods and beasts on a sorcerous sea. I am waiting for Ben. Old Italian men stroll by, arm in arm, smoking like chimneys. I am struck by a neon yellow Carlton sign on a nearby rooftop. In Australia that would mean beer. Here it is a nonsense. I think about Ben's conversations with people who ask what he is up to. He tells them he is walking from Rome to Pescara. At first I wondered why he doesn't tell them he has walked from Canterbury and is on his way to Jerusalem. Now I understand. It is nigh on impossible for people to grasp that he is walking from Rome to Pescara! The whole story would be so ridiculously improbable that kindness dictates he spare them the mental assault.

He walks into the train station at lunchtime and I hoof it up the mall to meet him. We drop his pack at my hotel. We eat. He tells me he saw the strangest thing he's seen since leaving England.

'I was walking along the road and high on a distant hill was *something* – I had no idea what it was. It turned out to be a four-metre-high monstrosity that looked like a cross between Pooh Bear and the Tin Man. It made more sense about 500 metres down the road, when I saw a metalwork factory that specialises in oversized monstrosities.

'The sunset over the mountains was magical! And while I didn't hold much hope for a decent bed, I was counting on a cheap restaurant for dinner. What I got was super-cheap! Pasta, pizza, wine and dessert all for six euros! Bargain.

'As I was leaving I asked around for directions to the road I wanted but all anyone would say was, "NO! Very dangerous. No lights." I wasn't sure about the "very dangerous" bit, but "no lights" sounded like a good place to camp. I soon figured "very dangerous" meant industrial area and "no lights" meant nowhere to camp. So I had no choice but to keep walking. After about ten kilometres I was back among farmland, so I was happy enough to sleep there.

'I got an early start this morning, opting for the road I was on rather than the highway, which would have been more direct. I thought the smaller road would give me a pleasant walk along the river. As it turned out there was no river to be seen and it was anything but quiet. I pushed myself too hard, but I've made great time.

'And now,' he says, 'I'm buggered!'

We wander down to the sea and there he sleeps, flat on his back on the esplanade beside the whitestone fountain whose saving grace is that it isn't hideous, surrounded by an assembly of old men smoking and young men peddling bootleg CDs. I keep an eye on the cameras. *Adriatica keeps an eye on me.* When Ben wakes, we catch a bus to the port to find out what time the ferries go to Split, our first port of call in Croatia. We call by a travel office and a very nice man tells us there are no ferries. We find this a silly thing to say and walk on down to the ferry terminal on the water. We slip through a narrow gap in the chained doors and find a ferry official, the only human being in a very big building. He tells us there are no ferries. He tells us they are seasonal. He tells us they stopped last week. No ferries? We ask again to make sure. No ferries. Other boats? No boats at all until the spring.

'March,' he says. 'There will be boats in March.'

The news doesn't bother me. I haven't committed myself to walking all the way to Istanbul. Or Jerusalem for that matter. North, south, train, feet. I'm just along for the ride. Ben takes the news well, considering. However I know him well enough to know when he's digesting information and it's best to leave him to his process. Now is one of those moments. He's digesting. He's processing. We are 150 kilometres from Ancona, the nearest port to the north, and 300 kilometres from Bari in the south. Personally, I don't mind the thought of walking south along the coast of Italy, of catching a ferry from, say, Bari to Dubrovnik. It's the landmine thing – *I'm wary of the Balkans (even though I'm counting on being pleasantly surprised), where neighbours so recently turned on neighbours (counting on being shamed by my narrow-minded ideas about the East) … the region may well be blossoming (while children get around with half-limbs) … as I said, I'm counting on having my stereotypes shattered (oh, poor choice of words, I think again of the children)*.

Ben decides to train it north to Ancona, because while he is committed to walking to Jerusalem, he has no problem taking public transport backwards. From there we will catch the ferry to Zadar. Great. My walk through the bombed-out fields of Croatia just got a whole lot longer.

We wander back towards a busy blackish road where we presume the buses will be. We um and ah about which one to catch and as we do Ben jumps aboard the first one that stops. I'm not quick enough. The bus pulls away and he leaves me standing. I am *so* pissed off. Not least because Ben has my ticket. I take a seat in the bus shelter and breathe my fury, which is loaded with all the left-behind fury of all time. My puppy sits tight on its lead, at my feet. Just as I recover, Ben comes grinning down the road. Clearly he's covered a lot of his own internal ground in the hundred metres between stops. We bus it back to the city centre together, with the hassle of having to find somewhere else to stay because Ben reckons we can do better than fifty euros a night and he's probably right.

We hoist up our packs and head into the evening, with nothing more than two addresses scribbled on a piece of paper that he got from the long-legged beauty in the information centre near the trains. Our little foray into the darkness leads us up a massive road teeming with traffic and into the backstreets medley of suburban Pescara. Three times we ask directions and three times we get different answers. We sit on a wall and rest, leaning against the wrought-iron fence surrounding a stately mansion overhung with giant trees. It is dark now. I'm over it. Ben leaves his pack with me and goes scouting. It is a pilgrim moment. He returns with a grin. I am leaning on the wall of the B&B we are looking for – as it turns out, the best little B&B in

Pescara. We buzz the intercom on the gate. No answer. We buzz the intercom on the side gate. No answer. Ben slips through the gate and knocks on the door. A very elderly couple invites us in. They lead us through their princely home, up the winding marble staircase past a riot of home-baked artwork to our room. It has a bath! It has a cat in the tree outside our window. It is thirty-five euros. We decide to stay an extra night.

We wake to a day of rest ... so to speak. When travelling, everything is a mission. Even the washing. I'm travelling with one set of spare clothes and they're all fine merino wool, even the undies. This means they don't stink. And when I want to wash on principle, I handwash and they dry overnight. Not so Ben, who has a huge bag of washing that needs doing. It's no simple task, bussing across a strange city whose inhabitants have no intention of speaking your language looking for washing machines. It's like playing a video game – from the inside. Eventually we find a laundromat, over near the port where we were yesterday.

I leave Ben to the machines and go looking for a post office, a half-hour expedition that brings me face to face with the kind of callow naivety that makes pilgrimages worth their salt. Wandering along the road past the local stadium, I duck into an internet café. There is a young man behind the counter, black as it happens. The colour of his skin would not be noteworthy were it not for the fact he is the only black man I have seen in Pescara working behind a counter; perhaps he even owns the small enterprise. The others, to my limited experience, roam around the esplanade and the mall selling bootleg CDs, DVDs and other paraphernalia. *I am not speaking here of the legitimacy of their endeavours.* I ask the young man behind the counter how much he charges for internet.

'Three euros an hour,' he says.

I am not willing to pay this, so I thank him and leave. I curve around the stadium wall, wandering merrily along a busy road to find the post office. On the way back to the laundry I meet a huge black man, young and handsome and charming and fit. Again, the colour of his skin is not relevant except in the context of place and culture. We smile. He tries to sell me some cheap plastic goods.

He speaks American-accented English. I don't buy his goods. He tells me he's hungry. I laugh, unsurprised this young man has a healthy appetite. I reach deep into my pockets and give him a handful of change that probably totals five euros or more. I walk on. I saw a movie once in which the opening scene was a washing machine falling from the sky. Falling. Falling. Falling. It lands on a woman in the front yard of her home. Right now, walking along the streets of Pescara's downside, that washing machine is a metaphor for one of my favourite belief systems: *give alms to all who ask*. It's a Gregory the Great thing I found on a Walt Whitman magnet which for years was stuck on my fridge:

> *Love the earth and sun and animals,*
> *Despise riches,*
> *Give alms to everyone that asks.*

Falling. Falling. Falling. Just as I curve around the stadium walls the washing machine lands. I would not give a young man, dedicated and motivated to working for his living, three euros for a service that I needed *but I would give a healthy young man almost double that for absolutely nothing at all*. Clang! Confrontation with my distorted and unconscious actions knocks my inner world sideways. And again, I am not speaking about the legitimacy of either man's purpose. *There is something dishonest about my giving*. I give to anyone who asks. It is a code. A principle. It drives my husband crazy. And yet somehow I have used giving as an excuse to abdicate from other responsibilities … *what?* I have been lazy … *how?* I pull my puppy in close. I am always uncomfortable when one class of people occupies a set place in a community, especially when that place is either on the fringe of a society or in domestic or sexual service to another class. I have a spine-prickling suspicion that my blithe act of giving in Pescara has kept one young black man in his place and denied another his opportunity for something *else*. I wonder if beggars are even asking for money. For what, I wonder, do they yearn? And what, in handing over the coin, am I truly giving? I suspend my alms policy.

I find Ben and we carry the clean washing home. We get off the bus and I nudge him.

'Look at that,' I say.

He is confused.

'What?'

'That!'

There is a laundromat at the bus stop across the road from the B&B.

Late this afternoon we are meeting one of Ben's *couchsurfing.com* contacts down by the sea. Couch-surfing is a 21st-century travellers' boon, an online network of strangers willing to extend their couch or their friendship to people they don't know. We agree to meet by the sea ourselves and I head into the mall to find the Gore-Tex runners he's been nagging me to buy. I try Foot Locker. I try Athlete's World. Anywhere else in the world in such shops I'd have a fair chance of finding a pair of Gore-Tex runners. Not Italy. Both shops are packed with customers when the stores around them are empty. Italians like their shoes. I have identical experiences in both shops. I ask for Gore-Tex runners. The assistant shrivels his nose and spits: '*Gore-Tex!*' I look around me at shelves and shelves of gold and silver runners … *so Italian!* I look at the feet of the people on the streets and conclude there is no Gore-Tex in Pescara.

No Gore-Tex, but a fabulous blue sky. Wall-to-wall computer graphic blue; all-day blue, no-change blue, east-to-west blue. It goes with the pace of life. Italians do not hurry. They make up for their lack of urgency in their speech. As for siesta, this afternoon I make a good go of it. Truly, it must be one of the sanest customs in the Western world.

I wake and wander down to Adriatica to meet Ben and Clarissa, the couch-surfer. Ben and I hook up, no worries. We are to meet Clarissa and her husband Arnaldo on the beach by the boat. We find the beach, but where's the boat? Clarissa rings. We walk towards each other. She points out the boat – she means the whitestone fountain whose saving grace is that it's not hideous. So it's a boat. Aha! A galley!

Clarissa and Arnaldo take us for 'the second best *gelato* in Italy' because the best is closed, and we sit together for a couple of hours by the shores of the Adriatic Sea. They are thirsty for stories about Ben's travels. And there's nothing like local input to sink a little deeper into a land. Clarissa and Arnaldo are great company They think they do not speak much English but to us they're walking talking English-speaking delight. Clarissa is native Pescara and Arnaldo impresses us with the news he is from Napoli, descendant of the great ones who invented pizza. He wants to be in Ben's movie. We film him. He is so funny he has us in stitches. Arnaldo is one of the *Carabiniere*, a class of cop that has Ben and me totally baffled. He tells us the *Carabiniere* are military police with civilian duties. Ben and I are no wiser, but at least we have some explanation for the range of uniforms and guns and attitudes on Italian streets.

We bid our new buddies farewell with promises to put their picture on our blog and head into the night for dinner. Funnily enough, we are craving pasta. It is too early. We find a bar that does not sell pasta. The chef comes out and says we can have pasta. She offers us local pasta or tomato pasta. Ben goes the local, I go the tomato. She offers us something else and we nod. We sit outside and wait. The waitress comes by with a tray weighed heavy with a pair of bright green cocktails. In an *aha!* moment, Ben thinks they're for us – he thinks the chef has offered us cocktails; I thought she offered us bread. The waitress lays the drinks at another table and returns to us, this time laden with a happy selection of tapas that neither of us ordered, neither of us wants to pay for and neither of us is hungry enough to eat. The carrot sticks, however, are too tempting to refuse, given their fresh food status. We order the very best of their wine. The waitress returns with our meals. Mine is delicious. So is Ben's, whose 'local' pasta turns out to be a crepe. The waitress turns to our untouched tapas, now revealed as the mystery offering from the chef.

'You do not eat like Italians!' she says.

Dawn at Adriatica. We rise in the darkness and tiptoe down the marble staircase onto the shadowy streets of morning. We run through the emptiness, feeling impishly like the only ones on Earth alive. We sit by the shore as fluorescent pinks light bushfire yellows and the silver half moon shines high above our heads. All the sky bodies are present: sun, moon, clouds and stars. The umbrella stalks of the summer past are stone-dark against the rising sun, conjuring the presence of the old ones and their stone circles. *Adriatica*. Ben films while I sit with the stillness of the morning. I look out to sea. I think, *First they came by land, then by sea, then by air. Now they come for the summer.* I wonder about giving my attention to the invaders, the ruthless ones for whom more is never enough. Simplistic, I know. I wonder if a woman such as myself might have stood by the shore long, long ago and watched the boats come – traders, invaders, big boats, wooden boats, mythical mystical boats. There is a priestess in my imagination calling to the clear still waters of the sea, her bare feet on the sand, her soft robes silken in the breeze, hers a world of white and the palest of blues. She watches. She waits. I feel forgiveness rising in my heart; forgiveness for myself and for mankind, my brothers; absolution for my inner war with the invaders and deliverance for the colonists, the rapists and the murderers; amnesty for humanity, prelude to peace. A long journey home. By the shores of an ancient sea a million miles from all that I know, I am released. *Dawn at Adriatica.*

As we pack for Ancona, we decide I need a computer. We are both tired of me waiting for Ben to finish with his before I can write my blog and it'll be good to have additional hard drive for the video footage. I reckon it's worth the extra weight. We drop our bags at the *deposito bagagli* at the train station and go Apple-shop hunting. Whether by fluke or destiny's hand, we find one nearby and in fifteen minutes I have my first Apple. Only we can't pick it up until tomorrow. Which means that the train to Ancona and the ferry to Zadar will have to wait. We have time up our sleeves. We find a couch in the corner of a bar, we order water, we roll around laughing as we watch video footage of ourselves on Ben's computer.

I remember a conversation I had two days ago with my husband. He was talking about his reluctance to make plans and I agreed that he needed not to make plans. He replied that this applied to me too and I had shaken my head.

'No,' I said sagely, 'Ben and I have no plans.'

In fact we did have a plan, only one, and that was to walk from Rome to Pescara and catch the ferry to Split. Within an hour of that conversation with my husband, our one simple plan was catapulted into the Pescara blue.

Ben takes a tip from the locals and curls up for a siesta. I wander down to the sea, to sit awhile with my beloved Adriatica. It has taken a few days to gel, but in Avezzano I experienced the first flutters of a new wave of deeply held hostility towards men, this particular story news to me. It was revealed through a subtle fear playing in my auric field like coloured ribbons streaming in the light. As I walked around Avezzano's unfamiliar streets, where only men have a public face, I felt the timeless contradiction of a woman alone: I wanted them to think me sweet, so they would do me no harm; and I wanted them to *see* me, to offer me recognition *as the woman I am*. Fear, either way. I am not enough, either way. A challenge to the masculine, either way. I think of my husband and my son, of the stranglehold of obligation to please that clings to me like a sticky, cadaverous web. *I can no longer stand before their judgement. I am tired of their chastisement. I am on my knees in the face of their inability to celebrate me for who I am – approve of me you bastards!*

I might hold my ground as a woman but I am perpetually drowning in it. And besides, holding ground is a monumental waste of good energy and it is not the truth of a salutary woman. Ironically, I am new to the pleasing game. I say ironically because I have been in rebellion most of my life and what is rebellion if it is not the flipside of pleasing? Mostly though, my rebellion has not been pig-headed. I have simply been well out of step with a significant social requirement for my gender: conformity. It never occurred to me to get married when I was eighteen and pregnant, for example. You'd think I'd shot the president the way the world carried on about it – 'or worse', says a friend who was forced to adopt out two babies. (It was the seventies.)

I might not have been pig-headed but I did get pleasure from being a lesbian for a while there, back in the days when sexuality was a political gauntlet. Feminism validated my world and my choices. Feminism made me okay when all around would punish me. Feminism didn't just let me have my babies, it celebrated my little family. For by the time I was twenty-one I had birthed a second child, a daughter Rebecca, because common sense told my fiery Aries spirit that as I grew older I would not revisit the role of the mother bound by infants at her breast. If I was to have a daughter, I reckoned one fine day in a park, and a playmate for the toddler who was demanding I push him on the swing, it would have to be before my boy was two. And so I did. She was born six weeks shy of his second birthday.

Being a lesbian enabled me to deny the masculine what he wanted most. Lesbianism enabled me to punish, sweetly. While those around me wore overalls, I wore short skirts on pretty legs. In my defence, I wasn't conscious of my little pretension at the time – and ultimately, of course, when we punish, we punish only ourselves. The trouble with feminism, however, is not that it went too far, *but that it didn't go far enough*. We've liberated women to behave like men. Great! As any self-respecting feminist will tell you, that was never the point. The point is we burned out. The point is that two generations of women risked ostracism and ridicule to change laws and lives and there was no-one to whom we might have passed the torch when we were limping with exhaustion. Our daughters' generation thought the world was won. We liberated women to behave like men but we didn't have time to uncover who we are as women, *undefined by the masculine*. Our victories are numerous and ought to be celebrated. We won political gains, legal gains and educational gains. These didn't spill into domestic gains, because the whole point went right over his head, so we won the right to the double shift. We won the right to judicial intervention; he knows he can't touch your arse in the tearoom because it will land him in court and could cost him his career and maybe even a lot of money, but *forty years on he still doesn't know why*. And while we won the right to enjoy sex, what we have is the right to perform sexually for men. Terrific. We can slide up and down poles shame-free. We can dress the whore. Yippee. *Who are we undefined by his fantasy about who he wants us to be?* And that leaves our spirituality. We might have reclaimed a whole lot of goddess myth and ritual, but this is a make-believe world out of step with our time and culture. Women weep on the inside. And this is what we weep for: our sexuality and our spirituality, undefined by the masculine. This is our collective anger, our bitterness, our rage and impotent fury, our sadness, our distress, our dismay, our powerlessness. Our compliance. We do not know who we are. And we are unwilling to risk his displeasure, or our homes and lifestyles, in order to find out. As for him, he is so sure of his ground, he is not so much unwilling to listen as *he doesn't know how*. My husband, who has the sexual finesse of an adolescent, spirited and hungry – although it wasn't always like this – tells me his previous lovers have only ever expressed rapture with his lovemaking. I tell him women do not tell men the truth.

The evening is cool before the darkening sky, the deepening sea. As above, so below. *As within, so without*. I call Ben. We find a wine bar and there we sit happily sipping honeyed wine while we roll the dice on the beautiful blue leather backgammon board. There is a mob of Australians at the next table and I forget we are in Italy. Ben wins the game. We have been tallying the score since leaving Rome. Things are not going my way. It is 8–0. Eight-bloody-nil. The only backgammon partner I've had in recent years is my eight-year-old grandson. I am warming to my game; it is only a matter of time. We move next door for pasta, saying 'g'day' to George, Helen, Henry, Jenny, Michelle and Dave on our way out. I love them for their interest in Ben's mission. We take our seats next door, we order, we roll out the board. I feel myself sinking into the game. At last I see only the board. I win the next game. And the next. Ben is starting to sweat. He takes the next game and calls it quits. At 9–2 we roll up the board and return to our wonderful little B&B.

We wake to steadily deteriorating breakfasts. On the first morning, as we dined among that cacophony of artforms – a museum of the uncontrived staring out the window through egg-yellow awnings at candy-pink walls – we were served scrambled eggs laden with freshly chopped tomato and a plate of toasted cheese sandwiches. Ben was in culinary heaven, while for me the loving service was compensation enough for the thin white bread and plastic cheese squares. As for the eggs, I cannot stomach an egg that is not free-range and so on day two it was cold toast spread with something that might be called 'cream cheese'. This morning, day three, the bread isn't toasted, although the lady of the house graciously makes Ben an omelette.

It's a lot like groundhog day as we head for the train, leaving our bags at the *deposito bagagli*.

The computer won't be in until lunchtime. Ben goes microphone hunting to improve the sound quality of our filming, while I roam down to the sea.

If you were to ask me where the mists of time might be, I would tell you, *'Adriatica'* – out there on the eastern horizon, where blue meets blue and, as you turn towards the light, fades to white. If you were to erase all signs of human habitation, forgetting for a moment the light poles and the umbrella stalks and the evenly spaced rocks, there is only a flat blue canvas. No hills or bumps, no greens. Just blue and the white-gold sands of the shoreline.

I wander back up the mall and along the main road, ducking into the backstreets. Pescara is an ugly city. Its narrow streets are lined with the square concrete buildings of hurried reconstruction. They are functional, I'm sure; yet they are not pretty, or even interesting. I wind my way down to the broken end of town, past the old cobbler tap, tap tapping on a leather sole, the old tailor bent over his cloth stitching time. Young men in grubby clothes hang in doorways eyeing my camera, though not so hungrily I feel the need to turn back the way I've come. I meet the river. As is the way with such places, the developers have already arrived. There is a new park, a new cement building with wavy lines, a new generation on its way.

My sweet Apple is ready. Ben rocks up and we take her home, so to speak. We're hungry. Ben's need to follow one more long shot for a microphone wins out over lunch and, against my better judgement, I follow him. We jump on a bus. We jump off the bus in Nowheresville. I look at the long brown tunnel of road to nowhere and tell Ben I'll meet him back in town. He stands at a bus stop on one side of the road, me on the other. His bus pulls in while I wait. And wait. And wait. There in Nowheresville beside a barbed wire fence on the edge of the long brown road, I wait hungry and tired and weighed heavy by the new Mac. The bus comes. I board and think I hear my name. I think I hear my name in Australian. I decide I am delusional. Ben jumps up from a seat at the front. He has been chasing shadows; the bus has brought him full circle. We dissolve laughing and go get lunch. And what a lunch! Our best meal yet in Italy: roast vegie stack, barley with chopped tomato and white cheese, circles of cheese-stuffed ravioli. I take my husband's advice and with an eye to nutrition drown it all in olive oil. There is nothing more I might have asked for before getting on the train to Ancona.

We rattle our way north, through more functional ugliness tormented by an occasional audacious relic on a hill. For long stretches Adriatica keeps us company. Our packs sit beside us on seats of their own. From the train I look into people's backyards. I see their junk and their washing and what in the world they don't care for. Out the front is their public face and, inside, the soft underbelly of their lives. The train window is a cocoon for the voyeur with the legitimacy of a paid ticket. Staring into backyards is a bit like surprising a woman in her nightie in the middle of the day: when we meet her later we pretend we didn't see.

We pull into Ancona just on dark. It's gorgeous! We're pretty sure the ferry to Zadar doesn't leave until tomorrow night, but we catch the bus straight down to the port anyway, just to check. Ancona's old city is still standing, high on the hill overlooking the harbour. I am stopped in my tracks by the blue of the sky above, dazzlingly bright-dark for a cluster of moments before dark. It is the blue of the heavenly domes. We bus back up towards the station, to the cheap end of town, and find a hostel. It's clean. It's warm. Ben heads out into the night to find an Irish pub. I tell him he's dreaming. I tuck up between another set of clean white sheets and anticipate exploring Ancona with our cameras in the morning.

It is in Ancona I finally meet *Italia*. The bustling port is heavy with the business end of the Mediterranean, giant cranes overshadowing the old customs house that might once have been anything from a temple to, well, a customs house. The town is full, generations of Italians strolling through the central streets and square. Lured by the pull of a great green copper dome, we clamber up the cement path to the Cathedral of San Ciriaco, the thousand-year-old church calling to us from the heavens above the harbour; it is only from the hilltop that we discover, way below us in the distance, the striking Arch of Trajan, a huge white marble monument that for two millennia has marked the entrance to the Roman Empire's greatest Adriatic port, the harbour claimed by Julius, the Caesar himself, soon after crossing the Rubicon. And that's not even the beginning of Ancona's story. Of course, we didn't know any of this at the time. We learned it from our friend Paolo, whom we met when curiosity got the better of us and we stuck our cameras inside a very old doorway in a very narrow cobbled street. Paolo Principi is the tour guide at the paradoxically named *Galleria d'Arte Moderne*; I say 'paradoxically' because the building itself must be at least a thousand years old. Paolo speaks six languages and is more fluent in English than anyone else we've met in Christendom who has picked up the language from five books and thirty-seven tapes. Although, as an aside, I think there are more Italians per capita speaking English in Ancona than anywhere else in Italy ... or perhaps the rest make a point of not trying very hard. 'Like the French,' says my Dutch husband scornfully when I speak to him on the phone.

Paolo makes sure we understand that his name means 'little prince'. Little Prince Paolo of Ancona. He tells us he spent two years in a coma after he was knocked down by a car. He wears a wooden cross around his neck and leads us to lunch through a small door, up a narrow winding staircase and into a bright, airy and very crowded restaurant. Over pasta and bottled water Paolo offers us his religio-spiritual philosophy with one line and a chuckle: *'We are all sons of a never-ending love.'*

After lunch, Paolo shows us his favourite Ancona landmark, the *Santa Maria della Misericordia*. We have already been there, have already been captured by her faded stone markings that tell more than a Christian story, her air redolent with the breath of the feminine, stories of the ages embedded in the stone and indivisible to us, son and daughter of a new world. With his trademark chuckle Paolo tells us the stone angels were stolen from Constantinople a millennia ago. I am pleased the little church is dedicated to Mary, but I am irked, as usual, by the linguistic knavery of the priests who string together 'Mary' and 'Misery' as if they are synonyms in sisterhood. Paolo tells us that Pescara was not bombed in the Second World War and was not previously a city, but a small fishing village expanded for expedience by the Fascists, around the same time as Americans began rocking round the clock. Ancona, he tells us, was bombed in the war, then rebuilt and restored. I forget to ask whether he thinks Pescara was sacked by Romans or raided by Lombards or conquered by Rainaldo Orsini and Louis of Savoy et al, all of which I gleaned in a bored moment yesterday from Wikipedia. Stories. Lenses. Prisms. We farewell our dear prince and find an internet café to bring the new Mac up to speed.

My final consumer act in *Italia* is to succumb to the purchase of a comb. Okay, I confess, as well as travelling shampoo-free, I have been travelling comb-free, relying on my fingers for grooming. After three weeks without a comb, well, my hair's a bit rough. And how much can a comb weigh?

We hurry to get to the port before six, to salvage our bags from *deposito bagagli*. We settle in for a long evening at the terminal waiting to catch our ferry to eastern Europe, a night crossing to the darklands, when, joy, I find a fabulous restaurant up some obscure stairs outside the terminal and we treat ourselves to a fantastic farewell supper: pizza with anchovies and roasted eggplant, salad as fresh as the garden and, joy of joys, a celebratory *tiramisu*. We are a bit drunk by this time, as well as high on pilgrimage and light-headed about leaving the known world. All of which explains the small globs of *tiramisu* gliding down the front of my shirt. 'Don't tell Mum,' I say to the camera. And we laugh so hard we cry. There's nothing like a dose of delirium to keep things sane.

I wake early on the ferry to windows so dark it looks as if they've been painted black. An old woman has her face pressed to the glass, scanning for morning. It isn't long before the window closest to the bow is more blue than black. Ben is dead to the world on the long turquoise lounge across the table from mine. I sit up. We are surrounded on three sides by orange lights on the shoreline! We are here. We are near Zadar! I don't know how we manage it, but we are the last to disembark into the new morning, tumbling onto a street that would be empty if not for the crooked old woman dressed all in black, standing incuriously beneath a tree; she is part crow, remnant of time and place.

We walk into a small square beneath the haughty rectangular tower of a very old church and there we find a bar, just open. We down packs and stop for coffee while we get our bearings. Ben is a wireless fiend. Wherever we are, whatever the time, he's opening his computer before his bum is on the seat. And we're in luck. We hang around catching up on blogs until morning proper arrives and we discover, contrary to what Ben was told late one night in a pre-Pescara bar, Croatia does not accept euros. We promise the barman we'll be back to pay for our coffees.

Zadar is beautiful. The cobbled streets of the old city are so clean and shiny I wonder if an old woman runs over them with a mop each morning. There are magnificent signs of the ancient ones everywhere. Strangest of all, to my ignorant mind, is that everyone speaks English. Fluent English. I am disappointed. A culture is transmitted through its language and besides, I'm still using pidgin-Italian, an odd mix of *si*, *si-si*, *buongiorno* and *grazie* to get me through and I'm sounding ridiculous.

I sit beneath a lamp post in the middle of a bigger square, minding our stuff and watching Zadar come to Sunday morning while Ben reconnoitres the city for a bed and a shower. Like many coastal towns in Europe, Zadar's summer season has ended (she says with the know-all experience of four days in Pescara). Bed, therefore, is a long way away. We find a taxi. We ask for the *hostal*. It's by the water, but it's expensive and flimsy-bunk-bed horrible. We walk back up the road to the camping ground, where a locked gate stands between us and a paddock of lush green grass. We look at each other, we look around, up and down the wide tree-lined street, and there across the road we spy a small sign on a private house offering rooms. It's wonderful. Clean white sheets and a clean pink bathroom. We're home! We shower. We're hungry. Really hungry.

We walk up the road and duck down a lane to the water's edge. We are directly across the harbour from the terminal, our ferry tall and white still berthed outside the old city. We walk until we find a restaurant on the shoreline and there in the darklands of my imagination we feast, Ben on 'wild animal in wine sauce', relishing the intrigue of the mystery meat, and me on a huge plate of delicious fresh handmade *gnocchi* at sea in a tomato sauce of delicacy and substance. We drink delicious wine. Our young waiter tells us, in impeccable English, that he has been all over the world, even to Australia, and Croatia is 'the heaven on Earth'. We humour him. We play backgammon. Ben takes just one game in four. The score is 12–7. I pinch myself that I am in Croatia. I remind myself this is the old Yugoslavia.

I remember the 'wog boys' who played a strange game called soccer on the high school oval at lunchtimes. I remember the teenage girls who had a disastrous time navigating the cultural commands of their parents and the 'freedoms' of the new country. The politics of a time I was too young to understand has seeped into my bones. I look into the faces of the old ones around me now and, in my ignorance, wonder how a generation robbed of its music and ideas is coping with the fresh breeze that blows through the lives of their grandchildren. I wonder also whether, along with the fresh wind, oppressive pre-communist social strictures have also come tumbling down, leaving everyone freer than they ever were. And I marvel at the ability of the human spirit to recover. These thoughts, and others, shade my eyes as I wander the streets of Zadar, a city whose name you can purr – Zadarrrrrrrrrrrr.

Cultural ambassadors that we are, we head home for a siesta for the afternoon, waking on dusk ravenous for the night. We wander into the old city, laptops and cameras in tow, winding our way around the harbour towards the people and pretty lights on the other side of the water, Adriatica's darker shore. We cross the bridge over the harbour and enter the old city, through the old city gate in the old city walls. I fancy I can hear the clop, clop, clop of horses of ages past on the cobblestones; catch the flash of the red cape of a horseman from the corner of my eye. We find a café and make ourselves at home. When we've had our wireless fill we wander home in the darkness along the harbour's edge, the lights of the old city keeping pace with us most of the way. We walk past stately old homes and offices bulging with waterside commerce, past small jetties and sweet marinas, past solitary white dinghies moored in the grey water, past young women alone and comfortable with the night. We take a shortcut we discovered earlier in the day and experience what might be considered a 'famous last words' moment: I announce that the advantage of walking on a peninsula is that it's difficult to get lost. Immediately we are without our bearings. We wander strange streets in the dark. Fortunately, the advantage of being lost on a narrow peninsula is that you can't get too lost. Tucked up at last between our clean white sheets we play a final round of backgammon for the night. I do an extremely competent job of colonising Ben's gammon and manage to turn a ridiculous strategy into a face-saving loss. The score is 13–7, to Ben.

I wake early and write. As Ben begins to stir I set up the backgammon board. He rolls over and winces, justifiably given the escalating pace of my game; or perhaps he's just recoiling from the gentle light of a new day. He declines the third game. I am closing in. The score is 13–9. We enjoy a lazy start to a day with lots to do before we head down Adriatica's eastern shoreline. We look for breakfast. We find coffee and orange juice and, strangely, ice-cream. No food. I feel like a cat, looking for a spot to curl up in the sunshine. Or a woman seeking a hammock and fresh dates.

The dark moon is coming and I wonder if I will bleed this time around. I feel discomfort in the depths of my belly, my ovaries heavy. I haven't bled since my husband returned from Thailand, three moon cycles ago. When he and I met a year ago my bleeding stopped, suddenly, and did not return until four cycles later, when it made a quick appearance before vanishing again, only to return in the month when one of us had to go. *I bleed only when I am not with my husband.* I wonder if marriage was such a shock to my system it scared my eggs away. My mother's menopause kicked in when she walked out of her marriage; she never bled again. Mine seems to have kicked in the moment I walked into marriage. I wonder if there's a connection?

I sit beneath the tower of the old, old church drinking fresh orange juice. The priests emerge from a side door in the timeless stone, their black dresses lit red with crimson sashes and serious buttons on the march down the underside of their sleeves, swirling with the business of morningtide. A very tall man walks by with the exaggerated gait of a giant, *fe fi fo fum*, pleased with his reflection in the shop windows. A woman with a sturdy brown pug on a lead lets him piss on the wheels of a pram. I down one orange juice and reach for the second. A child walks by with an awkward gait and legs the colour of doll skin; she is one of a picture perfect family – mother, father, daughter, son, well dressed and well fed. I wonder again about landmines.

My feet are cold. I change chairs and shift into the sunshine. I soon tire of chasing the sun and tell Ben I'll meet him at the back of the old church, now revealed as the *Sveta Stosa*, the Cathedral of Anastasia.

I sit in the sunshine on the edge of jagged rocky ruins, almost too hot beneath the almighty walls. Colossal and curvy they mock the tower, telling a different story to the cathedral's public face out the front. Little kids drive electric cars round and round a labyrinth of ruins two millennia old. I'm delighted by the ease with which the people of the old countries live in their heritage. I sit on the remains of the Romans beneath the handiwork of the Byzantines and breathe the dust of the Illyrians. It is strange to be in the old Yugoslavia. When I was a child I had a hard plastic pencil box with a map of the world on the front and two interlocking wheels that turned together, giving me the name of a country in one window and its capital city in the other. I loved the names of these countries and their cities, but I always thought Yugoslavia an ugly word. Forty years later I sit in a square in a fabulously named city called Zadar and toss up two words in my mind – Yugoslavia, Croatia. Yugoslavia, Croatia, Yugoslavia, Croatia. One is light, even as it speaks of difference. The other is off-key and harsh, conjuring a place I have no desire to visit. Actually neither are places I have had any desire to visit.

Ben rocks up and we play two fierce and fervent rounds of backgammon on the stone, leaving the score at 15–10. We go for a walk, roaming aimlessly around the old city looking for money changers and a Croatian SIM card for Ben. I don't know why it takes so long, but eventually we realise it's a public holiday. We abandon the city for home, walking happily along the harbourside, bellies hungry for gnocchi and wild animal and good wine. Like a city-sacker of old, more is not enough for me. Not today, not when fresh homemade *gnocchi* swimming in the best *arrabiata* sauce in Christendom is mine for the asking.

I look across the harbour to more open waters, where small islands lend the day a sweeter serenity. Adriatica is different here in the east; she is dauntless and intrepid. Over there, on her western shore, she is soft of blue and call-to-me still, while here she is deep and dark and certain. Here it is the sky that fades to white the closer you get to the light; there it was the sea. Here the fishermen wear black t-shirts; over there, though I did not see them, in the romance of my imagination they wear white. We play backgammon while we wait for lunch. Even though, at 15–10, the numbers are slipping and they're not sliding my way, Ben is a worried man. The games are getting tougher and he has his mother's own luck with the dice. Double fours are the only throw that will give him the game and they do: 16–10.

As we walk on home, full and content, Ben tells me he is concerned about our progress from Rome. When we set out we had 230 kilometres to walk and a ferry ride to Split. Two and a half weeks later, we still have 160 kilometres to go to Split. He is worried about crossing Turkey in the middle of winter. I have no idea what any of it means. We wander on in the late afternoon sun. I think of the old people I have seen in Zadar, Croatia, *Yugoslavia*. The faces of the old ones here look as tired as they do in my own country, where in my growing years they were the faces of the fruit pickers and factory workers, the cleaners, the labourers and the fishermen. Only in my country the old ones laugh a lot more, at least among themselves. We go three more rounds of backgammon before bed. This time I have my own luck with the dice. Double twos will steal the game and they do. I rest easy on 17–12.

We wake in the dawn light to the excitement of being back on the road. It takes us a good half-day's slog to clear Zadar's industrial corridor and then clod our way through the riot of new cement works on the edge of the city; new freeway, new footpaths, new blisters. Now why am I doing this again? After a week of hotels and trains and ferries my biorhythms are not cooperating. My shoulders scream as the extra weight of the computer pushes me beyond anything at all I consider acceptable, even though I've posted home everything superfluous, even face cream. Right on the fringe of the habitation wasteland, we hear the most terrible meowing hastening from the weeds. My heart sinks, certain a cat is about to present itself with half its legs run over. Rather, it is just an extremely hungry ginger kitten, starving as much for human company as it is for food. Ben opens a tin of tuna and offers it gently to a very grateful little puss.

Half an hour later we take our first rest beneath a small palm with the Adriatic Sea just metres away. I hobble over to the only sign of civilisation this side of the road, a concrete jetty, and there I lie flat on my back among the dry seagull poo. I look vaguely at the sky and give my attention to the wind. It blows harder. I allow the news it brings of other worlds to sink into my bones. I shade my face with my fingers and through the gaps I watch the birds. I like to think they are swooping and soaring just for me. I am in the altered state of the pilgrim: it's called Delusional.

We press on. Today is agonising, of spirit as much as anything else. I feel as if I'm dragging a sack of bones along the bitumen and indeed I am – my own. It is the time of the dark moon. I should be in my hammock. We walk in the noonday sun. It is too much so we stop awhile in the shade of a small tree near the water's edge. Ben's great. He is happy to rest when I need to. There by the shores of Adriatica he gets internet! I harmonise effort and ease, and sleep.

We walk on, the heat of the day gone now. There is a row of houses selling produce on the street. We buy tomatoes and a string of dried figs from an old bent woman dressed all in black. I leave Ben to finalise the transaction and walk on. He hollers for me to come back. He's not paying thirty kuna for figs and two tomatoes, not when he's just feasted on a massive plate of spaghetti bolognaise for the same price. I want the figs. They might be so common I scrape them off my bootsoles, but figs are quality dried fruit and, besides, I'm presuming she grew them herself – or at least scraped them off her own bootsoles. I pay her for the figs.

Civilisation gives way to a two-lane road south, bound on both sides by low, dark green scrub. The romance of the Adriatic coastline buckles under the weight of the rubbish that keeps pace with us. I think seriously about buying a donkey. Then wacko-the-diddleo! We make Sveti Petar. Out of the Adriatic blue, here we are. And there's a camping ground to meet us.

We pitch our tents in time to sit on the rock wall by the shore, dangling our legs over the water, watching the sun go down behind the islands on the western horizon. Surprisingly, my feet have held up okay. Sure I have new blisters. But they are *new* blisters. The old ones have held steady and I can walk at sundown without feeling as if my bones are poking through the skin of my feet. It is a beautiful evening. A pilgrim's evening. The sun glows yellow orange through grey clouds. Shadows and light play on the water, as well as the jetty, the islands and the low slung sun. I listen to the water lapping at the rock wall and gaze into the soft lime green of the rocks beneath the shallow waters; my spirit walks the shining golden pathway on the water to the sun. Ah yes, now I remember: *this is why I'm doing this again.*

We wake to a cloudy day, the benefits of which are threefold: we pack up dry tents, we walk in a heat-free day, and Ben gets up early and thinks it's late. I crawl out of the tent to see my towel, the red-dirt colour of the Australian desert, hanging on the branch of an olive tree beside the Adriatic Sea. *Ah yes, this is why I'm doing this again.* We ease into the walk along the roadside, cars and buses and trucks coming at us at ungodly speeds. I mean that – *ungodly*. Speaking as a pilgrim, getting about life at those speeds is ungodly. My shoulders are screaming with the weight of the pack. My feet are screaming harder. I announce I am taking the bus to Biograd, the next decent dot on our map, and will meet Ben on his way through. We round a corner and without warning Sveti Petar is behind us. No bus stops. No buses. I give way to the war within. The biorhythms are no more interested in this walk today than they were yesterday. I am totally engrossed in my torturous pain when Ben says something very simple: 'Isn't this beautiful.'

My attention switches from the enormity of my agonies to the blue-bound west, where sky and sea are one watery colour and inkblot islands come and go like ghosts. I realise I have nothing to lose by surrendering my crescendo of pain and turning my attention to beauty. I sip the yellows and purples of the tiny weed flowers on the roadside. I delight in a rare crimson. I breathe deeply the bright brown of the freshly turned earth. I marvel at the shiny black backs of the low-flying crows. My shoulders straighten out and my feet find their rhythm. The pack isn't as heavy as it was. I begin to see beauty in ugly: the rich blue swish on a bag of rubbish, the orange scrap of ribbon that might once have held a gift.

We walk Croatia's tourist strip, where *Kamps* (caravan parks) with English names – Suzy, Tim, Anita – offer insight into who the summer visitors might be. New developments are everywhere: new houses, new paint jobs, new jetties. The European Union's latest money funnel. Although that could just be my ignorance talking. Unlike in my own country, prime agricultural land has not been completely sacrificed for profit. Nearly every one of those new houses boasting rooms for rent with an Adriatic view has a front yard dripping with olives, oranges, grapes and tomatoes, and bulging with the coming winter's potato crop. We walk through the new seeking to settle for the simple – a supermarket, a post office, even a bar for coffee would be good.

And suddenly, just like the end of Sveti Petar, shiny and new gives way to old-as-the-hills, and we stumble through Turanj's stark new town into its age-old *centra* on the seashore, just as the first drops of rain hit the dusty ground. We find a bar. We collapse on shiny aluminium chairs out the front. Surreptitiously I unlace my boots and peel off the sock on my left foot, ignoring for the moment a blister on my little toe bursting yellow from its bandaid. We dodge curious non-stares from the locals and order coffee from a happy woman about my own age. This is a woman content with her place among her own. The world, her world, comes to her. She takes a seat at the table beside ours, pulls white cotton gloves over her fingers and begins to peel pomegranates. She fills a bowl with the crimson seeds and then offers the bowl to us.

'Vitamin C,' she says with a practical smile. 'Very good for you.'

We accept her offering with big smiles, as grateful for the welcoming gesture as we are for the morning vitamins. I decide to pay attention to the blister, wincing as the Betadine does its work. I strap it up again and tuck my feet back into their boots. We load up and limp on in the rain, calling by a small supermarket for bread and cheese on our way out of town and stopping at the bakery for a slice of cold pizza.

I breathe deeply as we limp into the distance, our sights set on a lakeside campsite marked on the map, about ten kilometres down the road. We take a dirt backtrack that runs between the highway and the sea, a sandy corridor of scrubby wilderness. We are surrounded by the faded purple beauty of clipped heather. I have my ears peeled for motocross hoons. The track is on the map, although the forks in the road aren't particularly well marked. With a good deal of debate and common sense we make it through to Pakostane, stopping now and then for little feasts of chocolate and figs to keep us going.

We wander through the backstreets of Pakostane, which are darkening with a looming rainstorm, and, strangely, find a tourist office. I want to ask for a larger scale map and directions to the lake road. Actually I want Ben to ask. He gives me a blank look, raises his eyebrows and says nothing. He's not asking. I want him to ask because he has more patience for such matters than me. Sometimes I think the whole world has more patience for such matters than me. He's not asking. I don't want to stumble blindly through the backstreets of Pakostane. I do not have one step to waste. He's not asking. I go myself. She has a small toy map. She tells me there is no bus. I say that's okay because we're walking. She tells me we cannot walk. I tell her we can and we are. She tells me we can't. I ask her where the road to the main road is. She tells me it is six kilometres. She tells me it is too far to walk. I ask again for directions to the road. She tells me it is six kilometres. She tells me we cannot walk. I smile and thank her for her map. Now I know why Ben isn't asking.

We make it to the main road and walk straight across the hostile bitumen to the lake road. And there we are promptly abandoned by our map. Left or right? It is impossible to tell. The road is a couple of hundred metres from the lake shore. I bow to Ben's experience in such matters and we go right. We cut through a farm in our efforts to get to the lakeshore, wading knee-deep through the brittle scraps of the summer's harvest, boots clumping with damp earth, surrounded by farm dogs barking hysterically. We abandon this idea and head towards a nearby pine forest, seeking the path the map is so certain circles the lake. As we shortcut through a paddock we set off more farm dogs. I am landmine wary, preferring the open ploughed fields to the cover of the spindly forest. Farmers with dogs and shotguns I can deal with. Landmines? Well, there's no dealing with a landmine. We take a breather on the edge of the pine forest, leaning up against our packs on the soft needles of the forest floor. I stretch out my legs, alert, discomforted by the explosive soundtrack in my head. Prudent or foolish? I cannot tell. I do not know. We stuff ourselves on a feast of crusty bread, cheese, fresh tomatoes and great ham, unconcerned that we've lost our way. We roll out the backgammon board. Refreshed and happy, we walk on.

We find the track and it's a bastard! The bureaucratic vandal who authorised the dumping of sharp and slippery white rocks on the path around the shoreline ought to be forced to walk it on his or her knees. The rocks costs me what pleasure is left in the day. They are a killer on my feet. I limp. I moan. Ben walks on. I think the least he can do is groan with me.

It takes us an hour to find a campsite, a high paddock of bare earth, hard and lumpy and not freshly ploughed, beneath a string of olive trees along its lakeside edge. I reason that where there has been human activity there will be no landmines. The wind whistles off the lake as we put up the tents, three trees apart. I am nervous. We are once again in the middle of God only knows where. The paddock doesn't feel hostile but nor do I feel welcome. The tents flap in the rising wind. We stand at the edge of the paddock and look over Croatia's largest lake into the dying day. *Vransko Jezero*, wide and windswept and grey. And there in the night in the howling wind I meet the murderer within. It starts with two words: Ivan Milat. In my country he is known as the Backpacker Murderer and he gave the Belanglo State Forest a very bad name. With an ice-cold shudder I recall that Ivan Milat is Yugoslav. Or perhaps I am making that up and he just looks Yugoslav. I toss and turn in my sleeping bag, warm and uncomfortable. I think of Ben in his tent three trees away. I get up and piss on the earth in the wind, squatting awkwardly on the uneven ground in the blustery dark. I cannot see Ben's tent, black against the black night. I scramble back inside, physical exhaustion no match for a coffee-stressed mind. The wind snaps at the tent. I think of 'Mr Brooks', the stupid movie I knew I shouldn't have watched on the plane to London. A good twenty-five years ago, when my kids were little, I lived alone with them in an old stone cottage in Adelaide. Night after night I'd wake to every little creak and mutter in the house, listening in my sleep for intruders at the doors and windows. And night after night nothing happened. *Nothing happened.* I grew very, very tired of waiting for nothing to happen. And so I turned off my television. No longer would I watch women being raped and murdered, whatever we wore wherever we went, week after bloody week on the TV. And a miracle occurred. Very quickly I learned that I live in a safe world. Random violence was so rare in my sphere I decided I had an even chance of winning Lotto. *I've never experienced either so I'm free to tell myself it must be true.* Then I go and watch 'Mr Brooks'. Cold and cold and cold Mr Brooks. Random Mr Brooks. No good reason Mr Brooks. No trace, fear-sucking, normal, respected and respectable Mr Brooks whose saving grace was that he targeted everyone, not just women. And in reality that made him worse because like women all over the world my DNA is attuned to the war against my kind. *I know that enemy.* Mr Brooks was a newcomer to the battlefield, not the devil we know.

I wonder who owns the paddock. I wonder if he … for I am certain this dark night that it would be a he … I wonder if he would resent us camping beneath his olive trees. I wonder if he has guns or knives. I wonder if he and his mates have been drinking and are looking for backpacker sport. Ivan Milat. Mr Brooks. The wind blows. The rain pours. The tent flaps and snaps. Contrary to movie myth, I feel safer on stormy nights, for what murderer in his right mind would be out on a night like this? Tonight, this is small comfort. It is not until my mind has Ben strung high from a tree at the end of the paddock, swaying in the morning light – a barbarian prank for an unsuspecting mother who dared camp with her son beneath an olive grove on the edge of a windy lake – that finally, finally, it has had enough bloodsport for one evening and allows me to take the reins of my own sanity.

Visibility to men frightens me; invisibility distresses me. Perpetually, in the back of my mind, the faintest of soundtracks is weighing up whether this man or that is a threat or no threat. Always I err on the side of caution. There in the darkest of nights in the wind and driving rain I ask who among them can I trust? I have learned to trust my Steadying Hand. Exploring this a little further, I identify two reasons for this aberration: 1. *he* values *my* trust. It helps him define himself as a man and as a 'good' man; and 2. I pay him. Not so long ago I trusted my husband. I am on the brink of knowing this is the wrong kind of trust, that it's Cinderella trust and Cinderella trust is always doomed to dust. Do I trust my son? On this journey there is no other man I would rather have by my side. Yet, also, my insecurities around him quiver the blood in my beating heart. Through the tremors of self-doubt I weather what I perceive to be his arrogance, his judgement and his ridicule – like father, like son, rolling down the patrilineal line. These qualities surface in neither son nor father very often, but when they do they are scathing and the women around them are on notice. In this way they keep us hedged off, unsure of our footing in their world. This pilgrimage is a journey towards trust between mother and son, thus enabling the healing of the relationship between his parents. A journey into visibility and acceptance, of seeing and being seen, *as I am*. I don't sleep well, but I sleep.

I wake glad for morning and pleased to see there are no bodies swinging from the trees at the far end of the paddock. Ben stumbles into a world washed clean. We break camp, surprised the tents are already dry. This morning I do not indulge in wondering why I'm doing this walk. I am struggling with pain and it's not my in my feet, nor in the weight of the pack on my shoulders. I feel utterly sick and have dreadful cramping pains in my belly. Bafflingly, it hurts to sit down. I walk. And I walk. And I walk. The detestable white stones give way to a sandy track. Every so often I have to sit down to let the nausea pass, but I cannot sit for long for the excruciating bolts of pain that shoot through my anus. I have never experienced such idiosyncratic symptoms. Lessons 1 and 2 of the road to Santiago are my guides: *keep going* and *this too will pass*.

We rest as often as I need to, which isn't much help – not only because it hurts to stop, but because it's cold this morning. Winter is on the wind. The grey and glassy lake of last night has become a turbulent green pond. We walk past plantations of old olive groves, tiny territories marked by ribbons of grey stone walls. There is a big brown sign beside a ragged wall that makes us laugh and lifts Ben's spirits higher than the helicopter he's wondering if he should call for his faltering mother. It says *Municipium Civile* in big white letters, but it's the hand-painted crusader, sword raised high above a bright red cross emblazoned on chest and shield, that in a heartening and mysterious way validates our bearing on this land. '*Via Apia*', says the sign, heralding the infamous Appian Way; and below that, two white arrows point in opposite directions: 7,001 kilometres to Jerusalem and 1,245 kilometres to *Roma*. Clearly, humanity has passed this way before. Ben's soaring spirits are sideswiped – by his calculations he should be less than 5,000 kilometres from the Holy City.

We roll on. It feels like forever, but eventually we hit the main road, surprised to find it's relatively quiet out here, the closest we're likely to come to coastal wilderness in this part of the world. We amble along the edge of the bitumen, listening out for cars; five kilometres of low-lying scrub rises to small patchy hills in the east and a stunning island coastline to the west; no developments in sight. We have our eyes out for Prosika, where I'm counting on a bed with clean white sheets and a tender breakfast. We spot an abandoned road leading to the coast, clamber over the silver guardrail blocking its flow to the traffic and sit in the middle of the crumbling black asphalt for breakfast: bread and cheese and the last of the tomatoes and ham. I've taken a couple of painkillers and the pain is slowly ebbing from my body. I take stock of last night's sleeplessness and know that I am done with coffee. It might give me stamina by day, but its price is fingernails-on-blackboards nights. I am beginning to suspect the pain in my belly is constipation, all this fluffy white food taking its toll, or maybe I ate too many figs.

We walk on, down the deserted road into a town dead for the winter. We think we are in Prosika, the tiny dot on our map before Pirovac; wherever we are, it is nothing but a collection of empty buildings, a crystal-blue Croatian ghost of summer.

We walk on, sticking as close as we can to the shoreline. When I think I can go no further I notice I'm projecting memories of past pain into the future. A question becomes my mantra, sometimes with every step: *Are you okay now?* Yes. I take another step. *Are you okay now?* Yes. Another step. And so on.

We make it in to Pirovac, my salvation. Bed. Shower. Food supply. Sleep. Recovery. In that order. Ben will walk on and I'll get a bus to catch up. Pirovac's centre is miles from the road. I begin to resent the new developments with their rainbow of ice-cream-cake houses and no bloody infrastructure in between. No rooms. No food. No transport. Just rows and rows of fancy cement barns, some inhabited, others not; some three-storeys high with no railings round the balconies to keep the inebriated or the children from tripping over a pot plant and crashing to the building site below. The Department of Occupational Health and Safety in my own country would have a field day. We make it into town, me blinded with pain. There are two big bars on the waterfront and no bloody food anywhere. I sit on a bench and cry, just for a minute. We find out there is a bus stop back up on the main road. I grit my teeth and we walk up the hill out of town. Ben puts me on the bus to Sibenik and waves me on. We'll catch up again tomorrow.

The passengers on the bus are curious about me. I think the conductor short-changes me and the woman across the aisle helps us across the language barrier. The bus weaves its way along the coastline, past miles of red-roofed houses cascading down steep hillsides.

We pull into a busy station congested with people and buses and smoke and fumes. Everyone in Croatia smokes. More so than Italy. The man I ask for directions to a hotel is abrupt and rude. The woman in the tourist information centre on the edge of the port is abrupt and rude. The Canadian woman she puts me on to, who rents rooms high on the hill above the old town, is not abrupt and rude so much as a disinterested pain in the arse – although that might be because I ask her if she is American. I develop an irrational hostility towards Croatians and their stupid housey coastline.

The Canadian woman sweeps me up from the footpath and drives me to the house she shares with her Croatian husband, their children and his parents, way up high overlooking the city. She rents rooms on the top floor. I am pleased to see the room is dark. I dump my pack and head straight for a shower. For the rest of the afternoon I alternate between clean blue sheets and sipping hot water on the loo, biting down on searing flashes of pain so as not to disturb the Canadian's other guests. I have no luck expelling anything at all from my body, but the pain eases off late in the afternoon.

Taking advantage of the moment I go for a walk. Sibenik is a pleasure by the port, the old city so steep there are only stairs to get to and from the town, the streets no wider than I am tall. Cars wind through the narrow alleys, unapologetically pasting me to the wall. I grab a late lunch from a friendly café, a black risotto overlooking the sea from which it came, and get hopelessly lost as I wind my way back up the stone staircases to bed. My ovaries pulse. If I am going to bleed I hope I start today, while I am resting.

I pass the evening sitting on the verandah with a German tourist, a man who works with AIDS survivors in his native Berlin. With our feet up on the railing we skim red-tiled roofs and old towers silver-grey, looking out over the old city to the blue sea and green islands offshore. We watch the day fade to grey, delighted when yellow lightning lacerates the horizon. The German expresses wonderment about the travelling habits of Australians and New Zealanders, who seem to spend months at a time exploring the world. He wants to know how we can afford it. He wants to know how we keep our jobs. I tell him there is always another job, which is true if you're not weighed down by mortgages and credit cards. And besides, it's not so hard to keep the job we do have and take time off. Germans, I have been told by Germans, lose up to half their wages to social security schemes dreamed up by policy makers to shore up the future. Leaders in my own country often cite the Germans for their model social policies in the workplace, without mentioning the cost to the people whose time and effort is devoted to their provision. Besides, I tell the German on the verandah, I have a husband who very generously supports me. His eyes widen.

'Then why are you not in the hotel by the port?' he asks.

I laugh. 'Because my husband is Dutch,' I say. 'He is happiest when I cross the road to save a penny.'

The German roars with laughter. The tribes of Europe. I have just reinforced what everybody knows about the Dutch. My husband likes to tell a Belgian joke: 'How was copper wire invented? By two Dutchmen fighting over a penny.'

In truth, walking up the hill to cheaper accommodation is the best way I know how to express my gratitude to my husband for his support for this journey. Because he *is* Dutch and he does like to save a penny.

The German and I say goodnight. I slip into my dark room at the back of the house and slide between the clean blue sheets. I lie sadly, looking into the darkness on the ceiling. More than anything right now, I would love to lie with my head on a feather pillow in my husband's lap, bathed in tenderness and love. I blink the fantasy away. Beneath the pillow would be a hard penis steering tenderness to sex, wanting from me. My longing for tenderness is just that, longing. My husband is an honest man; he is also delusional: he only knows what he knows and he is honest about what he knows. He just doesn't know he doesn't know and nor does he want to. As for me, I am tired of my own 'honesty', tired of knowing what I know and knowing that I don't know, because it's all a story anyway, just a stack of delusional tales I tell to patch up what I don't know.

My thoughts roam to my son, to the awkwardness and self-consciousness I feel when I am vulnerable around him. He knows me as strong and independent and in need of no help. In reality, I am tired of doing everything myself. And I am not as strong as I was. And I will neither pretend otherwise nor hide it, not from either of us. That means I am constantly exposed to his judgement, to his ridicule, to my vulnerability, to the light. A few days ago I asked him for help in getting my imbecilic tent pegs into the ground. I have a great little tent, an outdoors take-me-to-the-mountains tent with pegs that buckle at the sight of a pebble. I was too tired to try. He laughed his ridicule laugh at my weakness and I wanted to burst into tears. Instead I took a deep breath and looked him right in the eye.

'I need your help,' I said. 'And I am tired of you laughing at me.'

He said, 'I was raised to laugh at people when they couldn't do things.'

He was raised to laugh at people when they couldn't do things? Is that true? I know we laughed at a lot of things, but laugh because someone couldn't do something? I wonder if he has confused laughing with scoffing. I would like to think I don't scoff. I freeze between the sheets: *but of course I do! Laughter at the misfortune of others was a childhood survival tool in the wake of my father's random violence.*

This is how my mother and her children preserved their humour. This is how I raised my children. I vow from this moment to show only kindness to those all out of reserves.

I wake early and wonder, as I lie in the dark between the clean blue sheets, just what exactly my husband does with his time. When we first moved in together he'd spend all morning and then all afternoon working on his computer, hours and hours and hours every day and still he'd stress because he didn't get all his work done, worrying that there was always more to do. Yet I would walk by and he'd be playing Solitaire or if I asked what specifically he had to do he would complain about the volume of social emails he didn't have time to answer. Yesterday we spoke for a while on the phone. He told me he's had a couple of business meetings lately and I'm sure he has, yet he shares nothing with me about who and what and the ideas, concepts and possibilities he has explored. And he asks me nothing at all about myself ... or perhaps he did and I couldn't find a way to answer him that sparked his interest or established a connection. Perhaps he really does do 'not much' in his day and maybe he really is 'very good' and 'oh fine' all the time. I do my best to make offerings and openings to deeper conversation. More than this, every day, every single day, I post a blog on the internet about my journey, yet he never mentions it – never asks a single question about anything at all that's happened, never wants to know more, never comments. Curiosity zero. I am learning not to be disappointed in another.

    I throw back the sheets and pull up the blinds, boil myself some water for breakfast and sip it on the verandah, overlooking the city and the offshore islands, a world that is red and green and blue. I leave my perch midmorning, loading up the pack and heading down the steep city stairways to meet Ben at the port. Through a miracle of pilgrimness, and no thanks to Miss Rude-and-Abrupt in the information centre, I finally see him through the haze of smoke in the bus station, stuffing his face with a well-deserved hamburger for breakfast. I'm feeling a whole lot better, having sipped hot water through the night and experienced a small degree of movement. Ben and I laugh when we see each other; a handful of impossible phone calls had failed to reveal our locations. Not even the information centre was able to help. Swallowing my pride I'd called by to ask Miss Rude-and-Abrupt for assistance. Our conversation went like this:

Me (pack on my back, pointing to the street): 'I will meet my son here – can you please tell me where we are, the name of this place?'

Her: 'Information centre.'

Me: 'Ah yes, where is the information centre?'

Her: 'It is here on the road.'

Me: 'Yes, but where is here, how do you name it?'

Her: 'Information centre.'

Me: 'Is this the only information centre in Sibenik?'

She stares at me, eyes rock steady with a corrupt, 'Yes.'

Me: 'What about the port then. What is it called?'

Her: 'It is the Gateway to Croatia.'

I give up. I call Ben. I tell him I am at the information centre. He tells me there are more information centres in Croatia than pomegranates. I tell him to meet me at the port. He tells me, after we find each other at the bus station, that the port is several miles long. I had presumed he'd come in on the main road, the high road. He did. He says the views were awesome, but that it was a mission finding his way down to the water. In an effort to help him navigate his way, I had texted him, explaining I was at the port near the great church, *Sveti Jacov*, the Cathedral of Saint Joseph. As I did so, I'd hit the wrong button, the '7' instead of the 'S' for 'St', but the message was sent before I had corrected or even finished it. When we find each other he wants to know, 'What the fuck is 7t?' I dissolve laughing. That was the mangled text I gave up on, figuring he'd know it made no sense. He'd been looking for 7t, getting so pissed off he figured he'd just go get some lunch and I could come to him. It worked.

He finishes his burger. We stock up on supplies. I buy three packets of dried prunes. We chat while I have lunch, our packs seated with us at the table. He tells me he's glad to see I'm up for walking, that the only way it gets any easier is to just do it. This is the closest he comes to showing me his own complaint. He tells me about a café owner who told him about Međugorje.

'Rumour has it that an apparition appears to people there and it's quite a destination for pilgrims,' he says.

'It's only a small detour – it's random things like this that keep the journey interesting!'

'Sure,' I say merrily, gagging on my salad leaf when he tells me Međugorje is in Bosnia.

I give the landmines in my head the scant attention they deserve, focusing instead on the ferries on the water. Ben does the pilgrim maths. We can walk sixty kilometres along the coast road or we can do forty kilometres through the mountains.

'Twenty kilometres,' he says, 'is one less blister.'

Personally I can't see the toss-up. I'll take a mountain any day over an extra twenty kilometres.

We load up and hit the road, hoofing out of Sibenik up a brief and very steep incline on the edge of town. I am walking hunched over, face to the bitumen, one foot in front of the other in the afternoon sun, feeling like an Egyptian slave hauling blocks for a pyramid. Three heartbeats later I'm flat on my back on the footpath laughing so hard I nearly burst an appendix (and not because of the slave humour). Ben had put his arm out to stop me walking into a post just as I spied it myself. What I didn't see was the sign attached to it. Thanks to Ben I don't hit it as hard as I might, but still it knocks me sideways. I grab the pole and thus prevent myself from being a total write-off, but the laughter sets in and my legs no longer hold me up and here we are, two hysterical pilgrims weeping with laughter as we roll around the footpath on the edge of Sibenik. The thing is, people do not get us. They Do Not Get Us. No matter how clean and tidy and pleasant and polite we are, we are incongruent with everything that exists in this world. Everything. So we are already ridiculous. And something like this happens, me rolling around on my turtleshell back, Ben in tears trying to give me a helping hand, laughing our guts out in the middle of the day on the edge of a town where stony-faced is the generally accepted term of engagement.

Once we have me back on my feet, heading for the spotted hills of Croatia, the pack is a whole lot lighter and my spirit a whole lot freer for the laughter. We walk along the roadside, keeping company with a concrete irrigation channel funnelling water to the vineyards on both sides of the road. We are in the country; we are off the tourist trail. The road is flat and not busy. We pass through small villages whose scant inhabitants offer only cool detachment. Strange spotted hills roll along with us, as if the same hill is racing ahead to get there before us.

As the sky lights yellow and the sun dips low, we sit on the steps of a little chapel all by itself on the roadside for a feast of bread and cheese and chocolate and mandarins, watching as the sun concedes the day. It is a glorious evening, still and bright; the white walls of the chapel are lit crimson-gold by the setting sun, the colours of roses. The chapel has a small bell on its roof and a squat cement cross on its tip, a heavy wooden door and tiny little windows. So far, it appears to have escaped the EU money funnel that's pouring concrete from one end of this coastline to the other – even the dogs have new kennels; yes, concrete kennels. High on *magnifico!*, we walk into the dying day, scanning the roadside for a camp. Heading down a steep hill, tucked tight into a curve on the tarred road, we slide down an embankment into a freshly ploughed grove between two rocky ridgelines. We pitch our tents on the edge of the paddock, hugging close to the embankment, out of sight of the traffic. Ben is annoyed that I pitch my tent so close to his. It's a landmine thing. It's a murderer within thing. I'm fine with his discomfort. I tuck into my sleeping bag and, deliciously happy, listen to the crickets and the bugs do their after-sundown whistling thing.

My phone beeps and glows in the damp cold of early morn. It is a text from my husband. He says he is feeling sad. I text back. 'Stay soft,' I say, offering him the return tide of his own words. 'Let it wash through with the rain.' (It is the wet season in Thailand.) 'Be cosy,' I say. 'Be true, and I will walk for you today.'

Moments later I feel ill. He will think I am telling him what to do. He will receive not an expression of my heart but of control. I shake his dreaded judgement from my body and scramble out of the tent. There is light behind the ridge. The tents are wet with the dew. By the time the sun pops through the trees we are ready to meet the day, sitting on our packs snacking on leftover bread and cheese, washed down with chocolate and prunes.

We hit the road around eight and make a headstart on the hills. I will walk for my husband today; I will carry his sadness and his burdens, for they are also my own. We climb and we climb up a long,

long ribbon of bitumen, figuring we'll stop a few kilometres up the road for a decent feed at Podine, the first town marked on our map. Walking into the morning, chasing shadows and light on the winding mountain road, an endless chattering assault on my mind begins, bringing my body and heart down with it. My vow to myself on this journey is to meet the voices in my head, no longer to deny or resist or ignore or turn away from the unconscious and subconscious messages relaying constantly from the depths of my being, stealthily shaping my world without discernment or consent. I watch the chatter. I bow low with the burdens of obligation and resistance, negativity choking the oxygen from my veins. I am furious with myself. *I told him I would walk for him today because I knew it would please him.*

The phone beeps in my pocket, a return text from my husband. Sure enough, he is pleased indeed. He tells me he is 'touched' that I would walk for him and that he feels my love. He sends me 'long tender kisses'. It is a loving text, but I peer at it as if from behind a wall, peeping over the top to see what's going on in a tableau that has no connection to me. I struggle with the obligation to receive his offering, to play my role in his theatre of whimsical romance. I am wary now of romance, because in our world it has no foundation; I don't mind being wispy with longing, but I am also *not that*. Given the unacceptability of my independent self, I can no longer summon the sweetness of surrender to sexual enchantment that romance requires, floating to him on innocent wings that must crash and burn. *Must.* Because I have impossible expectations and he knows not what he is offering, or, more to the point, asking. Long tender kisses are beautiful if long tender kisses have value as long tender kisses. In our case, long tender kisses are not enough; they are always a prelude to more. *I will walk for you today.* Our messages are a pretend game fuelled by ignoble poetry employed to please a distant heart. Our communication is not unlike shadow boxing in a ring with answers that are 'right' or 'wrong', where the prize is approval, or censure, and consistency is a wraith so cruel it is impossible for me to know where I stand. I walk on, furious with myself for shouldering my husband's burdens as well as my own, especially when he has no interest in mine. Am I not carrying enough baggage on this journey? I ignore the text. I will walk for him but I have no desire to talk to him.

I walk on, lungs heavy with mental exhaustion. I recall the invitation my husband created for me to join him in life, how much I appreciated that he asked nothing from me, that I was free to come and go without explanation or justification ... and that it didn't take long at all before he began demanding what was once freely given and, I presume, he believes is now his right. Me. My body. My service. I did not see any of this coming. I mentioned it to the Steadying Hand one day and he replied, a bit flippantly for my liking, 'Well, every man has his seduction technique.'

There is no respite from the steady climb; I am a walking thundercloud. What fool am I to accept financial support and expect to live a life free from obligation? But then what's wrong with accepting money freely given? Can money be freely given? What has love to do with sex not freely given? What is this troublesome historic connection between the two? And how the hell did I, the one who managed to avoid this toxic trap all her life, stumble onto such a noxious battlefield? Ignorantly. Romantically. Blinded by the warmth of my husband's fire, that's how; seduced by the soft cotton of his king-sized sheets. So now what do we do? This I ask with every step up the mountain. What do we do? How do I be true and free and loving and loved and be with this man? When do we begin to share our thoughts? His expression of sadness is a start. I would love him to email me with glimpses into the sadness that has him snared today. I reach for the phone. I take another risk. I text to tell him that I receive his love. I invite him to email me with thoughts on his sadness, so that I might have an opportunity to know my husband.

As I walk that endless road, I hear his voice telling me how to speak to him: *'Now if you would just say ...'*. My husband also likes to tell me how to live. He thinks he asks 'very nicely'. What he does is render me invisible in my own home. Or his home. The trifecta is complete with his obsessive need for me to view the world as he does, a world I love that he, with his clever conspiracy theories, abhors (hence our mighty row triggered by Rupert Murdoch). I begin to sing a song I have previously rejected as trite:

I'm young and I love being young and I'm free and I love being free
To live my life the way I choose, to say and do whatever I please.

I am in territory previously unknown to me and for this I give thanks; for I am more compassionate for having wandered into this shadowy land, briefed now on the incomprehensible choices women make, most obviously *to stay*. I stand among the legions of women who have surrendered their sovereignty in return for their keep; I am among the initiated, the ones who please when we are not pleasing.

My phone beeps again. Dare I glance at his message? I reach into my pocket for the phone. His protective walls have risen faster than the screens near a bank teller staring into the eyes of one who has come to claim what is not his. He tells me the sadness has passed, that he doesn't need to write an email because there is 'nothing to do but be', which is his way of claiming the high spiritual ground. Childishly, my lips parody his escape route: 'nothing to do but be'. I squirm. I am furious with myself for bothering and sick to bloody death of being married to someone who is not willing to share the journey. How on Earth does he expect me to open to him as a woman when he refuses to show himself to me? Just before we left Wilsons Creek we were sitting on the verandah together, the pademelons grazing the winter grass in the sunshine. My husband loved to watch the pademelons, the small round wallabies nibbling on the fruits of our domesticity, returning to the musty earth of the forest as they please.

'You used to trust me like the pademelons do,' he said sadly.

'You have created an invitation for the pademelon,' I said. 'She is free to come and go. How long would she stay if you demanded sex?'

He thought I was being smart. In fact, the metaphor wasn't far off. I can only imagine our marriage bounty if my husband could receive the beauty and grace of my gifts, our gifts, freely given. My husband bought a book online that he longed for me to read. Eventually, to shut him up, I complied. It was about a woman called Anastasia who lived alone in the wild forests of Russia among the mighty ringing cedars. A Russian man called Gregory 'discovered' her and attempted to force himself upon her in his oafish manly way. One day, when we were wrestling with our sexual despair, my husband choked on a horror he expressed aloud: 'I hope I am not like Gregory.' My heart went out to him. *Yes, my dear*, I thought. *You are my Gregory.* And you and Gregory are not alone on this Earth among tribes of impenetrable men who are blind to the reasonable possibility that they are lacking as lovers; who would not be lacking as lovers if they were available to receive the evolving truth of a woman.

I don't mind my husband being a Gregory. What I mind is his refusal to allow our sexuality to be a journey. I mind his unwillingness to recognise the reality of his own being and, consequently, his assumption that it's okay to use my body as a distraction from, or a dumping ground for, his own demons. And I mind his desperate, unacknowledged need for me – my beautiful body – to save him from himself. Because once he is high on his own orgasm, everything is right in his world. He is validated. He is loved. He is secure *in his own mind*.

As I walk up the mountain road I do my best not to run from my husband, not to isolate myself from him, not to withdraw, yet I know I am already a long way away – and that every step forward is a giant geographical step towards him.

There is no respite from the steady climb. I need to adjust a bandaid on my blister. Ben takes a seat at a small fork in the road, a dirt track marked by the smallest chapel in Christendom. We sit on its step, even then a head taller than the little white shrine with its plastic Mary and mantle of melted wax. I take off my shoes and socks and examine the blister, roiling with the voices of discontent and confusion in my head. I attempt to explain to Ben my chagrin that those closest to us seem least able to bear our vulnerability. My words are jumbled and my language insecure. Instead of offering him the clarity of my soul, he receives the sludge through which it must travel. He cuts me off with a flippant remark, dodging my vulnerability as his own. I can feel myself sailing into treacherous waters, can sense the distant rumble of a coming storm, but I do not have the strength to turn for home. I keep talking and without warning I am in the midst of someone else's squall. I hold back the tears. I turn from my son and look to Mary.

I walk on. And there in the morning sunshine on a long ribbon of mountain road in a foreign country recently recovered from war, the purpose of my pilgrimage slugs me in the heart: *I walk to free myself from the hostilities that live in me.* The perfection of walking my inner hostilities through this particular land is not lost on me. *As within, so without.*

We reach Podine to discover it is not a town but a 'town' and the only place 'open' is the local tavern. A husband and wife are cleaning up after last night's party. They sell us orange juices from the bar. They offer us their clean toilets. They allow us to charge up our cameras and computers. They let us sit out the front on their wooden benches in the gentle sunshine. I soak up the music drifting into the morning while Ben dips into Don Bruno's prized blue bible and learns about the importance of stoning to death the man who gathers wood on the Sabbath. We are shocked. We giggle. This is the book that sells more copies than any other on Earth. This is the holy doctrine that we in the West pound with moral fortitude as we pronounce Muslims evil. This is the book upon which we swear to tell the whole truth and nothing but the truth. God help us, because with this god we're going to need all the help we can get.

The tavern husband beams his curiosity at us from a sweet moon face. Neither he nor we have the language to describe for him who we are and what we are doing. We thank him and his wife and walk on refreshed, deeper and deeper into the mountains. Old men call greetings from rooftops, old women throw smiles from cabbage patches. In Australia we call them 'rednecks' and I wonder why we in the West find peasant folk 'quaint' when they are not our own, and offensive when they are? I begin to warm to Croatia.

The mountains are autumn patchwork. The air is fresh, the sky blue and the breeze cool enough to keep us from overheating in the sunshine. Every now and then we pass through a 'town' marked on Ben's map and, despite my insistence that the size of a dot on a map is only relative to what's around (a lesson I learned in the back country of South Australia thirty years ago), he is convinced that each new 'town' will deliver the pig-on-spit he's been drooling over since first sighting in Sibenik. We have spied the spit, no worries; he just hasn't managed to time it right for the roast to be ready. I am pleased to discover that hope, for my son, springs eternal. Personally I'd settle for a slice of stale bread. In the spotted mountains of Croatia, on the middle road between the motorway and the sea, there is no such pilgrim luck.

Today is one of the few days we have a plan: we'll walk about fifteen kilometres and have lunch, then I'll get the bus and find a camp about ten kilometres down the road. Instead we walk. And we walk. And we walk. We have no food. We are rationing our water. The good news is I have found my pilgrim feet. By midafternoon I see Croatia's red, white and blue flag flapping madly in the wind up ahead. A castle! There will be hot soup. There will be fresh bread. And, of course, there will be wild boar roasting on a spit. It is a tourist castle, I am sure. I've seen such things on the tourist strip near where I live. The flapping flag is our beacon, our lighthouse on a hungry sea. It's not until we are a few footsteps away that we realise our castle is a cemetery. A bloody cemetery! We slide down the wall and lean up against our packs, resting with the dead while we watch the traffic turn left and right at the nearby crossroads. We eat our last morsel of chocolate and play backgammon on the footpath. The score is 23–13 to Ben, and we agree that I make a great comeback game.

Ben is still holding out for one of these 'towns' to deliver. I've given up holding out for anything. 'Let's just see what's around the corner,' he says. Round the corner is four kilometres. We make it to a major intersection. The sign says STOP and I do. I sit right there on the corner, laying myself and my pack down in the dirt among the weeds and rubbish while I take stock of our situation. What might have been a café is another bloody church. Not quite the sustenance we have in mind. I sit with the packs while Ben checks out the settlement for signs of edibility. Note: *settlement*, not town. A shiny black wedding parade drives by, streaming white ribbons and honking horns. The throbbing in my feet marks time with a not-so-distant chainsaw; face to the wind my spirit keeps pace with the clouds racing through the clear blue sky. Ben is certain that because the next town has a railway station it will also have food.

We walk on, surprised to find we are still climbing. We rest. We walk on. I thought Ben's bet on the railway town was a pretty good one, but the wrathful Bible god must be with us today. A sweet old man calls out from his verandah and offers Ben a drink. I am out of water. I sit in the long weeds on the roadside while Ben fills up my waterbag.

We walk on. Onward ever upward. The thing about walking is that you never know what's around the next corner, never know what's ahead, not even when you're right there on the corner; realities are revealed when they are present and not a moment before. And so it is that we turn one more corner, just one, and we are face to face with a new world. The sea! A great big horseshoe of land and blue sea. My beloved Adriatica! Croatia's southern coastline. We are as high as we can possibly be. We can see Split. We give a whoop! It's all downhill from here.

We walk on, as if there is anything else to do. We walk on and on. My feet, which have held up so well all day, now feel as if the bones are spiking holes in the soles of my feet. Pad, pad, pad down the mountain. Pad, pad, pad. Pad, pad, pad. The sun sets glorious in front of us. Split, on the far eastern corner of the bay, glows orange. It is as if the god of glory is making amends for our hunger and pain. Pad, pad, pad. Pad, pad, pad. Split is now awash in a hazy pink. Pad, pad, pad. Pad, pad, pad. Darkness is upon us. Pad, pad, pad. We don our flashing headlamps. Pad, pad, pad. And then, in the delirious darkness, we see a great white house with a pizza sign. Please let us stay, I whisper to the god of glory. We collapse inside. We order pizza. We order wine. We have just walked thirty-six kilometres over mountains high and higher seeking food and shelter. I rub my darling feet. We eat pizza. We drink wine. There is a family of daughters sitting behind us. We ask for 'hotel'. The father tells us three kilometres. My face must say it all. The mother speaks to a man at their table. They rent rooms. They rent us his. He picks up my pack and romps it up the stairs of the shiny white palace. He changes his sheets. He moves his dirty dishes to the corner of the sink. He gives us fresh towels and bids us goodnight. Ben and I look at each other in the silence and grin. I take the bed, he gets the lounge. He turns on his computer. He has wireless! I hit the hay. Ben waltzes back downstairs to the bar, just in time to watch Croatia beat Israel in the soccer. It's a big night for the boys. Each to their own, our day is complete.

It takes Ben a while to get going this morning, which suits me just fine. We hit the road midmorning, stopping for breakfast and backgammon among the weeds in a supermarket carpark. We stock up on crappy bread and cheese and orange juices that are more chemical than juice. We walk into a steady stream of traffic through another industrial frontier. Although we cannot see or hear or smell her, according to our map Adriatica is a tantalising few blocks to our right – with no road to the shore. We walk on and on into the traffic until eventually … bingo! We are able to duck down a side road and weave our way to the coast. We ask a young woman holding a child on her hip for directions to the water. She runs inside for her husband, who speaks a little English. He is more interested in telling us about the 1,700-year-old olive tree that we must pass on the road.

We sit in the spread of the massive tree, gnarled and shapely. The sign says it is 1,500 years old … it must be a very old sign. And there in the dusty shade among pocketfuls of pips we eat chocolate and play backgammon. Today's score is 5–3, to Ben of course. We have made a bet that could go a long way towards evening things up overall: if Russia sold Alaska to the Americans, Ben loses half his 10-point lead; if the Canadians sold Alaska then, hell, I'll take Ben up on his offer of calling it quits on the current round and starting the challenge again.

We find the water's edge and roam along a magnificent waterfront shaded by sweet old trees, entertained by moats and castle ruins. A drover's dog could tell you why everyone who sailed into this bay in the last 2,000 years wanted it for themselves. It's not just sheltered and fertile, the islands and peninsulas jut out in all the right places. More than this, it is beautiful. The sea is aqua-dark, a watercolour unknown to me; deep green yet blue, black on the underside and living bright through and through. We lunch in a crowded café among holiday-happy Croatians. We figure it is probably Sunday. We play backgammon, calling it quits at 28–16. It's time to google Alaska.

Ben and I part company on the waterfront. We've been walking into Split for hours now and it doesn't seem to be getting any closer. Besides, I'm not convinced the wide open pathway tracing the shore isn't going to dump us at any moment onto a hostile roadway. I wander up to the main road with my fingers crossed there'll be a bus. It takes a while but I find a bus stop, and there I stand, alone and bus-wondering for a good half-hour, watching someone's necklace of white washing flap in the breeze across the road. Croatians, I have noticed, wash only one colour at a time. Soon a handful of locals gathers at the bus stop, which is always a good sign. I ride the bus into Split, glad to be off my feet, relatively speaking, given that the bus is so crowded I must stand, bothersomely for all concerned, with the pack on my back.

From the terminal I walk a few small circles until a kind woman points me into the old city, past a giant bronze statue, bulwark to the massive city walls. The statue is huge, decked in long bronze robes and sporting an arrow-sharp nose, a pointed cap on his head, a book of spells in the crook of his left arm and a vengeful right finger pointing to the sky. He is either a man of the Catholic god summoning the wrath of grapes or a wizard! Daughter of a new world, it is impossible for me to tell. He's pretty impressive either way and I wouldn't want to cross words with him ... or would I? I duck through the walls to discover they are not city walls but *palace* walls. A bloody palace! How fantastic is that! Rooms and alleyways and arches yellow-old still standing. What a wonderful surprise. The palace eventually spills me onto a waterfront alive with the great ferries of Europe trundling in and out of the harbour, but not to Pescara, and people wandering contentedly along the white polished-stone esplanade beneath shady palms.

I sit on a bench and wait for Ben. I watch the people. I watch the children. I watch the boats. I tease apart my relationship with my husband, wondering what more I can do. I can acknowledge the reflection: *here is my defensive persona gasping for breath, knowing she is about to die*. I wander through my body: heart, soft and wide, focused gently on the horizon, knowing all will be well; belly, unsure and longing for certainty – here is my sideways glance, my watchfulness for escape, my 'I'm outa here!'; throat, tight with longing, not just for the right words but also for ease of conversation; eyes, here are the tears uncried, but not so many; thighs, here is the tension of holding on, the longing for tenderness, the wishfulness of *please let me take my hands off the wheel*, let me rest in the cradle of marriage; arms, here is the longing to hold and to touch ... I watch the sun set and the new moon grow brighter as the watercolours on the horizon fade to darkest blue and vow that from this moment on my body is available only in service to love.

The silver sickle moon is my favourite. New beginnings. A fabulous time to start the journey proper, Split to Istanbul. I watch the lights of seaside settlements glow yellow around the bay. I'm looking back the way we've come, back towards the longest day, back towards Ben.

The moon tracks gold on the water. I wonder where he is. It is a stunning scene and I'm surprised how well it captures on film. The air grows chilly with the dark. The bench is hard. I do not know the way in to my husband. It's all very well for him to claim transparency; for me that's like looking through a shop window – if you're going to see anything but your own reflection, your face has to press up against the glass, hands cupped to block the light, and even then you see only what's on display. How hard does he expect me to work to see him? For even then I can see only what attracts me, or doesn't attract me. Is it my role to weigh worth, value, design, content? I would rather he meet me at the door, invite me in and show me around. *'Ah, this has value; this is old but I keep it because …; this I'd rather let go but can't quite bring myself to live without.'*

I text Ben. He is coming. I text him again. He's coming. I check out the price of rooms in the grandiose old hotels behind me. I text to tell him to check in if he finds a hotel on his way into town, because there's no way either of us is willing to pay the prices of Split's elite. A man with dark curly hair and well-worn green and purple trousers asks if he might talk to me. His name is Jacool and he wants to practise his English. He tells me he has a mental illness and cannot work. He tells me there is no support in Croatia for people such as himself. He tells me he would love a new pair of jeans because even though he likes the green and purple keepsakes, people think he is homosexual, including his parents. Jacool's disclosures open a doorway to the war, which until now I have been reluctant to discuss among strangers.

'No, no,' he says quickly, as if shamed by such distasteful business.

'Just three times we had to go down to the bomb shelter,' he says, 'and one bomb in the harbour killed three people. We live like neighbours – why they want to do that?'

He asks for money and I give him twenty kuna, which is about five Australian dollars. It is not enough. He wants the jeans. I wonder why I do not just give him the money … and remember the suspended alms policy. Ah yes, when I understand why I do not give him the money I will be better placed to hand it over.

It's well past dark. Just as I am shaking my head to Jacool's further outstretched hand, Ben rocks up. The road to Split, he says, never ends.

I'm glad I took the bus. He takes my pack for me. He has left his at the *hostal* he found on the way in. I love him for this. We walk out of the old city and hoof it a good fifteen minutes through wide and shady streets. Now and then, shadowed by my husband, my heart sinks, but not as far as it used to; and where once the mists of distress would have descended, blocking my view of the mannequins on display in the shop window, my step is light and my spirit steady.

The *hostal* is warm. It has wireless. It has clean white sheets. I make a new moon promise: *I will attempt to know my husband.*

Split is beautiful. I am speaking, of course, of the old city. Down by the water it is mountain still, even with the ferries and the people wandering around the esplanade. We are told that in summer Split turns up the volume, that it's Croatia's party town, crowded and humming. From a pilgrim's perspective, it's great not having to compete for food and shelter, yet I can't help but wonder if Split absorbs all that energy into her old walls and is mountain still in the summer, just the same.

Today is a productive day, a getting-things-done-ready-for-the-road-tomorrow kind of day. We have washing to do; Ben wants to print *partypilgrims.com* business cards to draw attention to his website; I need a headband to keep growing blonde locks from my eyes: simple things that cost us the better part of a day. An Aussie couple owns the laundromat and we're treated to the indulgence of speaking our own language while we do the washing. Between missions, I sit by the harbour, eating chocolate and wondering about Croatia … *who is this country swallowed by the mists of global treaty and how is it she never previously existed for me? And why do her people not speak her own name – Hrvatska?*

Like the land of the Persians, now Iraq and Iran, this world should never have become the domain of barbarians. *Not today. Not yesterday. Tomorrow promised so much more.* Yet here I am walking this bellicose country mindful of treading on unturned earth lest it blow off my leg. A ferry blows its horn. I breathe in the sunshine. I see now why people say Croatia is beautiful. Sibenik was just rude. Zadar fabulously old and keep-to-itself. Split is a mother's arms, a healthy woman with a sparkle in her eyes. Yet behind the old city, there is a drab hubbub with, it seems to me, more than its share of bent old women scouring rubbish dumpsters and old men sitting in grubby stairwells drinking from paper bags. But that's just a stranger's perspective, don't mind me.

I am learning to accept the deadpan faces of the Croatians, for I am discovering that if I rest awhile in their company they will warm to the stranger, however imperceptibly; although, having a radar for aggression, I can be startled by their anger. While the Italians were exuberant and loud and passionate in their speech, even appearing to argue among themselves, the Croatians have an edge that is without joy. There is a huge exception and that is the old men who spent their youth and middle years as immigrants to countries such as my own and America. These men have lights in their eyes and songs, sad or otherwise, still living in their hearts. I know this because they go out of their way to reminisce with us.

Split is not the Yugoslavia of my mind. Yet, and yet, I watch the people by the harbour, lingering too long on faces pancake-round or pencil-sharp, curious about scowling features and eyes too cold. Faces that lit up in the hills are frozen in the city. I have followed my son into Yugoslavia's hostile heart – and my own, of course. We busy ourselves with our preparations to leave, as if the journey proper is about to begin. I am walking Adriatica's eastern shoreline, even though the sea is calling my spirit west to the other shore, the one that looks to the rising sun. Adriatica is beautiful here and I sense her power, but she is not my home. I long for her tide to carry me away.

As the evening sun strikes red the bare hills behind the city, I sit in the window of a restaurant in the palace's harbourside façade, priming the backgammon board and waiting for Ben to finish loading footage onto his computer at the *hostal*. The new moon hangs rowboat sweet in the sky. Jacool wanders along the esplanade on the other side of the glass. He does not see me, beholden now to a world that excludes him and his purple-green trousers. We are not unlike beggars, Ben and I: dependent on the goodwill of strangers. A song snatches my attention, 'The Lady In Red' playing softly in the background. I have long loved this song, stirring deep within me the beauty of a woman loved for her place in a moment, that she is all and she is enough; more than this, there is his sense of privilege that she has chosen him. Ben blows in, full of apologies for keeping me waiting. We order seafood pastas and wine; we roll the dice. Even though I won the Alaska bet, we have called off the challenge, for now. We share with each other our delight with the palace, built by the Roman emperor Diocletian around the same time as the olive tree on the other side of the bay was striking its roots into the new earth. Ben says he still doesn't know who the big bronze statue outside the city walls might be. I tell him I do, because I asked a Scottish tourist with a guide book earlier in the day. I tell him it is Thumbledore. He laughs and says, 'That's Dumbledore, Steph.' I tell him that actually it's Gregorius of Nin, who did something famously biblical for Croatia, perhaps struck down a thousand Venetians with one dash of his pointy finger. I'm not far off. A thousand years or so ago Gregorius won the right for Croatians to hear liturgical services in their own language. It's nice to know that pointed finger had papal purpose. Ben wonders why people line up to stroke Gregorius's toe, which with all the attention is shiny as a copper coin freshly laundered in a can of Coke. I tell him it's a Thumbledore-for-luck thing.

We wander home through the dark and shady streets to curl up for our second and final night in Split. I lie in the darkness of night and list my perceptions of this land: brutal, barbaric, harsh, cruel, sadistic, sharp, curtain dark, shadowy, unseen, emerging, emergent; I wonder about the music and laughter of the dead; I make a note of landmines, as if for the first time, and promise myself no unturned fields and to be wary of forests. Here, then, are the hostilities of my heart. I roll over and try for sleep. I have been childish, insecure and unable to see what the adult in me might choose for her life. I will walk for the woman, the woman born.

We breeze out of Split midafternoon, Ben's fabulous new business cards burning holes in our pockets and me high on pilgrim's purpose. We leave the city via the nearest waterfront, stopping for lunch beside a marina close to the old city. I swear Croatia has more boats than fish in the sea. We play backgammon and feast on seafood risotto, conscious that each meal we pass may be all that's offered this day. We walk into the afternoon, around the shoreline towards the edge of the city, weaving easily through a scattered parade of rollerbladers and lovers.

Ten minutes into it, Ben says it's time to rest. We sit on the warm grey dirt by the water and he promptly falls asleep, flat on his back in the sunshine. I sit easy, arms wrapped around my knees, watching Adriatica's blue tide run. Church bells ring in the distance. A chainsaw purrs on a nearby building site. A woman plump and sunbrowned swims offshore. Two large boats float at anchor near a faraway island. Dirty smudges of cloud hang low on the fine line between sea and sky. I have lain on a thousand coastlines just like this.

It's late when we rise from the dirt and load our packs onto our backs. We leave the coast when we run out of sand, turning away from jagged rocks and water to stumble through strangely quiet suburbia, past boys too young who skid dirt at us from their bicycle wheels, only to be called into line by barely visible elders sitting on logs beneath spindly trees. We make our way to the highway and spend the next hour walking along the main road into Split's grumbling peak hour traffic. We spy a sign for a camping ground five kilometres out of the city, knowing this will be far enough for us today.

We choose campsites on the far edge of a well-ordered pine forest beside a small estuary and pitch tents on ground so stony that we have to dig holes for the pegs. We make a fire on the stones from pine cones aplenty and a slim branch long enough to keep us warm well into the chilly evening. We eat bread and cheese for dinner by the fire. The sickle moon sets low over the headland, flat and narrow. The lights of Podstrana sketch orange and blue crayon stripes across the water. A puppy comes sniffing in the dark. We welcome her to the fire. She squirms and wiggles, lying low, as if waiting to be told off – and we soon find out why. I turn around and she has demolished my tent, her small black face peering out of the billows. She is scouting for food. We laugh and shoo her off. Sitting around the fire I catch my son's eye and realise I rarely look him in the eye, at ease and tender in spirit. And I realise that we, all of us, can only start from where we are; we can only get there from here. Ben crashes early, leaving me to the fire and the moon and the water.

I wake early and crawl into a glorious morning, pleased there's no dew on the tent. The last of the sunrise is colouring the horizon. The world is soft. I pack up and snack on Toblerone and mandarins by the water, waiting for Ben to surface. We hit the road and make good time, stopping in a roadside grove that borders the sea for a picnic feast of bread and cheese, chocolate and mandarins, resting on the soft dirt between the grapevines in the midmorning sunshine. Ben reckons he can see the weeds blowing puffs of smoke. Mirage or miracle, he witnesses it over and over. Stare as I might, they do not puff for me.

We walk all day along Croatia's party coast. The summer has long gone and it's wall-to-wall apartments and restaurants, all closed for rest or renovations. We walk along the single lane highway, Adriatica's blue water wonderful compensation for the rumbling inconvenience of the road. I stare at the shimmering sea and wonder again about Yugoslavia and Croatia and the dark years before war liberated the coastline. I wonder if the sea sparkled as brightly in the darkness … was the water quite as blue … did they hug their children as tightly … I wonder about forgiveness – and its alternative; about the young men and women who fled the dark tide and raised their families in a land so distant it was barely imaginable to the ones who grew old without their grandchildren. And I wonder about the C-like curve that is modern Croatia and whether it was ideology or geography that created such a strange shape for a new, once old, country.

We stop along the pebbly shore and play backgammon in the shade of the overhanging pines. Ben is keen to start a new challenge. I tell him, 'When I win three in a row.' My game is improving, we're breaking even. Nonetheless, I'm holding out for three in a row.

We walk on through iconic fishing villages, peering into waterside sheds stuffed with old wooden boats and nets, dangling our feet over splintered jetties into the shimmering sea.

We ride the day to Omis, twenty kilometres south, where Ben has teed up a couch-surfing bed for the night. Here we meet Ivan, a reporter for the newspaper in Split and the only person in Croatia who doesn't smoke. Over beer and the biggest pizza we have ever seen, we learn some very important facts about Croatia, such as the world as we know it can thank Croatia for the common tie. According to Ivan, the soldiers of oldentime rode off to war wearing red ties, and each year Croatia celebrates Tie Day. Even old Gregorius of Split gets a red tie. And we owe it to Croatia for the pen. Mr Penkala, a Croat, invented the pen – not to be confused with the Hungarian Mr Biro, who invented the biro, which is now commonly known as a pen. He tells us about the Bora, the Adriatic ice-wind that blows from the north and is due any day now. The most exciting piece of news, to us, is that Omis (pronounced Omish) is home to the infamous Kacic family, the best known pirates on the Adriatic, east or west. My heart skips a beat. Adriatica's darker shore is suddenly a little more interesting.

Ivan gives us a soundbite lesson on Yugoslavia. He tells us Croatia is known as the Christian Wall, gateway to the Christian west. Serbia and Croatia, he says, are Christian countries, Bosnia is Muslim. He tells us, with a shrug, that Tito, anti-fascist resister and Yugoslavia's best known prime minister, was a Croat. He tells us about a Macedonian pop singer – and as he talks I note how he pronounces the 'c' in Macedonia as 'c' for cat, leaving off the tail-end of the word as I know it, making it *Macedon*. I roll the new word around my mouth as I recall various maps we have seen. Makedon. Massedonia. Macedon. Ivan says the pop singer was killed in a car accident yesterday, a young man called Tose Proeski who is mourned throughout the Balkan states. 'This is the first time we have been unified for some time,' he says with another shrug.

I say, 'Perhaps this is the purpose of his death.'

Ivan is shocked. I get the sense that for him there is no good purpose in death, at least not for the young and the loved. I think of Princess Diana and Australia's crocodile hunter, Steve Irwin. I think of all those funerals I attended over the years for teenagers killed in car accidents, reporter on a country newspaper admitted to grief's inner sanctum. There is purpose in death. It brings us closer to love. More than this, when death is in the room, we are unmasked: *there is only love*. Ivan leads us into the Omis night and delivers us to couchsurfing luxury in the holiday apartment his mother rents to tourists in the summer, underneath their house. For Ben and me it is a pilgrim heaven moment and we sleep with the power of innocents.

We wake to the first breath of winter and, honouring a promise we made to Ivan, agree to farewell Omis in style with a visit to *Konoba U Nased Marina*. Forgive me for thinking we are looking for a 'marina'. We wander around Omis, a walled town held close to the water by a sheer face of rock that is Gargantuan, searching for *Konoba U Nased Marina*. Wherever we walk we are in the rockface shadow, awed by its presence and overwhelmed by the cold. The weather has turned. We meet a surprisingly wide river spilling from the other side of the rock. Were it not for our packs and the distance ahead of us, we'd have bowed to curiosity's naked charms and explored the back country. Instead we wander along a small harbour weighed heavy with big boats at anchor – *pirate boats!* – wondering all the while about the stone battlements carved high into the rock face on the other side of the river. We ask for directions to *Konoba U Nased Marina* from the locals, all of whom either roll their eyes or shake their heads, until a kindly stallholder in the market drops what he is doing and leads us through the narrow alleyways of the old town into what is either a cave or a very old stone cavern. A tavern. In a cavern. We duck through the doorway into a dark room full of seagoing treasures, including a few old buggers in for their morning swill. *The pirates' lair.* We down packs on a faded rug in the corner, aware all eyes are on us. I sink into a nest of cushions covered in faded tapestries, a rusted anchor on a chain on the floor nearby, while Ben steps up to the bar to order the salted fish recommended by Ivan. From where I'm sitting he looks like an intergalactic stranger in a Star Wars bar.

'Are you serving food yet?' he asks. The barman tries to take Ben seriously. He says something to the locals and they all laugh.

'No,' he says. 'Just … ' (makes drinking motions).

'Then we'll have two hot chocolates thanks,' says Ben.

The barman says something to the locals and they chuckle.

'Nothing hot,' says the barman.

'Coffee?' asks Ben hopefully.

More laughs.

'Beer or whiskey,' says the barman.

I can see Ben weighing up his options. He peers into the glass of a man beside him.

'What about that?' he asks.

They laugh louder.

'Beer or whiskey or that,' says the barman.

'I'll have one of those,' says Ben, delighted with the opportunity to lean his elbow on the bar and toss down the hearty black herbal brew favoured by the locals, all of whom look as if they've spent the night in a nautical time warp.

Our promise to Ivan fulfilled, we roll on, stopping at a bakery for dry and boring pastries to fuel us up for the road ahead. *Up* being the operative word. The road south from Omis is straight up – as in uphill all the way into the spotted hills of Croatia. We are on the dark side of the mountain and freezing cold, whipped by a wind that can only be the infamous Bora. The chill is driven away by the risen sun on the clifftop overlooking Adriatica's silent blue and Omis, now far below. We stop for bread and cheese and backgammon, the sunshine warming our bones at last.

We walk steadily through the day, the party coast giving way to the holiday coast. Instead of wall-to-wall apartments and restaurants, all closed, we walk among pockets of apartments and restaurants, mostly closed. The road stays high. Adriatica's tide runs a darker blue. Wild pennyroyal, crushed underfoot, vents familiar minty vapour.

Ivan rings Ben. He wants a photo of us for a story he is writing for his newspaper. This means we need internet. We look around. Nothing but us, the sea, the road and the spotted hills of Croatia. And a tunnel up ahead. I have an aversion to tunnels, especially those with no light and no end in sight. As we're wondering whether the dusty road down the steep hillside will lead us around the tunnel, a Croat in a battered van pops over the rise and sweeps towards us, covering us in yellow dust. He invites us to stay in his caravan park, down the dusty road. I ask if the road takes us around the tunnel. He says yes. I ask if he has internet. He says yes. Now we're interested. He wants us to hop in the van and he'll drive us down. Ben tries to explain that he is walking and it is not possible to ride in a car, even down a dusty driveway. I hop in the van, just to spare everyone the trouble of explaining the inexplicable.

Milan introduces himself and offers Ben his office computer, which is old and unused. First we need him to take our photo so we can send it to Ivan. Milan insists on serving me morning tea. I settle on water and a doughnut. 'Kamp Sirena' is a vertical caravan park whose only guests are a dumpy middle-aged English couple soaking up the last of the sunshine down by the water's edge. Milan's hospitality is generous and insistent. He keeps us too long. We head off into the afternoon sunshine, despite his ministrations for us to stay and his warnings about wind and rain, and without him marrying off Ben to his daughter, the very gorgeous and sensible Marija.

The road stays high above spectacular blue-green water. Slowly the vista widens, becoming a Mediterranean-style postcard with the highway racing along beside a wild blue ocean. From a tourist sign we learn the river that runs through Omis's spectacular gorges flows behind the giant rocks above us. An amazing sight, we're sure, for the backpack-free. The sun shines all day. Small white clouds gather in the afternoon; the Dutch call them 'sheep clouds'. Soon the whole flock is an amorphous white.

We play backgammon overlooking Adriatica, now silver-grey, like an evening dress that shimmers silver when you know it is really grey. I grow tired. This morning I woke groggy and clumsy, my eyes puffy and my eyesight poor – facts I can no longer ignore. My feet have begun to rub around the heels and toes. There is a tug in my thigh muscle with every step, as if I have bumped the corner of a table. I've had enough – which in pilgrim land is a major 'so what?'

We walk on. The high road winds around steep hillsides tumbling into the ocean below.

We walk on. The sun begins to set. It's beautiful.

We walk on, both of us willing to forgo dinner for a campsite. A big white building promises food and, pilgrim heaven, it delivers! Mushroom soup and salad, topped off with rissoles for Ben. It's long dark by the time we're ready to move on, our sights now set on a bed in Brela, way down below on the coast. *Brela*, a name to be whispered.

We walk in the dark, zigzagging down Brela's perfect roadway into night empty streets, down a long concrete stairway and onto the promenade by the beach. We veer away from quiet waterfront restaurants and wander out towards the headland. Near the end of the pathway, below the magnificent homes of Croatia's retired elite, we find a shadowed patch of pebbly beach beside a large wooden dinghy and a few plastic roller boats, shelter from prying eyes. We pitch our tents, such as we can in the dark on the pebbles, me tying the tent ropes to the dinghy to compensate for the crappy aluminium pegs. My tent is a saggy puff of nylon but it will do for tonight, because I am all out of reserves, physical and emotional. We wave at the high half moon over the water, the lights of an unknown city glowing orange behind the headland, and say goodnight.

I lie in bed, rough on the pebbles, exhausted and fighting tears. I am beyond my limits. Unwilling to risk my son's disapproval or buttoned-up arrogance, I did not speak my need to stop earlier. Or I did but didn't do so clearly. Or I did so clearly and he failed to hear me. I no longer know. What I do know is I am tired of the energetic darts he fires my way in lieu of speaking, absolving himself from responsibility for his thoughts, or needs, yet clearly telling me *something*. I'm also really, really tired of reading about myself on his blog, hurt by his perceptions of me and pissed off that he speaks for me. I feel misrepresented. I feel betrayed. With enormous effort these past days I have focused on my own experience, allowing him his, not-speaking my disquiet with his blog-sport. And now, terror of public exposure and ridicule snatch the breath from my lungs. A self-defensive fury rises in my limbs and I cry out as the pointed fingers of anonymous judgement tell me who I am and what I am like. This is an old war. And it has nothing to do with my son, other than the fact I want him to protect me from judgemental forces that can only be unknowable and invisible to him. And I want his approval. I just hope I haven't trashed my feet. My right knee aches and there's a pinched nerve in my bum. I close my eyes against the sagging nylon, just millimetres from my face. In truth, give or take the odd war, I am content and warm, tired and cosy on Adriatica's eastern sands, the lap of the little waves on the pebbly shore rocking me to sleep.

Within moments I wake to the plop, plop, plop of raindrops on the tent. It is a beautiful sound. I listen in the dark-light to the sweet pat, pat, pat, keeping a weathered eye on the saggiest part of the tent, now down near the foot of my sleeping bag. Lightning flashes white and brilliant. I count the seconds. Eight. Thunder rolls around the bay. I weigh my options: will it pour, won't it pour ... stay here soaking wet or seek relative dryness, even if it means sitting up all night?

At the next round of thunder, I settle on affirmative action, packing everything into waterproof bags and me into Gore-Tex raingear. Thunder circles the bay. Rainburst bruises the tent. I unzip and brave the watery night, on mission for alternative shelter. The world outside is wild and magnificent. Lightning snaps the blackest of clouds white and yellow and grey. Big rain rides the water. Ben's tent with its magnificent red alloy pegs is holding up fine. I can only presume he is sleeping, in which case there is no need to disturb him. Bowed low into the storm I trot back along the promenade, seeking out a stone bench in an alcove I spied on our way in. It's there and it's wet, not as sheltered as my mind-in-a-storm recalled. On the way back I check out a gated entry-way to one of the great homes on the hillside. It would do if the rain was driving the other way. And then I notice what I didn't see when we pitched our tents – change sheds! Three concrete cubicles. One is clean and dry in the far corner. I run across the crunchy wet pebbles to the tent, which is now a soggy mass of wet nylon, and drag out the pack and sleeping bag. They get the driest cubicle. Thunder and lightning pummel the night as I bundle up the tent and shove it into the cubicle next door, along with the raingear. I leave one cubicle for Ben, just in case he bails out later in the night. The thin blow-up mattress fits tight along the back wall of the little shelter. I prop up the pack as a cushion and wriggle into my sleeping bag, and there I sleep in the shape of a V, feet up against the wall, body up against the pack, in a patch of dry concrete three feet long and two feet wide, waking often to watch the storm blow the bay and Ben's tent, billowing madness both.

Needless to say, we are on the road before the sun ceases colouring the dawn. And there we meet the Bora Ivan warned us about. We name him *Boreas, God of the North Wind!* Now we thought we tasted the Bora wind of the north yesterday – that icy chill in Omis was nothing compared to the blow-you-down-roar that rolls us along the highway to Makarska today. No wonder the trees around here grow at forty-five degrees. We hug the shore as we head out of Brela, wandering along the sweetest little marina, the sky above wild with the washed-clean fury of bright greys and blues and whites; the odd local wandering about with nowhere to go in another no-breakfast town; our cameras mesmerised by a handful of coloured balloons dancing on the water in the morning light; the wind plucking the rigging on the boats, playing the ropes like an angel harp. We walk up a steep hill back to the highway and as the ground levels out turn straight into the wind. We are laughing as we walk. This wind is crazy! I turn around to speak to Ben and Boreas throws me over the low concrete wall beside me, pack and all. We laugh but we are also nervous. This wind is hardly good company for walking into oncoming traffic or, as it turns out, around sheer cliffs on the roadside or, as it turns out, across high-strung bridges.

We walk around the coastline, great gusts of wind challenging us to stay earthbound, occasionally forcing us to hang onto railings for support. The road runs high above toybox towns beachside, way down below. Every little town is the same: a cluster of creamy-white walls and red roofs beneath a clock tower, or bell tower, depending on the priorities of the moment.

We make it into Krvavica for breakfast around lunchtime, where for the first time since stepping foot in Croatia I share spontaneous laughter with the locals, entertained by the turtleback strangers doing their best to remain upright with almighty Boreas blowing in their faces. Boreas is compelling and cheerful but he has a serious bite and we're wondering how long he likes to hang around.

We walk on to Makarska, curiosity drawing us into a Mary sanctuary on the outskirts of the city: Vepric, a shrine in a cave. Plastic Marys and flowers and coins and ribbons litter a damp cave dripping with water and the roots of ancient trees. It strikes me that the good bishop who founded the shrine might have worshipped Mary mother of Jesus, but he was well aware that the Earth was his mother. We film Ben, party pilgrim doing his level best to take the Catholic Church seriously, and walk on into Boreas's jocular draft, through the wide backstreets of Makarska and into another splendidly fabulous old city by the water, too tired to explore the ancient stone edifices across the harbour and the 'pirate ships' docked cityside.

We might have been content to rest awhile on her esplanade beneath shady palms, but Boreas's biting chill drives us into the internet café for the afternoon, where once again I am confronted with Ben's blog, stung by his reference to 'pilgrimage being hard at the best of times – try travelling with your mother'. I do not understand where this comes from. In my world we are keeping good company. Why would he choose to write about the thirty seconds we grate on each other's nerves?

And now we're chasing apparitions, turning away from the coast, heading over the spotted mountains to Međugorje, Mary country – a small detour to Bosnia on our way to Dubrovnik. We load up with bread, cheese, chocolate and mandarins, because according to our map there are few settlements between here and there, although at least one overpass, which experience has taught Ben makes great shelter come rainy, windy nights. We turn up a quiet narrow mountain road and stop on a hillside in the sunshine, laying out last night's rain-soaked tents to dry over large tracts of wild weeds. Taking advantage of the moment, we also air sleeping bags and damp socks and anything else that might have soaked up last night's moisture, laying them bare on the warm hill overlooking Adriatica's darker shore.

We pack up late in the afternoon and walk up the mountainside into thinner traffic, to three times as many honks of encouragement from motorists. Aha! The penny drops. The populace around Makarska is used to people making the pilgrimage to Mary, which Ivan told us is the third most visited shrine to Our Lady in Christian lands. And even though we smile about starring in the 'Honk If You Love Mary Show', I am deeply touched. I am neither Catholic nor religious, yet I am humbled by the recognition of fellow travellers who know we also walk for them. Consciously or not, my pilgrimage has led me here.

The road climbs steadily into the spotted mountains. We gaze down the frilly sapphire coastline into the mists of perpetuity, and over the rooftops of settlements large and small across the sea to *Hrvatska*'s blue islands. The view is spectacular.

The sun dips low and streaks the evening yellow. At the top of the highest mountain, we spy smoke pouring from an oven in a restaurant built from the mountain itself. Heaven! Ben has finally arrived in time for his pig-on-spit. We enter the restaurant on sundown, the sun a dying blaze of gold. There is a family in the room and Ben makes a great show of admiring the oven and its sizzling supper. Something's not quite right, but we have no idea what it is. We take our seats in the wide empty room at a window that stares right into the sunset. We glance at our menus, Ben scouring for his roast. We are confused. They are confused. They bring us wine. I ask for pasta with tomato. The mother nods. No-one can make sense of Ben's order – until eventually we realise that the pig he has his heart on is chicken and not only is it not on the menu, the restaurant isn't open! We have gatecrashed the family dinner. We laugh so hard there is nothing else to do but accept their hospitality and wish like hell they'd ask us to stay the night. We play backgammon and drink brandy while Boreas terrorises the mountainside. We roll the dice until good manners tell us we have outplayed our welcome.

As we pull on hats and scarves we have a map moment, a terrible sinking confusion that we are on the wrong road. The longer we stare at our folded paper guide the more it looks like Tupeci, the first village on our road over the mountains to Bosnia, is on the coast. Then I remember Ivan's 'good son, bad son' story: Croatians, he said, are hill people (it's a pirate thing). They did not live on the coast until tourism lured them down from the mountains. Good sons, he said, traditionally inherited hill land; bad sons inherited the coast. The upshot of this tale is that: a) bad son didn't do so bad; b) there are coast towns and hill towns with the same names; and c) while there is a coastal village of Tupeci, we are in the right place – the hill village of Tupeci.

Rugged and gloved and cling-wrapped in Gore-Tex we head into the dark of night. It's late. There is no-one else on the road. We walk into the wind for about a kilometre, eyes peeled for the national park marked on our map. Its gaping entrance greets us on a sharp bend in the road, along with a sign indicating bears and deer. We're impressed there are still animals in this country.

We kick around on the stony ground at the entrance, looking for a relatively private spot to camp. We do okay, although my tent pegs are looking more like twisted scraps of wire every day. I wonder why a company who makes a tent called 'Outer Limits' would include such pathetic go-nowhere pegs – especially when a product as fine as Ben's go-anywhere red alloys is available.

I lie in my tent in the dark in the wind and listen for the creaky footsteps of the murderer in my mind. He has been with me ever since I realised one human being had the capacity to take the life of another; that is to say, since I was about eight years old and a girl my own age whose name I have never forgotten disappeared in the Blue Mountains when I was on holidays visiting my grandmother in Sydney over forty years ago: Vicki Barton. Perhaps that is the way for all of us, fear of the murderer, the human survival story. I wonder about his connection to the aggression I am walking in this old-war land. Stricken looks must dart across my face when we pitch our tents, because Ben proceeds to tell everyone about my fear of camping in his blog. In my world I am a model mask of 'everything's fine' but clearly Ben sees something enough to write about.

I do not tell him that I do not fear camping in the night, but what camping in the night may bring. I lie in the dark in the wind and trace the terror that courses through me. In my own country, I would meet the devil I know; cultural familiarity would give me an edge that eludes me here among strangers, whose particular brand of violence and madness are unknown to me. I wonder, how am I like this? Where is the murderer in me? And do you know, I find her. She is the one who wished her father dead, night after night as she lay in her bed going to sleep as a child; and she is the one who wished death might steal the ones who made her life difficult, hoping for the easy way out of relationships, respite from responsibility – the indulgence of one who has never experienced the death of an intimate. The murderer within. This terrible knowing that someone, a man, always a man, will get me. I lived with this terror for the first seven years of my children's lives, fearing I would answer the door to my father and he would shoot us all, dead – until he died and I was free to listen to a soundtrack I hadn't even known was playing. Stories. My father with his hands around my mother's neck. Family realities unspoken. Unacknowledged. Story-fears having their wicked way with our hearts and minds. Here is the 'see-me, don't see-me' seesaw game of hostility and resentment that revealed its hand in Avezzano: fearing the displeasure of men and despising them for my fears. Here then is the key to my liberation. Am I safe now? Yes. Am I safe now? Yes. Recognition. Acknowledgement. Release. Which story do I choose? If I am to tell stories to shape my life, then let me do so because they are real and present. *As within, so without.*

We wake well before the sun, in tents cold with the night. Boreas didn't let up all night, blowing the tents so hard in sudden gusts they cringed flat to the earth, like dogs who've been in the rubbish who know they're in for it. We hit the road early, eyes streaming with the cold, still climbing the spotted mountains that nudge Adriatica's eastern shore. We have walked with these mountains since taking the inland shortcut from Sibenik to Split. We photograph them, but we cannot capture their presence. In our pictures the mountains are always the backdrop, yet in reality they are ever-present giant rock-faces that leave very little room for the coming and going of humanity. If the country were a palette, the coastline is the painter's brush-stroke, just one soft and wavy line down the landed edge.

We walk steadily upwards, directly into the freezing cold breath of a certain wind god, each bend promising the top and revealing … another bend. The bare tops are great grey walls of rock, either pat-a-cake smooth or scratched, as if big cats have sharpened their claws on the sheer faces. They are spotted with spindly, dark green vegetation, such as that which grows in high vertical places whipped by wind gods. The sweetest of blue skies lights the morning below us, pretty white clouds sweep the world above, and mists lie low over the islands at sea. Heavy lorries rumble by, blowing the scent of the roadside pennyroyal into the morning.

We walk on, mesmerised by the beauty of the islands below us, until at last the road turns inwards and we turn our backs on Adriatica's darker shore, parting company with, if not the known, then the now-familiar, heading inland through mountain passes to God, or Mary, knows where.

After seventeen kilometres of up-mountain road, a quarry greets us at the top. This is good news, because it means the steady stream of trucks might back off. Even way up here the EU concrete funnel has poured new houses and kerbs in settlements few and far between. I guess the Croatians deserve something for the unreciprocated fishing rights their pending-EU status has delivered the Italians – don't mind me, it's just something I heard in a pizza bar. The old ones must wonder why Croatians went to so much bother to free themselves from one master to forfeit their autonomy so quickly to another – I heard that in a bar too. And, while I'm passing on the gossip, I also learned in a bar why Croatians do not call themselves *Hrvatska* in public – it's another EU thing.

'Not everyone is happy with it, but if they need us to be Croatia then that's who we will be,' said a young man. 'We do it for the money.'

We rustle our way along the mountain tops, still wrapped in Gore-Tex to keep the chill from our bones. We rest on the roadside among the wild sage and the thyme, peeling the juiciest, most delicious mandarins in Christendom and eating them with triangular bites of Toblerone. We wander past a big stone oven roasting a pair of unidentified animals on the edge of a small settlement called Dugi Nijve, but we're too early for the feast. We wonder who on earth they're feeding, as there are so few people or settlements up here; at least that's how it looks to a pair of strangers from another world. Ben's taken a liking to the black herbal brew favoured by the pirates. He throws one back for every pig-on-spit that's not ready and for every oven that's not roasting. Three, in total.

And then we meet Fila, an old one with long grey hair, clothed not in black but in a riot of rags, who beckons us inside her ramshackle home with drinking motions. Ben is not one to refuse hospitality. We sit at her kitchen table, a parade of Mary perfume bottles watching over us. Fila offers us wine or coffee. I ask for water and nearly choke on the clear rocket fuel that lunges for my throat. For Ben it is a hallelujah moment, because I tip my 'water' into his cup as soon as Fila's back is turned. Everyone needs a Ben at moments like this. He eats and drinks anything and he can hold a conversation with anyone in any language, his pidgin Russian getting us by in this particular instance. Her balloon body now wrapped in a blue and white chequered pinafore held together with a string of white plastic rosary beads, Fila unwraps a round of sheep cheese from a dirty tea towel, gets an unidentifiable meat roll out of the small fridge, shoos the flies from a loaf of stale bread on the bench and hacks into all of them with a rusty old knife from the sink. Ben hoes into the feast. I am a seesaw of concern about health regulations and manifest ingratitude, longing to be released from the restrictive control that prevents me from embracing the kindness of strangers *unconditionally*. I manage to nibble on the cheese and, indeed, it is good. Loaded up with rocket fuel to spare and a tatty Mary message for the Croatian community in Sydney, within the hour we are on the road again.

Then Ben mentions the 'B' word. *Bosnia*. Bloody Bosnia. I am here in the mountains of Croatia because I am following my son to Istanbul. I am following my son who is summoned to visit Mary Disneyland in Međugorje, with its little cross on the 'd', even on the road signs. Therefore I am following my son to Bosnia. As we walk into the late afternoon, tired and hungry for more than bread and cheese and chocolate, I ponder our proximity to Bosnia, the Balkan backwater basketcase that pushes all my survival buttons. Forgive me, my ignorance is like the current fashion in petticoats – worn on the outside. My thoughts are especially embarrassing given my wonderful friendship with a woman whose parents are Croatian. She deserves better than this from me. As we draw closer to the border I am a riot of internal wrangling, struggling to make sense of the vineyards and rubbish heaps and stone cottages from where children are driven to and from schools invisible to our pilgrim eyes; worlds of antiquity and modernity, hand in hand. I forget that distance is relative, depending on whether one is walking or driving; that nowhere to us is a twenty-minute drive to civilisation for others. Hands stuffed deep into my pockets as the mountain begins its downwards slide, I am surprised to feel a softening in my heart, an emerging compassion for the people of an ugly word whose landmined children are without limbs. My pilgrimage is bringing me closer to hostilities left over from old wars, simmering or otherwise, without and within. My emerging compassion sings for those ahead of me; its warmth is for me.

After thirty-plus kilometres on the bitumen in the mountains, I am limping and tragic, hunched over and near-blind with delirium. As the sign for Vrgorac comes into view nigh on sundown, the countless ones lost in blizzards over millennia come to mind; the ones who have walked all night seeking shelter in a town only to be found dead the following morning, hunched up and covered in snow beneath the sign that marks the edge of town. Now I know why they do this. It's because their destination was the sign, not the warmth within. Day after day on this pilgrimage the sign has come into view and what little energy I have left is drained from my being, right there and then on the roadside, content as I am to sit beneath the sign and take not another step.

Yet I do. And in Vrgorac that leads us to the first bar we find, Restoran Tin, which like most other establishments in Vrgorac is dedicated to an elderly man with an interesting face and a burning cigarette between his fingers. We never do discover who Tin is, or was. An intellectual perhaps? A man of ideas? I get this notion from two black-and-white photographs hung one above the other on the bar wall, one of the interesting face and the other of a single bed in a simple room with a desk piled high with books.

We collapse in the bar and I take off my shoes, rub my feet and moan. I order a brandy to warm my bones, knowing in those same bones that I am not taking one more step. Boreas has begun to blow again and his great gusty puffs rattle the windows. The thought of heading out into the night, into that cold and blustery dark to find a camp, is too much. I'm not taking another step. I tell Ben. He laughs. Boreas blows. Ben laughs again. He doesn't want to be out there any more than I do. He runs down the road to check out the hotel. They want an outrageous price. 'Did you tell them where we are?' I ask. We laugh. It's not funny. We ask the barman where we might find a room, Ben's pidgin Russian coming in handy for the second time today. He suggests the hotel. We shake our heads. Given our state he neither shrugs nor argues; rather, he offers me a gentle brandy, makes a dozen phone calls and comes up trumps.

As we sit in the dining room playing backgammon, surrounded by noisy locals in for their workday meal and waiting for our own pastas to arrive, a young couple rocks in and announce in sign language that they have a room for us. We roll up the board, put dinner on hold and follow them into the night. They lead us up a pathway behind another bar, just down the road, up iron stairs and into a clean room that has been packed away for the winter, biding its time for the summer season that clearly hums annually in this region, judging by the tourist sign on the edge of town – the one with the stick figure hunter in one frame pointing his rifle right into the hearts of the stick figure hikers in the next frame. I was too tired to notice, but Ben took a photo.

I wake distressed, though not obviously so. My humble gratitude of the night before has gone with the wind. The bed is too cold. The pillow too high. There is no hot water and no toilet paper – and to think I've been known to complain about the 16th floor of the Marriott! What's more, we wake to a cacophony of Christian bells colliding with each other, like a tray of kitchen plates and cutlery dropped all at once on a tiled floor. I am distressed at the thought of walking thirty-plus kilometres today, all the way to Međugorje. I do not have it in me.

And yet I do! By the time we're on our way out of town my step is spirited and I swear the pack is getting lighter. We stop on our way out for a paper. Today is the day Ivan's story is supposed to appear in 'Slobodna Dalmacija', the daily newspaper that comes out of Split. We find the paper in a pocket-sized supermarket, the only sign of life in Vrgorac, and step into the cold outside to rifle through for our moment of glory. I'm a journalist, versed in industry pragmatics. I have no expectations about Ivan's offering, however generous and well meaning, because one drowning baby whale and we're yesterday's news without ever seeing the light of day. But it is a wow moment. We have the whole page. There is a big photo of Ben and me with our packs on. There is Ben's Google map. There is a whole page of text, not a word of which we can understand. And there is Ben's phone number. Within moments, the phone rings with encouragement from a stranger. We buy a handful of copies of the paper to send home and walk on. Ben's phone beeps with text messages of goodwill, tidings and support from the people of *Hrvatska* that keep coming all day.

We rig up in full thermal regalia, prepared for Boreas, who strangely seems to have taken a breather. The road is Sunday still, the morning relatively warm. In no time we stop and peel off our gloves, hats and jackets. We wander through the mountains – boar country, deer country – taking the high road around the rim of a wide, open valley below. A small river runs the length of the valley floor, carving up fields of green, yellow and brown. The houses are all white with red roofs. Skinny poplar trees streak the landscape; willows gentle it up. Smoke pours from chimneys. Dogs bark. Gunshots ring out from a distant blue mountain. If we turn our eyes to the horizon, we look into the hills of Bosnia, shades of rolling blue. I try to imagine what it might be like to be a country at war. I wonder what it is to have war come, as if war is a thing, *a noun of independent substance*, and then have it go away again.

As the road begins to roll downhill into the valley, we come to the border crossing. It is deserted, a couple of white portable boxes with shredded flags dripping from the top. Ben is disappointed. He likes his passport stamps. He films me crossing. I make the mark of the cross on my chest as I walk up to the white boom gate and pretend to twirl on my belly around it, like a child swinging on a horizontal metal bar, my pack making the gesture an impossibility. I walk around the boom and Ben calls out, 'How do you feel?' I throw my arms to the sky and cry, 'I'm freeeeeeeeeeeeee.' This is the moment the guards decide to emerge from their boxes. One from each. A man and a woman. A Croatian and a Bosnian. Our foolishness drifts into the morning. We hand over our passports. In this moment we count ourselves as two among the uneducated and the ill-educated, the ignorant and the arrogant.

'Aah,' says the man looking at my passport, *'Australian'*. It's my guess they've seen the likes of us before.

We wander into Bosnia, of all bloody places. Surprisingly, it is different to Croatia. The new houses have a little more flair. The old has not been demolished but co-exists with the new. The faces in the *caffe* bars are a little more wary, the distance between our reality and theirs is greater than that between us and the coastal Croatians.

The crones wear serious black and herd sheep. The roads are not EU new. I'm a little more careful about where I walk, pissing on flat rocks rather than putting my feet on the dirt. The country is a Mercedes Benz museum, the whole lineage from the original to the brand spanking new showcased on the roads. Perhaps driving a Merc here is compulsory, or perhaps it's the company's emblematic peace sign.

We stop for pizza in a big bar with a big warm oven and wireless! A young woman with earrings in her nose, studs on her belt and purple glue in her hair makes us welcome for the afternoon, as we rest and catch up on our blogs. A text comes through from Međugorje offering us a room in a hotel for the night. It brings tears to my eyes, that others can see the miracle in us.

Midafternoon, as the storm clouds gather, we load up and walk on. I feel a great deal of love and surrender as we walk through the countryside to Međugorje, along the highway in the small rain, past the road signs with their little cross on the 'đ', past tourist signs pointing to various shrines on the Mary Queen of Peace trail.

It is dark by the time we make Međugorje. I romp into town with lissom ease; at last, I think, and how fitting that I should do it for Mary. We stop in a crowded bar and ask for directions to the Rosabel Hotel. Pilgrim timing is with us – the man who owns the bar lives next door to the Rosabel. He makes a call to our hosts and settles us in with a drink while we wait. And there we learn that we are not in Bosnia at all but Herzegovina (!), which yesterday, to the alarmist on the inside, would have been a more dastardly thought than Bosnia. Nikola, a quiet man in his forties, comes to pick us up and drive us to the Rosabel, a gorgeous little hotel all sunshine yellow and white, and there we encounter grace in the kindness and company of strangers.

Snow comes in the night. Nikola and his wife Mira, our hosts, ask nothing from us, other than how many days we would like to stay. We tell them two. I lie in bed in the morning light and feel my uneasiness with receiving such generous hospitality.

Later in the day, I walk awhile with Mary in the rain. We wander around the hillside, a wheel of red and gold with the turning season, and sit in a grove amongst the wild thyme and soft mosses of the high country. I am out of sorts, bothered by my ordinariness, *my three dimensionality,* among other things. Međugorje is gentle and sweet, understated in its glory and gaudy in its commercialism. The streets are lined with the iconography of Christendom, mostly cheap trinkets, and I wonder whose face was plagiarised for the statues and cards of Mary, for they are all the same. The taxis ferrying people up and down Apparition Hill, where Mary first appeared to the children of Međugorje back in 1981, are: a) unroadworthy in my own country; and b) driven by madmen through the narrow streets. The Grand Prix was on TV last night, perhaps this explains the driving.

I am loving being among the people of Herzegovina. It is easy to play the fool in ignorance, when the politics of difference leaves us peering in from the outside; not so now the strangers have come for me. They have fed me. They have kept me warm. They see the miracle in my son and me and for that, well, as a pilgrim I can show my colours – my humility is scrambled with unworthiness.

Mary still appears at twenty to six every evening, these days to just one of the six 'visionaries' who first met her on the mountain twenty-six years ago. The local church is packed at this time, as cult Catholicism echoes around the chamber inside and is broadcast outside, where loud speakers rumble chanted Latin into the ice-cold evening. Now and then they break into song. Eventually I can sing along to an anthemic 'Kumbaya'. I stand at the back of the church, shoulder to shoulder with humanity in all its European colours. The chanting calls my awareness to my feet, which have no interest in standing for two hours on the hard stone floor, yet the hymns make the effort worth my while. Christian hymns are magnificent in chorus. *Ave Maria.*

There is snow all around us on the mountains. Big snow. White snow. Bloody-cold-out-there snow. *We-have-to-walk-through-those-mountains-tomorrow snow.* Ben and I have woollies enough to put on everything and be warm, just, at midday. Add a sleeping bag and we're hoping we'll be warm enough to get through the night – if we can bring ourselves to leave the Rosabel Hotel. Mira and Nikola are impeccable hosts and the Rosabel is the prettiest hotel in town. We rest for two nights in warm beds in a warm room and feast on three-course meals three times a day. The food is the best I've had since leaving home. The Rosabel's loving hospitality is worthy of, well, the company of

Mary, Our Lady, herself. And amidst it all I am a melting pot of reflection, insight and realisation. Herzegovina is breathing warmth into the hostilities in my heart. Even though I feel as if my son uses me for blog sport, I'm not sure he really believes what he writes and instead I wonder if he has not the language or even maturity to express himself clearly. And then, over dinner at the Rosabel, between delicious spoonfuls of creamy mashed potato in a dining room packed with a gaggle of lively Italian women devoted to the cult of Mary, I see it! The reflection: just as Ben has been using me for blog sport, I have been making blog sport of the people of the Balkans, casting them in roles that have no bearing on their own lives, telling stories that suit my theatre of the moment.

This forces me to get real about what I think Ben is expressing in his blog when he talks about 'travelling with my mother'. I relinquish my hurt for insight, recalling my attempts to show him my vulnerability in exhaustion, to be truthful in my 'had-enoughness'. Perhaps he feels responsible. Perhaps he feels powerless to fix things. Perhaps his acts of love, in attempting to make things right for me, are scrambled with the torment of making sure no harm comes to his mother. I still wonder though, accounting for all of this, why it is he blogs me for all the world to read but does not speak to me? Of course! This way it's easier not to take responsibility for his feelings. Maybe he's using the blog as a way of communicating with me.

I would love to share the situation and my feelings about it with my husband, yet I cannot. For he will not offer me confidentiality, will offer me no assurances that he will not speak out of turn. I feel I should not have to ask my husband for his loyalty, for safe harbour for my thoughts and emotions. I will not discuss it with him again. Besides, he's not interested. When I speak my heart he thinks I am being clever. When I am defeated and silent he is convinced our marriage is improving and there is hope for us. When I think he is listening it turns out he is being 'patient'. There is no point talking to him and I rarely do, most often lately ignoring the texts and rings on my phone.

I am acutely aware of resistance riding me ragged, as if there is an internal 'somewhere' I must reach, an etheric 'there' that is an ideal inner state I must attain before arriving at a geographic 'there'; and my husband is integral to this journey. I tell myself I have three months to walk, that I am free to enjoy what's here. I sink into this thought, releasing all resistance in my body, allowing all of time to be with me, in me, here in Međugorje. And this is how I discover freedom is a way of being – it is not a thought.

I wake to a day highlighted by two delightful meetings, the first being breakfast with the good Fathers Ruairi and Tony at the Rosabel Hotel, Irish Catholics from Dublin and the Kingdom of Kerry respectively. Father Tony is pink and forgetful, an older man whose breakfast is three slices of white bread with the fluff ripped out of the middle and jam smeared onto the folded scraps of crust. He wears a wedding ring and makes mention of a daughter ... I am curious and forget to find the right moment to ask. Father Ruairi, a young man in his forties, is one of the most intelligent and funny human beings we meet along the road to Istanbul. We laugh with the good Fathers and we share war stories, our own and others.

We get a late start to the day: slow because Ben is running on the minimum allowable sleep for a pilgrim, having spent the night drinking with an Irish lad he met in the church who assured him he was in town only for religious purposes; and cruisy thanks to the company of the good Fathers. We're on the road by midday, leaving Međugorje by way of *Krizevac*, Crucifix Hill, where adult children of a Catholic god do penance by climbing to the top with bare feet.

We wind our way through the hills of Herzegovina, just my son and me walking in steady rhythm along a clean sweep of bitumen, dark and stark against distant blue mountains capped with snow. I am inspired, by all that is my life at this moment. I text my husband: *Raising my heart to the divinity in my husband.* I have no idea how he will receive such a message. It doesn't matter. I am beginning to feel the first flutters of what it is to be married *and* a sovereign woman.

The afternoon is sweet. We walk on, down the hill into the long slow town of Capiljan, fifteen kilometres from Međugorje, where we run into Nikola and his son Joseph, the only locals in all the hills of Herzegovina with whom we are acquainted. Timing is everything, isn't it? Not least because they weren't around when we bid farewell to Mira, the Rosabel Hotel and Mary, enshrined life-sized in the corner of the lobby. Nikola is picking up Joseph from his maths college; he is worried about us and warns us, not for the first time, to steer clear of Albanians. We wander on, puzzled about why we spell Herzegovina with a 'z' when they spell themselves with a 'c', as in *Hercegovina*, and even more puzzled by signs telling us we're in 'Herzevacko'. We wonder if they even call themselves Herzegovina?

I am not a vengeful person, for this I am thankful. What is done is done and I have a natural ability to move on. This is one of the finer traits I share with my mother. So it is that as I sit with my son on the footpath of Capiljan, for want of a rest and an open bar, leaning up against our packs beside a grubby wall overgrown with weeds and blooming with rubbish, the backgammon board between us, when my inner world abruptly tilts, a bolt of ancient aggression ripping through my equilibrium. *Irena!* I have not thought of Irena for years, yet here she is, walking with me from Međugorje to Dubrovnik. She is a woman who rightly belongs to another lifetime, her place in my present world irrelevant. Or so I had thought. Yet here she is, stirring from the mud of subterranean reality, ascending into consciousness to eddy and swirl with the voices in my head.

Irena, not just bitch but *Yugoslav bitch. Yugoslav bitch with her bull-dyke hips and pancake face*; fascist bitch who, with one strike of her avenging tongue, had me facing ten years in prison for social security fraud. Bloody Irena. Ben rolls up the board and we walk on through the quiet streets of Capiljan, me watching closely as an unhealed past plays bitter in my heart. I let it run, entertained by the emergence of hatred denied; relieved and somewhat embarrassed to find a personal source of mistrust for the entire world that currently surrounds me. Long ago, when the people who knew me wondered what I was going to do about Irena, I would say, surprising us all with the peace in my heart, 'There is nothing to do – the universe will take care of Irena.' Yet clearly I have internalised her embittered righteousness and buried her poison in my belly.

Irena traded a job with the Department of Social Security for my scalp, dobbing in a single parent who worked while she studied for failing to declare extra income to the department. I do not know why she did this. I do not know why my colleagues found her charming enough to share her bed. We employed her because we were good feminists with a commitment to working collectively, believing it was our philosophical duty to have an immigrant worker and an indigenous worker in our women's shelter, so that Aboriginal and immigrant women might feel better supported leaving violent relationships. They were token positions, this we knew; but it was well-meaning action and the best we could offer our times. The indigenous worker was troublesome because her family and community demanded so much of her time she rarely showed up for work; the immigrant worker was troublesome because she was an untrustworthy bitch who used sex as power and was never, ever going to accept our wicked political ways. We were young, we were idealistic, we were radical and we were a please-ourselves nightmare to the system. Worse, we were really, really confident. We, most of us, were excited not only that we had an immigrant worker, but that she was an immigrant *and* a lesbian. And only myself and one other understood that she and her overbearing pelvis were horribly, incorruptibly dangerous.

And after all is said and done, the federal police dragging me from my bed early one morning with their pounding on the door, facing a judge who might deem me worthy of that decade in prison, risking a hard-earned cadetship on a metropolitan newspaper ... after all is said and done, I have never regretted not declaring the extra income. It was 100 dollars a week. It paid the rent while I studied. It meant I could afford to go to university and not raise my children in a dump, in the days before middle-class welfare gave everyone who bleated an extra dollop of cash, with the exception of those for whom the system was created – the elderly and disabled. Don't get me wrong, I have long bowed to the citizens of my country, who place high value on supporting a woman and her children regardless of what we think of her circumstances. And I bow to the judge who said he would dismiss my case were it were not for his concern that the department would appeal, and handed me a suspended sentence instead. In a strange way, I have been grateful to Irena for tying up for me what would have been a loose end. I used to think of that money as a loan from the Australian community and now, thanks to a punitive lesbian immigrant who needed a scapegoat, it has been repaid. Although I would have preferred to repay it in my own way, offering financial support to another young woman seeking to educate her way to a new life. *And of course I still can.*

The church bells of Capiljan ring Irena from my body, releasing me from her psychic assault. We take the back track out of town, walking along a deserted road alongside high barbed fences. The footpath is a crumbling cement track through a parade of weeds. If anyone works in the decaying buildings behind the fences, they have left for the day. Somehow it is right that I should be walking a wasteland as I deliver myself from the hold Irena – and whatever she represents for me – has on my life. I breathe her out with every step, feeling the sadness of her impact on my life, the betrayal of my colleagues, the sense of unworthiness that no-one thought to stand for me. Here is my confrontation with the world, my enemy within; here is my exhaustion from standing up to 'authority', my compulsion for defending the underdog, my susceptibility to making the personal political; here is my longing for approval and my need to rest. I thank Irena for playing the role I have clearly defined for her and for playing it so well. And I give thanks for the completion of this journey, two decades long. It is done.

The sun is just setting when we decide to call it a day, pitching our tents in a perfect little campsite across a field on the other side of the railway tracks, just outside the small settlement of Gabela. There among the shoulder-high reeds, we find a small bright green patch of freshly sewn yarrow with ground so soft that even my bent pegs find firm footing. We sit on the ground and watch evening come to the village on the distant hillside; lights on, dogs barking, smoke curling from chimneys. The moon rises behind us. I am glad to be camping in Herzegovina, privileged to be here among her people. I have learned these past days they consider themselves to be Croatian. Why then, I asked a man in a bar, are you Bosnia Herzegovina? He shrugged. His friends shrugged. No-one knows. Just like the border with Bosnia, no-one knows where that is either. These men fought in the recent war and they agreed they would fight again if they thought it would deliver them independence from Bosnia. War. It comes. It goes. People die. Borders shift. Someone, somewhere, knows what it was for.

I lie in bed in the light of a new dawn, listening to the stillness of morning cold. My husband has ignored my text. I'm amused by the reactions whipping through my body, like the train in the night whistling down the track behind us. There's a whole emotional thesaurus playing out inside me, ranging from the distant rumble of an 'oh well' shrug to anxiety that has a rip-roaring name: *I am in trouble*. I pull the sleeping bag up tighter around my chin and lie in the peace of morning, belly fluttery, throat tight. *As if having expressed myself, I am open to danger.* Irena. My father. Men. Me. I am them. It is a long journey home. Now that I have walked Irena through, she no longer has a charge. But she reminds me of Adelaide, triggering other memories from this time, exposing a hidden grief for my daughter, my little girl, the baby who wouldn't let me out of her sight and the child who would sing to me the theme song from 'Beaches' before she fell asleep at night:

Did you ever know that you're my hero, and everything I would like to be? I can fly higher than an eagle, for you are the wind beneath my wings.

The world that housed Irena on its fringes was, at its heart, the world of our world. For seven years we lived in the whirl of hope and love, enthusiasm and enterprise that was the Adelaide lesbian feminist community. Melissa Etheridge, k.d.lang and Martina Navratilova played and sang on the world stage while we, the greater community of which my little family and I were a part, played and danced in our own little cosmos. We were feminists and we meant well, all of us. We gave life our championship best during feminism's golden days, when two decades of extreme ideology finally yielded mainstream traction, at which point our daughters' generation took the money and ran, literally and figuratively.

Westerners, it seems to me, have no idea that corporate, political and social benchmarks we now take for granted are rooted in a word we scorn and a tenet we mistrust and malign: *feminism*. And we have forgotten, if we ever knew, that not so long ago it was legal to deny a woman entry to university. And we have forgotten, if we ever knew, that bankers, on principle, did not lend money to a woman without her husband's permission. And we have forgotten, if we ever knew, that until recently it was legal to rape your wife. And we have no idea that a plethora of simple fair management practices, community consultation for example, are based on the collective experiences and experiments of feminists, women who were willing to risk *everything* for change. For a better world. *For everyone.*

These were days when anyone who did anything at all in our private world was a woman – bureaucrats and teachers, doctors and nurses, builders and mechanics, musicians and acrobats and sportswomen; when a thousand women turned out for the annual women's ball and Adelaide had a swing band thirty-women strong. These were pre-IVF days, when lesbians almost never had children and mine were a rare and precious commodity. As feminists we partied and we debated and we raised stakes and standards. Time and place were on our side.

And while my son was served very well by these days, for he attended a mainstream school and I did not deny him the culture of his time or gender, but measured it with the circumstances of our private world, my daughter struggled with this life; not because she wasn't loved and not because she didn't have a wonderful time, but because I turned my back on our natural relationship with the best of intentions to do the right thing by her. I put politics ahead of who we were.

All my life I had longed for a little girl. I had dreamed of dressing her up. I dreamed of brushing her hair. I practised on my dolls. Where my son and I stood side by side to face the world, my daughter and I faced each other. I brushed her hair, I tied it in ribbons. By the time it was long enough to plait I was in feminism's embrace and my interpretation of the politics of our time encouraged me to keep her hair short. In this way, I reasoned, she would be spared a mother obsessed with how she looked. My rationale was reinforced by the mothers in the playgrounds who interrupted their daughters' play to tidy their hair, making sure they were consistently cute and pretty and pleasing. My daughter would be spared her role of decorating a patriarchal world.

Reason stilled the longing in my heart: my daughter could have long hair when she asked for it. As it turned out, my daughter spent her childhood wishing she had long hair but thought she wasn't allowed and, pleasing me, did not dare to ask. It was our missing expression of love, mother to daughter, and it breaks my heart that her confidence was undermined by something as simple as longer hair; breaks my heart that the little girl with the raggedy blonde locks might have thought herself less than beautiful; breaks my heart that I did not live my longing to brush my daughter's hair. Perhaps I am making my own point about the social value of a woman's hair. My great grandmother used to say that long hair sapped a woman's strength; as a woman who has been valued for her long blonde hair, I know why.

Here in a paddock of yarrow, green and fresh, in a country not long emerged from the shadow of war, I can feel the liberation of a middle way stir in my bones. Not that, nor this. Not ideology, but truth. Truth of a moment. Truth of a woman. Truth of humanity.

I'm up before the sun to discover ice on the tent. I rub freezing-cold air between my hands, breath misty with morning, as Ben and I chuckle through his tent walls about the convulsive blast of the trains in the night. We pack the tents wet and walk around the dawn through Herzegovina's misty morning farmland ringed with snowy mountains. Three times we take the wrong road. It annoys Ben. It doesn't bother me at all. We're walking anyway. It makes no difference to me whether we walk this way or that. Not today. We cross the border back into Croatia. Again I am struck by the incongruity of lines in the sand: one day you have neighbours up the valley, the next you need a passport to visit them.

We walk along the river to Metkovic, a grey and grubby city that seems to offer not much at all in the line of pilgrims' aid: not food, not directions; but plenty of coffee, though not for me. We are looking for the turn-off to a shortcut to Dubrovnik that will keep us off the highway. Although the road is marked clearly on our map, no-one I ask seems to know where it is. Ben sits in a coffee shop near a park, doing his refusal-to-ask-directions thing, while I ask a man in a television repair shop for the way out of town. His customer shakes his head and tells me the Bosnian border on this road is closed. He shows me the turn-off up the road and shakes his head. 'They do not like strangers,' he says.

I return to the coffee shop and relay the news to Ben. We find it silly. As we do the lines in the sand, which are such that the Croatian coastline has a five-kilometre interruption called Bosnia, just north of Dubrovnik. The back road that no-one seems to know about leads through Bosnia. I am feigning confidence. Neither of us is interested in taking the long way round, especially if we can stay off the highway.

We find the back road, me ignoring the explosive landmines in my head. We wind our way through charred hillsides ringing with chainsaws salvaging what little wood is left from the summer's fires. We walk and we walk around the winding country roads, the subject matter of the voices in my head morphing from landmines to the random violence of barbarians with guns. I vow that by walking this road I will free myself from the irrational world of 'what if'. And if walking this road costs me my life, if choosing freedom from an irrational future costs me my life, then today it is a price I am willing to pay. Even if I catch a bus back from the turn-off, just the act of walking onwards down this road towards Bosnia challenges the grip of 'what if ...' on my life.

Metkovic in the distance is now white and red-roofed. I wonder what happened to the grey city we visited an hour before? Our road meets another, not on our map. We walk on. At the top of a rise a silver car stops and a woman speaking easy-English asks if we need a lift. We explain to her and her trio of curious children that we are pilgrims and we are walking. She throws her name out the window as she drives on, an invitation on the wind.

We are hungry. Ben is still holding tight to his illusion that towns marked on maps mean food. We wander into Bijeli Vir, past ready for a good feed. As is the way with miracles, the moment we decide to find the woman in the silver car we realise we are standing outside her house – that's her car parked out the back. Tereza makes our day. She invites us in and sits us down at her kitchen table. She cooks us lunch and serves us wine from the family vineyard. We swap travellers' tales while she makes the children lunch. Tereza grew up among Yugoslavia's privileged classes, travelling the world while her comrades marked time. She married a farmer's son and has met her agrarian in-laws halfway – she will farm when she is home and she will please herself when she is not, with and without her children. Tereza's gift is that she saw not bedraggled strangers on the road, but travellers in need of food and rest. *She saw the need and she responded unconditionally*. I wonder if there is any greater gift one human being can offer another?

Eventually we must be on our way. Tereza and her children send us packing with a CD of Dalmation music and bags of mandarins and pomegranates from their orchard. I carry the CD. Ben gets the fruit. Tereza tells us if we have trouble at the checkpoint to call her; she has a friend who works on the border.

We wander on, following the road out of Bijeli Vir through small stone villages along the edge of a lake, which Tereza's children tell us is called the 'white lake'. The road is a back road's back road. Villagers sit in the sun passing time on small plots of land they've claimed from the water, laughing when they see us and making exaggerated gestures about heavy loads. I get the feeling they are familiar with the weight of such burdens.

Tereza's teenage son pulls up in a car driven by his aunt. They tell us we cannot pass at the border. Tereza has rung her friend in the police office to check. The crossing is for domestic workers only, not internationals. They tell us to come back with them and Tereza will drive us to Metkovic. I am snared by their urgency, trying not to be too excited by such an easy Bosnia out. But Ben's not going anywhere. He's not returning to Metkovic and he's not taking the long way round. He will find a way across the border. I can feel Ben trusting the mystery of the knowable unknown and I take a breath, holding true with him. I am curious to see what will unfold. We thank them and wave goodbye, continuing on around the white lake.

Ten minutes later Tereza blows in, a blare of demanding dust on the roadside, adamant that we must allow her to help. Ben asks her about an alternative road through the mountains. She makes a phone call and laughs about our lucky day. A new road was carved into the mountains six months ago. The turn-off is a kilometre shy of the border. We smile and wave goodbye for a second time. We walk on, spirits high, thankful for the initiative of peasant pragmatists who refuse to be thwarted by idiot bureaucracies. It is a beautiful day. It is a pilgrim's day. It is one of the best days we've had so far, out here in the wild places, just us and all that is right with the world.

We rest on the edge of the last village before the border, lying back on our packs in the fading sunlight, eating Tereza's pomegranates and watching the sun dip below the mountain on the other side of the lake. We can see our road at lake's end, high up the mountain face.

We reckon we can make it to the top by dark. The road is chalky-white and stony. The light fades fast. The lake reflects the last of the sunset. The moon rises at our backs, a great silver disc of light so bright we are casting shadows on the stones. I stop and breathe it all in. When you are in a car, beautiful places are a moment; if you stop the car, they are a cluster of moments. When you walk, beautiful places are an eternity carved into the soul.

A small white chapel greets us at the top. We are ecstatic. It is locked. We are bemused. We have forgotten to dry our wet tents. We hunt around in the dark for a key, turning over stones, digging under logs. We pitch the tents on the white stones and let them 'dry' in the chill night air. It's amazing where you can pitch a tent when you have to. It is a gorgeous night. We sit on the chapel steps, rugged up to billio, eating bread and cheese and chocolate and mandarins for dinner. We can see the lake below. Village lights glow orange around the water's edge. The occasional dog barks into the valley night. I leave Ben to his computer in the shelter of the chapel doorway and burrow into my sleeping bag, resigned to a night on the stones.

We wake before sunrise beside the little white chapel on the hill to discover that, as well as the lake before us, the ocean is behind us. Light comes to the day in soft colours, watery pinks and blues on a snow-white canvas. Just as we're eating breakfast, chocolate and mandarins if you please, the sun breaks through the clouds, clipping the tips a brilliant orange. The clouds a little further around the sky-line are ablaze with a billowing yellow fire. The lake is dark, the ocean dark blue. It's a chilly morning and it's beautiful. We load up and wander down the other side of the white stone road to meet the highway that skates along the coast, and that's where we spend the day, all day, walking into a steady stream of traffic on the main road to and from Dubrovnik, ducking through that five-kilometre stretch of coastline called Bosnia on the way.

I am beginning to detect a distinct difference in our wellbeing at the end of the day depending on whether we've been wandering the back roads or chewing up the highways. The main roads require a particular focus that rarely lets up. We're in our own zone for sure, cars and trucks and buses racing by as we wander along in the small space between the white line and the gutter, the advantage of the trucks being that at least they blow a welcome breeze our way. My world is reduced to the minutiae of the roadside, an abundance of wild sage and thyme; blackberry brambles and fennel, thinner now than they were further north; crocuses, purple and white, and tiny sprays of pink snow-grass flowers bursting from cracks in the bitumen; rocks and streaky sand-coloured stones of all shapes and sizes; and rubbish, the flotsam and jetsam of modern human existence washed up on our bitumen shoreline, most commonly cigarette packets (Marlboro man is still riding in these parts), orange juice cartons, disposable nappies and, new as the day they were bought, wedding ribbons – pink and yellow and white and cream and peach – rosettes that the Slavic peoples tie to their cars for their honking, tooting wedding parades. Now and then I rest my eyes on the skyline, to the low hills in the east and the islands in the west. The world turns.

We walk and we walk and we walk. People honk and wave like we're friends. Of course! They recognise us from Sunday's newspaper article. We eat cheese and bread and mandarins and chocolate. We play backgammon. We have our first argument, about whether or not the dice landed on the board. The world turns.

We find a patch of sunshine free from rubbish and spread out our tents to dry on the clipped bushes. We lay back on our packs to rest amongst the thyme and the dark green mosses, the white stones and the stalks of last summer's weeds. We are two metres from the roadside and we lie there for all the world as if we own the joint. And perhaps, for a moment, we do.

We walk on.

A bus hits a blue car, which ploughs into a roadside shop. We don't see the accident but we walk by soon after. The world turns.

We pass abandoned stone dwellings, crumbling city walls. Tide in, tide out. Moon bright, moon dark. Sunrise, sunset. The world turns.

We walk too far into the night, seeking shelter that doesn't show. A spectacular full-bellied moon rises before us. When there's a lull in the traffic we're in paradise – moon, ocean, mountains, night stillness. When there's not, it's crazy to keep going on the road. We stop at a house that has rooms advertised in a town that's not on our map. Like just about everything food or shelter related in this country, it's not open. 'It's not the season,' Ben reminds me. The woman who owns the house leads us through the old stone byways of Banici (at least we think the town is called Banici) to an equally old woman who has a room. We are grateful. We take the room. There is no hot water till morning. 'It's not the season,' I tell Ben. He is not amused. It is three days since we have showered. I cannot remember the last time I combed my hair. Funny how easy it is to curl up unwashed in our tent in the wild places, and how horrible it is to sleep grubby between clean white sheets. Not sticky in the mountains, sticky in civilisation. The world turns.

Some days are for climbing mountains and others ... well, they'd be hard work even if you laid low on the flatlands. Today I could have lain down beneath one of those old olive trees and slept for a thousand years.

Thunder rolls as we leave the town we think is called Banici; we walk into the highway traffic beneath a darkening sky. Five kilometres on, all thoughts of breakfast in Slano are abandoned when we meet our turn-off into the mountains just before the town. It's not an easy call. We have only the last of Tereza's pomegranates, a ball of old bread and three mouthfuls of chocolate in supplies, weighed up against: a) heading into Slano for the *possibility* of finding breakfast; which means b) sticking to the highway for the rest of the day, because psychologically it is impossible to backtrack.

We take the turn-off, heading up. And up. And up. Soon we are high above the blue islands off the coast, dormant she-dragons, protectresses of an ancient tide. We wander through mountain passes between the fertile lowlands and the spotted hills, through villages lucky to escape the summer fires that have scorched the landscape all around.

For me, it's a one-step-at-a-time kind of day. It's agonising. It's pathetic. Ben is incredibly patient, waiting here and there along the roadside for me to stagger by. We pass through villages that haven't seen a stranger for, oh, at least 200 years. We're so high up in the spotted hills that we're not walking through them so much as *we are them*. The villages are old-stone gorgeous; well kept and productive, alive with flourishing vineyards and olive groves, vegetables and newly turned fields. No rubbish. No people either for that matter, no more than you can count on one hand all day. And even fewer cars. We walk rims of spectacularly lush and fertile valleys on roads that ought to be goat trails. We reckon we're half a hill away from Bosnia. A red and white Croatian flag painted high on the face of a rock wall gives us our bearings, extreme art for wayward tourists.

I walk into the wind, making a game of surrendering the purposeless thoughts weighing my spirits. I let the wind blow through me, separating all that holds me together. I am the spaces between the strings.

Walk-wise, this is the worst day of the pilgrimage; ironically, visually and tranquilly it is among the most stunning. Many times I lie flat on my back on the road, unable and unwilling to take another step. My pack feels like it's weighed down with boulders and every step is like walking in treacle. It's a bugger of a day to misread the map and head up when we thought we'd be heading down, not that we'd have chosen a different route had we known. Strangely, physically I'm in good shape. My feet and shoulders are fine. It's the spirits that are dragging the load, the weight of obligations and a chattering mind telling stories. 'The Sound of Music' theme song might have picked up my spirits on previous days, *The hills are alive* etc ..., but it does nothing for me today. Contrarily, it's a fifth-grade recorder tune thrumming my beleaguered bones, *It's a long way to Tiperary* (or Dubrovnik) ... over and over.

We hold out all day for a decent meal. Ben does his usual routine of believing each village is about to feed him, specifically pig-on-spit. No dice. We sit beneath a tree alive with the yellow-gold of autumn and eat the last of the pomegranates, me admiring the beauty of the crimson seeds and Ben high on the sharp, juicy taste. I have given up all hope of ever seeing civilisation again. Ben talks of finding food in the village that meets the highway. I tell him to be more specific. He says there's no need, that any food anywhere will do. It's my turn to paint a miracle. I tell him we need *an establishment*, somewhere overlooking the water where we can relax and enjoy a *great* meal: a tall order in post-summer Croatia.

I struggle all day with voices and resistance and then I turn a corner and poof, they are gone! What is it that has made the difference? I lie under an olive tree in the most beautiful soft green grassy grove, old as the hillside itself, the weathered rocks alive and soft as the grass, and there it comes to me: no past. Peace now = no past. Only now. Only here. I am lighter, so much lighter, as we walk the back roads into the village, where there's a bar that doesn't sell food. A bus turns into the street and all the cars have to reverse out to let it pass.

We walk on, into the rising darkness, over a headland behind the town to avoid the highway, climbing too high for comfort. We head down, down, down for the second time today, eyes peeled for a campsite. We meet the highway and I'm done. I sit down on my pack and refuse to walk another step – and there behind me is the miracle, the Restaron Babilon with its lights on and tables set and its mussel risotto and fresh tomato and mozzarella salad dripping in olive oil and its fabulously fine wine *overlooking Adriatica*. We take our seats, for all the world as if we're dressed properly for dinner. We toast the miracle. Life, dear friends, is divine. When we're full and done we roll out the door, across the road and down a small laneway to a bed we spied from the Restoran Babilon, pitching our tents beneath scraggly pines on a freshly mown lawn walled on three sides beside the sea. Adriatica is returned to me, her lightness, her allure. Perhaps the darker shore can deliver lightness, too. There is a flutter in my belly, a different sensation to that which greeted me at Pescara.

Today I do what pilgrims do best – I accept the simplicity of the hand dealt to me with patience and goodwill. Which on this particular morning takes the form of standing in the rain for two hours waiting for a bus. These days, I am allowing myself to be two people: one who loves the physical actuality of life on Earth, walking the turning seasons beneath rising moons and settings suns, exhilarating in the challenge of the mountains and sleeping on the ground at night; the other who loves to lie in the old groves, fresh dates and cheese and chocolate within arm's reach, reading good books in the gentle sunshine.

After yesterday's fabulous display of resistance, there is nothing else to do this morning but let the one who likes to rest and ponder take the bus. We are six kilometres from Dubrovnik. Ben walks and I, eventually, ride the bus around Adriatica's eastern shoreline into a sweet and contented township that for centuries has stood right where she is, surefooted and strong. Everyone says Dubrovnik is a beautiful city and everyone is right.

I hang out at the port, waiting for Ben. He texts me to say he's at the internet café next to the pizza shop by the south gate of the old city wall. I walk up the hill to the old city, thinking I may as well have walked from the freshly mown lawn below the Restoran Babilon. The simplicity of Ben's instructions is a nightmare. No-one I ask knows anything at all about a south gate. Eventually I sit by an old fountain and text to tell him it is up to him to find me. I am not walking up and down any more old stairs. Contrary to the rest of the country, everyone in Dubrovnik wants to offer us a room. Ben rocks up with one room scout and I have been claimed by another. We meet and they tussle over us. Mine speaks English and has business partners in Australia. And besides, he's not cranky. We allow him to lead us away.

Our room is at the front of a big pink house overlooking the old fortress, the ocean below still pounding her walls after all these years. It's great to be still, to know that for two days we're not going anywhere. Having a room is like finding childcare for the packs – we get to go out alone in the city.

Dubrovnik is the last of our known world until we reach Istanbul. From here we are well and truly in the unknown. Croatia is now familiar territory, no longer an edgy doorway to darkness; welcoming, not frightening; or perhaps Dubrovnik is my lighthouse in a coming storm. *As within, so without.*

Now and then, my mind still tumbles with nonsensical conundrums about identity; about yesterday Yugoslavia and today nations that I, daughter of a new world, have never heard of (relatively speaking); about a personal resistance to Yugoslavia and, embarrassingly, a softening embrace for the more exotic Slovenia, Albania, Croatia – Bosnia's stretching it – shadowed each and every one by humanity's capacity for darkness and division and good neighbourly murder. I wonder if a visit to other splintering blocs and hostile-pact nations would have had this effect on me? There is something about Yugoslavia, the vocabulary of new-Australian politics entering my consciousness at a formative time in my life – legendary betrayals and nervous friendships, a timeless hall of mirrors of perceptions, assumptions and suspicions that have worked their way into my bones. *Whose stories are they anyway?* Old curiosities and resentments are playing out on Adriatica's darker shore, them and us, dare I whisper the word? ... *barbarians* ... which them? which us? which lifetime? ... *as within, so without.*

I think of Mira at the Rosabel Hotel in Međugorje. Mira who is the wind. Mira and her husband Nikola whose children, according to the fingers on my hand, must have been born into the war. Mira and Nikola who run a hotel but whose business is Love. Mira. I never did ask her about her life. To do so would have been like catching the wind – *once you have it, you no longer have the wind*. Yet the breeze and the gale-potential that is Mira will stop for Love. For the love of Mary. For the love of a child. For the love of meeting the miracle in others.

In Međugorje, among a sea of Catholic hearts and minds, unified in their devotion to Mary mother of Jesus, I witnessed humanity's one common thread: we worship goodness. Even the ungood worship goodness. And nearly all of us, regardless of the values we hold, will pay homage to life. And most of us will seek comfort, for the heart and for the spirit, from *the all that is* or God, by any other name. In Herzegovina I learned that kindness is more than being nice. It is to Mira I bow my head in gratitude for this teaching.

I wake to Dubrovnik's discordant church bells ringing in a grey day – and a deep throated dog howling along to the bells (*pause to reflect on this sound …*). We are awed by the sight outside the window, the old fortress walls elegantly curving into an angry blue ocean smashing at her feet, the line between sea and sky blurred by the mists of a rainy morning. Ben goes scuba diving while I spend the day wandering around the city, surrounded by Australian accents. The woman who dries our laundry has me pegged. She says the last two summers have been full of Australians. Personally, I don't think it's just the accent. We're the ones in trackie dacks and t-shirts while the other tourists are show-pony chic. We're the ones who've flown all the way around the world and we haven't come for the weekend.

As I walk along the clifftop pathway between the old city and the laundromat, I get the feeling Dubrovnik belongs to no man. This is an ancient city eternally young. Draw lines in the sand around this one as you will, hand it over to this nation or that, impose your identity as you like, Dubrovnik is a free spirit, unchained and unclaimable.

I am reminded of a picture in my mind that captured my attention as I entered Dubrovnik's old city yesterday: a gaggle of crocodiles snapping their jaws and me squealing, *I can't, I can't*. It strikes me that this image represented a fear of being all I can be. And I wonder about realisations and their connection to place, in this case to a city who knows who she is.

From Italy's Adriatic shoreline, staring into the mists of time, I was the priestess on the golden sand at sunrise, watching the ships of the invaders come for the city. Here in Dubrovnik I am the empress on the high cliffs looking west, and the ships sailing in from the dark horizon are coming home.

I sit awhile on a bench looking out over the dark sea towards *Italia*. The parting words of the Steadying Hand come to mind – he told me my son has to forgive me for birthing him. It's all a bit psycho-babblish for me, but I wonder … I think of him out there in the cold near-black water and wonder if what I perceive to be his arrogance or hostility is perhaps simple frustration. I often feel as if I am playing the same role for him as that required from me by his father, and also my husband; that is, to express not just the anger that eludes them but also their feelings. I think about our first fight, about whether or not the dice was on the backgammon board. I recall how tired I was, walking, walking, walking, wanting to rest, Ben clearly unimpressed with the spot I first chose but not saying so, ignoring me and walking on – and me not having the courage to upset him by expressing my needs, because I am so tired of people's pointed fingers telling me I am 'too … ' – until I simply downed my pack on the roadside and spread out the tent to dry. I wonder if my son simply cannot cope with the vulnerability of a woman. I am tired of feeling judged by him. Perhaps, returning to the words of the Steadying Hand, his arrogance is actually contempt for his mother because he has difficulty reconciling that she is also a woman.

Looking out at the storms at sea, I think of the day before yesterday, of buckling under the weight of my own resistance in the mountains, of my son's derisive voice in my head even though he was a model of patience and goodwill – and recognise the story is just that, an un-reality playing in my head – the un-reality of a weary heart spurred on by the weight of obligation to him, the mistrust of wondering what he will write about me on his blog, the towns promising abundance and offering nothing, feeling so terribly hungry and being offered nothing, the weight of sexual obligation to a husband who financially supports my journey. Out there in the mountains I burned and I burned and I burned. And then I turned a corner and experienced an embarrassingly simple epiphany: no past – *there is only this* (the mountains, the vineyards, the sunshine, the road).

Only here, only now; no past no future no stories no resistance. Only this – and a wonderful lightness in my being. I think of Yugoslavia. I think of the war. If only … if only Croatia and Bosnia et al could be here now, only here, only now, no past no future no stories no resistance. *As without, so within.*

I wander down the hill towards the old city and find a restaurant for lunch. The food in Dubrovnik is fabulous. I mean *tiramisu*-two-nights-running fabulous. Wonderful service and presentation, fresh salads and soups and extraordinary main meals are everywhere. The restaurants are superb. I would go so far as to say it is years since I've been anywhere that's offered such a choice of quality restaurants. What's more, it's impossible to spend more than forty bucks on eating and drinking everything our hearts and souls desire – and that's for two of us! *Indulge me, I'm a woman who's been on a diet of cheese and bread, chocolate and mandarins.* Over mushroom pasta and delicious white wine, a man walks in who reminds me of a man I know at home: Karol. And another man: Zvone. Hard men, humourless men, steer-clear-my-tender-heart men. *Yugoslav men.* How strange then, when I think of them as Slovenian, they become exotic, charged with mystery.

Later in the day I sit in a wine bar on puffy white chairs watching evening come to a peaceful city beneath a stormy sky. I'm waiting for Ben to return from his deep sea dive. I think again of my epiphany in the mountains. Dubrovnik, I realise, embodies this lightness of being. She is a city who answers to no master; a city whose women fill her streets at night: a city humming with visitors from all the nations on Earth; a city whose youth wear no badge of resistance.

Ben shows up shivering with cold. To warm his blood he orders the pirate liquor he discovered in the tavern in the cavern in Omis. Feet tapping to the hits of the 90s, we laugh till the tears run as we play backgammon well into the night. I beat him convincingly. At last. We have dinner. Ben refuses to pay for water and takes his wine glass to the toilet to fill it from the tap himself. He doesn't make a fuss about much, my son, but when he does it is always about admirable and incontrovertible matters of survival-related principle. Water is a human right and he will not pay for it. The waiter surrenders the fight.

Dubrovnik is a vertical city, sliding straight up a mountain that meets the sea. We climb the hundred stairs to our room. I settle in for the night and Ben heads out again with his camera. I lie in bed in the dark and listen to the night outside my window. In Dubrovnik, I have forgotten I am in Croatia.

Dubrovnik is a city that looks after its cats. Morsels of cheese are left here and there on stone walls; bags of dry food are tipped into corners by rubbish bins; last night's stew, still in its baking dish, is left on the roadside for happy healthy street cats. We leave town by the gentlest slope we can find, keen to avoid the twin main roads way up high on the spotted mountain. Neither of us is in the mood for a vertical hike or the highway traffic. We find a beautiful walk around the ocean cliffs that turns out to be the old road and, hallelujah moment, it meets up with the highway a few kilometres down the road. This is a coastline created by a god whose primary purpose is to showcase the colour blue. We pass stray cats lined up along an old stone wall, occupying Adriatica's premier real estate, eating from their own dishes. The mystery of their luxury is soon solved: up ahead is a woman walking with her black Labrador, feeding the cats as she walks by. She has also laid out cushions for them in a sheltered hole in the wall.

This morning I walked the walls of the old city while Ben finished his blogs. Apparently Dubrovnik has the finest example of complete medieval walls in the world. Daughter of a new world, I was blown away by thoughts of the tales they could tell. I hesitate to demonstrate the extent of my ignorance ... but I had always thought fairytale castles were just that, castles conjured from the imaginations of storytellers. I didn't know that real castles looked like this. As I wandered around the wide greystone battlements, past cross-bow slits and smooth black cannons aimed across the sea, my mind's eye conjured trysts and sword fights, death and camaraderie, naughtiness and nonsense. I'm sure these walls have seen it all over the centuries. Yes indeed, Dubrovnik is a beautiful city.

It is not easy being on the road again. Two days pack-free in warm cosy beds and we're soft already. For some reason, rest eats into the stamina. As we wander around the coastline I'm aware that until now we've always had a destination, even if it was a few days away – Avezzano, Pescara, Zadar, Split, Međugorje, Dubrovnik. These have been our lights on the hill. Now there is only Istanbul. We are truly entering the unknown, geographically at least. I wonder what it means for the spirit and the heart?

We manage about seven kilometres before darkness blots out the day. Summer's-end is official with the winding back of the clocks and the day's early close takes us by surprise. There are people in my own country who scoff about the impact of daylight saving on the length of a day. They do not account for the rhythms of life and their relationship to workday sync.

As darkness falls I am shrouded in a crisis of confidence. Self-loathing and distress set in. I do not want to sleep in ugly places. *I am more than this.* I long for my husband's love and attention, realising in a moment that I am imagining my husband to be the man I need, not the man he is. Ben wants to walk into the night and I tell him, 'No, I do not need to be reckless,' surprising myself with the firmness in my voice and the surety in my heart. I tell him I am happy to walk the small roads by night, but I will not walk the highways. It is a beautiful moment. A personal moment. He receives the truth of my words, just as they are transmitted. I tell him I am willing to let the journey go if he needs to frogmarch through the night to Istanbul. I tell him I am in no hurry. At first I feel only release. Then the loss of this pilgrimage floods in, all that I have yet to do, a landslide of imaginings and fear as I return to the present. *I do not need to sleep in nowhere dark places.*

We are sitting on a lump of land under a fruit tree in a small orchard beside a rubbish dump behind a row of ugly buildings. It is the only camping spot we can find in the dark. It is too early to burrow into our tents. 'Let's find somewhere to eat and come back here later,' I say. It is a good idea. We find a pizza place. We open our computers. The voice in my head is rattling on. *Why am I doing this pilgrimage? Because I do not want to be with my husband.* The reality of this bites hard. Then the pure white light of momentary right swamps me: *get a room.* I do not have to sleep beside a rubbish dump. Why do it hard when goodness and all-I-need is everywhere? And why am I waiting for Ben to offer me this? *Because I am buckling to his need to save money.* I do not need to save money and I am surrendering my authority to his disapproval. I guess it's an adult-child-of-an-alcoholic thing: tired of playing the rebel, tired of 'fighting' for my needs and 'rights', I am without the resources to define and claim my world. I leap up and tell Ben I'm going room hunting and, surprise, there's one next door. It's closed for the winter, of course; but they let us in anyway. I make an agreement with Ben. I will pay for the rooms when it's important for me to have one. He can contribute what he feels is appropriate in the moment. We slide into sleep, Ben excited about tomorrow. Montenegro is on the horizon.

We walk steadily all day and cross into Montenegro about an hour before dark. We walk along the main road and, mercifully, the traffic thins out the further we are from Dubrovnik – or the closer we get to Montenegro. We stop for a bread and cheese breakfast overlooking Adriatica. We stop for fabulously fine hot chocolates in a messy town. We stop for lunch in a café that sells nothing but petrol. The shop assistant kindly allows us to eat our bread and cheese at her tables. We roll out the backgammon board at every stop. For most of the day we are walking through scorched Earth, where the summer's fires have sucked the life from the mountains. A couple of hours from the border the spotted mountains shift a beautiful valley away from the road and autumn wheels through the valley floor, all the shades of red and orange and yellow.

As in Herzegovina, it is difficult for us, son and daughter of the new world, to know whether buildings are in a simple state of decay or have been bombed. *Are we making up stories? Surely bombing is the realm of six-year-olds with plastic toys pretending to blow things up?* As we draw closer to Montenegro, it is clear that the buildings – homes and farms – have been destroyed. They don't proclaim their ruined status to an attention-seeking world. They sit quietly, stark yet barely visible, shaded by autumn and new life slowing down for the coming winter. This is more than television.

About a kilometre from the border we turn a corner and Montenegro comes into view; a great valley, long and wide, skirting a puddle of ocean. The sky is a massive watercolour wash, a pretty blue-grey. Montenegro – my unpainted canvas. As we pad, pad, pad down the steep hillside between the Croatian checkpoint and the Montenegran checkpoint, I feel light and sweet in the face of my own beautiful darkness, mirrored by the world around me. We have that conversation again about the name we call nations and the name they call themselves. What, we wonder, is Montenegro in Montenegran? We don't wonder long, for there is a sign between the borderposts and the *republika* announced there is unpronounceable – *Crna Gora*. We walk well into the darkness before finding a very smoky restaurant, the only food in sight. The meal is well-cooked but nothing I particularly want to eat, especially at the big euro prices. Through the nicotine haze I eat chips and a pancake and a fair whack of Ben's tomato and onion salad that he didn't order. We rise to leave and the bill is exorbitant. She's ripped us off, fair and square. Ben is not one to argue. As soon as there's an irresolvable matter he goes to get the police to sort it out, in this case because no-one is speaking the same language and he's too pissed off to remember he speaks pidgin Russian. Personally, I can't imagine he'll have any more linguistic luck with the coppers, if he can find them in this strangely withdrawn country in the dark. I sit quietly among her regulars and wait for his, or their, return. The longer he takes the easier it becomes for me to pay her and move on. Ben comes to the same conclusion and gives up on the cops.

We walk into the night, past boggy fields and rubbish, neither of which I am willing to camp on or near. We walk into Herceg Novi, a long town that becomes a city, knocking on doors that advertise *sobe* (rooms): we either receive a 'no, no, no' (it's not the season) or give a polite 'no way' (robber baron prices). We walk on through streets dark and dozy. This is one sober town. The only women on the streets are those scurrying home. The men in the bars and meeting places have little life left in their faces. There is a shimmering fear in this world. And an awful lot of mud around. And then, the miracle. I ask a man loading goods from the boot of his car into his garage if he has a room. He does! He gets his wife, a woman of middle age who has life coursing through her being, a welcoming smile and a loving greeting in her hands. More than this, they want a wonderfully fair price for their room. We unwind the packs from our backs and collapse onto chairs, feet up on the beds. We've been on the road thirteen hours, walking for about eleven of them. The woman brings us each a shot of Ben's favourite pirate brew. She brings us pancakes. She bids us goodnight. And then a wild thunder rattles the windows and the skies open and, well, we're very, very glad, for many things really.

We wake to roaring thunder reverberating all around us. It's a dark, grey day and we get an unhurried late start, mainly because we have internet access without leaving our beds. When we do finally hit the road, we find a map of *Crna Gora* in a strange bookshop, having left the old one behind in a pizza bar a couple of days ago. By midday we're sipping cappuccinos in lieu of hot chocolates over breakfast. *Crna Gora*, or, depending on the vowel preference of the signwriter, *Crne Gore*, has no more taste for breakfast than its northern neighbour, so once again we have bread and cheese and chocolate and mandarins. The rain holds off and it's surprisingly warm. The best news for me is that my pack is finally feeling lighter! These last days it's been so heavy, as if the straps are two hands pulling down on my shoulders. Amazing isn't it? There's nothing extra in it, no noticeable changes in my physical abilities, yet there you go, out of the blue the pack's heavy and impossible to strap on properly, and then, hallelujah, it's not.

There is sadness in the people around us. And fear. And lots of new houses. And destruction. We walk around the coastline on ratty footpaths. In the parallel world of my mind, I am walking the back roads of my childhood: I see beauty in the weed flowers amidst the destruction and rubble; blooms of kindness shining brightly in a pockmarked landscape of unkindness and fury. Within a couple of kilometres we meet a no-footpath, no-end-in-sight tunnel, so it's up and over the hill for me. Ben waits to see if I make it over. I scurry breathlessly through the bush, straight up a small track to a magnificent view of the coastline back towards Herceg Novi. Ben can't resist and follows me over.

An hour later we strike gold, walking past a restaurant that delivers Ben the feast he's been drooling over since we landed on Adriatica's eastern shoreline: pig-on-spit. We're on time and in luck. The roast is shriveled. It's probably not pig. It's ready to be eaten. We sit in the restaurant in the dark because the power is out. That doesn't affect our feast. While he's in lamb heaven, I'm in chip heaven. Fast food entrepreneurs will have a field day when they discover *Crna Gora* still has old-fashioned, bloody delicious, greasy homemade chips. These are pre–trans fat days and jeez they're good.

We hit the road again and the thunder makes good its promise: it pisses down for the rest of the day. It's lovely walking in the rain, knowing we're in for a warm bed as soon as we've crossed the inlet up ahead on a ferry. That said, one of the most dangerous things a pilgrim can do is make assumptions about what's ahead; yet all is well. By day's end we're warm, not particularly well fed, content. And for the first time, I arrive 'home' on dark not trashed. Life is turning around now I'm taking responsibility for my own bed, choosing the best that life has to offer, moving beyond survival. Today I watched closely the relationship between how I play backgammon and how I live my life: not taking enough interest in what's happening at home, not taking the time to bring home my most distant pieces, exposing myself to the vagaries of others, not bothering to protect or at least consider my options and always, always, always making a comeback – I play a great survival game. I change my tactics, I take my time, I watch the parallels. There's no doubt that when I am fully present with the board, I am at my best.

There is something delicious about rainy days in cold countries that quickens the heart and lightens the spirit. We're on the road early, the mists lying low over crowded mountains backing up the inlet, the water choppy and grey, smoke curling from weathered chimneys. The rain is holding off, for the moment. We walk the few kilometres into Tivat and by the time we've stocked up on supplies – bread, cheese, chocolate and, sadly, no mandarins, because the quality of the fruit and veg in Montenegro is awful – the rain is a steady downpour.

 We walk all day into the traffic in the driving rain. We pass the brightest red bush we have ever seen, way up high on a mountain. It looks as if it is on fire, alight with the turning season – the beauty of dying reflected in a red bush. I wonder what is dying in me? We get the feeling *Crna Gora* is a nation just recovered. Like most developing countries, rain means mud as water pours through stopgap infrastructure and barrels through the streets, carving new fissures as it goes. As for her people, *Crna Gora*'s folk, as we've met them so far, are extremes of lights-on or lights-off. Those with the lights on are the strong-hearted, their spirits full and present and glowing, their faces alive with love and welcoming smiles, theirs the surefooted confidence of knowing who they are. They are a minority in any culture; it is heroic that they are here among the war-ravaged. The others have foreheads creviced with confusion. They have frozen stares and eyes of stone. I see a woman with lips so tightly pursed it is as if she has sucked in all her breath and the wind has changed, leaving her face poised with a sudden and terrible and never-ending grief. I tell myself it is because of the war and then I wonder, which war?

There are hostile hearts amany in Montenegro. Yet there is also a softening peace around us ... and madness on the roads – forty-kilometre speed limit, blind bend, unroadworthy car – *yeah mate, gun it why don'tcha, there's plenty of room to overtake!* Sometimes, this is how I play backgammon.

The road today is hard work. Reckless winner-takes-all driving is one part of it, fumes from a plethora of barely functional vehicles is another. We look for photographic subjects and realise we have come to expect the beautiful or the extraordinary from landscapes and architecture; ordinary is no longer enough and this stretch of *Crna Gora* is either bog ordinary or ugly.

As we walk the narrow edge of the wet road, Ben a hundred metres behind me, I think about leaving my marriage. I am consumed by the loneliness of a world that contains no-one but me. *I would rather die than go through being single again.* A heartbeat later I slip on slime in the gutter, the weight of my pack hurtling me into the path of an oncoming car. The car swerves and I regain my balance. I turn around and grin at Ben. We are both acutely aware how close the call. I walk on, unsettled now by the timing of my slip. It was as if the one we might call God had just tested me, *You'd rather die than be single – is that true?* No, actually. It's not. It's not true at all. When I die let it not be from self-pity. Rather, let me find a new way of living.

Late in the day we find a back road that cuts through the mountains into Budva. It is such a relief to allow the spirit to rest as we walk, grateful for the respite from the eternal vigilance of the main road. Dripping wet we find a hotel at a great price with a heater to dry our clothes and a man with a soft smile to welcome us at the desk. We are in wet pilgrim heaven: warm bed, clean sheets. Budva has an aliveness we've not found elsewhere in *Crna Gora*. People have a spring in their step, even if the sight of the turtleback strangers does bring them to a sudden halt. We trail through the city in the darkness and the rain, searching for the seafood restaurant recommended by the man at the hotel. We find it down by the water, amidst a tired summer circus closed for the winter. We order, fish for me and a feast of meat for Ben that is preposterously prehistoric. Over wine, our conversation turns to our darling Lily, who funds her fabulously five-star lifestyle by climbing poles for men who are drunk on grapes or control, and dancing topless in their laps. Lily is beautiful and she is highly intelligent; more than this, she is skilled at negotiating with the men who govern global finances. Hers is a world in which women are paid to create an illusion and they are paid according to how much they can bleed from the wealthy, the drunk and the lucky-at-the-races, a world in which the truth of a woman's sexuality has no place, a world that burns her out and to which she returns over and over again. After all, where else can she earn two thousand pounds a night? I can tell from the look on Ben's face that he thinks I'm moralising. I call it observation. I remind Ben of the young woman he flew to our resort on Koh Samui the year before, a bar girl from a region of Thailand that produces crops of girls like Australia produces wheat. Ben rolls his eyes. This was the one and only time my life has been touched by the perfidy of one human being purchasing another. *My son bought a woman.* Humorously, to me, at the time he was reading a book called 'Sex Slavery in Asia'. Humorously, to me, at the time he failed to see either the connection or the contradiction.

'Men are not interested in the truth of a woman,' I say.

Ben laughs.

'You want the truth of a woman?' I ask. 'You believe she comes to you by choice? Then give her your money and set her free to please herself about how she spends her time.'

From Budva, according to our map, civilisation is about to thin right out as we turn our backs on the ocean and head for the mountains of Albania and Macedonia. I am reminded of a quote I used to carry around with me when I was young: *In order to discover new oceans, we must first have the courage to lose sight of the shore.*

After dinner, Ben heads out into the wet night seeking more lively local company. I lie in bed and ponder courage. New oceans are always exhilarating; so too, when you stop sweating it, is losing sight of the shore. Courage, I decide in a warm bed between clean white sheets, is conscious action. It comes with the territory of life on the edge. Courage is feeling the heart beat a little louder and holding true as it pounds harder. Courage is the 'yes' of life, the blood of love. It is an absolute refusal to settle for mediocrity, to barter the spirit's longing with the desire to tell stories about why things must stay as they are. Courage is the willingness to square our shoulders and bare our breastbone to the sun, the wind, the rain and the storms of life. Courage is an open heart. And steady eyes and an open heart are the only armour we need as pilgrims of life.

I wonder how I might tell the difference between courage and bravado. The answer is immediate and simple: my wishing self. Pay attention to the wishing one. Because if it's not here now, it can't be here. It can't ever be here. Because wishing is wanting and wanting is clawing at a perennial future. There is only one thing that stands between wishing and reality – truth of this moment and cache of all I desire – and that is myself.

Wishing has been my anaesthetic. It has tricked me into thinking my mind knows my heart when in fact it is putting me to sleep. Wishing is not the voice of the heart. Wishing is the voice of the mind, the rambler, the apologist.

Longing is the voice of the heart.

So what, I wonder, straying from my own point, is so bloody difficult for me about my marriage? What is so life-numbingly impossible about my husband? The answer is this: the absence of interest and enthusiasm and friendship; the wanting, wanting, wanting from me; the obsessive rigidity and control. And the only question left for me is this: how does this reflect me? How do I play this out in my own life? This is the purpose of my pilgrimage, to recognise my face in my husband's reflection. For there is not one step I have taken in the past five weeks that has not been accompanied by the overwhelming and vexatious unholy war between my heart and mind about sex and money and obligation. It is an old war. A vicious war. A war that takes prisoners. And I long to be free from its entanglement, knowing that I must burn in this cauldron of fire if I am to prevent it from surfacing over and over again in my life. The enmity is age-old and its narrative labyrinthine; it is beyond my own time and place. More than this, it is the propellant in a gender war whose solution is as simple as, well, peace in the Balkans.

We wake to a clear morning and a slow, lazy start. And then, as we're finally making our way out of town, we discover the Kangaroo Motel. Of all places. And of course, with its walls lined with murals of a great ship called *Endeavour* and its helpful sign telling us we are 17,000 kilometres from Perth, we can't resist. We sit with hot chocolates as black and thick as the dirt the cocoa grew in and take advantage of wireless galore, catching up on our blogs and emails. Take two and we're on the road by midday.

We wind steadily upwards around the coast; the mountains and the blue water with us all day and the sunshine a shimmering pathway all the way to Italy. The first two hours are wonderful, the traffic so slow we wonder if someone has died. And then, well, it's business as usual for the invincible on the narrow roads of *Crna Gora*.

The mountains here in *Crna Gora* are more ragged and rugged than the spotted mountains of Croatia, which we left behind at the border, and there are more of them, leaving even less land between them and the sea. On our first evening in *Crna Gora*, as we walked into Herceg Novi, to our right was a magnificent stretch of towering mountain rock lit by … settlement lights? A dying moon? It was a great transparent monolith streaked sideways with translucence. It was not of this world. And then, the following day as we walked to the ferry, we were startled by red fire on the not-so-distant mountain tops, like flaming lava flowing down the rock. And that was on a dark and cloudy day. Rock or foliage? We're still not sure. We could only imagine that mountain lit by the sun.

We walk on, the winding bitumen rising steeply to give us steady views over Budva and the long blue coastline. Resting on the roadside, high over Adriatica's darker shore, we are again amongst olive groves. They've been missing from our lives these past days and these groves are as old as an olive grove might be, massive trees ballooning grey-green over the earth, the air beneath and between them so very still. I long to spend the night with them. We roll on. Around the next bend we meet a small grey-white church, the steeple a little rounder on the top. Across the road is a café. Ben's coffee is now froth-free. Slowly, imperceptibly had we not been walking this land step by step, we are moving closer to 'the East'. Or perhaps the East has come for us.

The days are closing earlier as winter draws near and this creates a source of tension between Ben and me. He's calculated he needs to walk close to thirty kilometres a day if he's to cross Turkey before the coming winter. Once again he is agitated by my refusal to walk into the night. And I am unwilling to walk busy roads in the dark. I am also not interested in trashing my physical body by working her from sun-up to whenever. She needs, and has earned, and loves, her rest and her time to ponder. I will not walk the main roads at night. At four o'clock I down pack at Beljurice. There are no more towns to speak of within striking distance before dark and we are hungry. If we don't eat here, there will be no dinner tonight. And if we do eat, we lose our last hour of daylight. I'm eating dinner and there's a pub to supply it right here in Beljurice. As we wander through the small shop-free gun-barrel settlement, past a tree laden with mandarins in someone's front yard, we're edgy with the unexpressed strain of meeting our own needs whilst considering the needs of the other. The mandarins in the shops these past days have been horrible. I decide to raid the tree, helping myself to as many mandarins as I can carry in my jumper, leaving a handful of change on the letterbox in return.

We take our seats at a table in the smoky pub, which fills quickly with the company of working men calling in for their dinner. I'm aware that neither of us, Ben nor me, is being honest. We do not know how to speak to each other without risking offence and, in my case, my son's contempt. I had thought my need not to walk the main roads at night had been clear and I'm confused and annoyed that I have been either misunderstood or ignored. Ben's way is the way of men: not-speaking. Our intentions in keeping the peace are beautiful, as well as cowardly. The situation is difficult because our needs are not reconcilable and they have to be addressed. In my case, my concerns are also loaded with a blind rush of paranoia about Albania, about walking the darker shore. And besides all this, I do not trust myself to speak gently. Oh, I vow to do so, speak peacefully and confidently that is, and in my mind's eye I do, but when it comes to speaking my needs, my throat is tight with the grip of illegitimacy and my belly already winded in anticipation of accusations of selfishness and aggression.

We unfurl the board and roll the dice. We speak in the spaces. We make easy peace. We do the best we can. We agree we will not walk at night. Again. I feel no victory, but I do feel a little more sure of myself. A little more legitimate in relation to my son. We wander into the night, meandering along the middle of Beljurice's cold dark street, for in reality there appears to be only one, wondering where we will sleep. A small sign announcing *sobe* from behind a large wrought-iron gate yields a small room with rickety beds in a big old house owned by a middle-aged man who speaks great English and lives with his mother. By way of explanation for his scant circumstances he tells us he is divorced.

From Beljurice we make a crack-of-dawn start, tiptoeing out of the house and down the stairs, climbing steadily out of the valley and around the coastline towards Bar. Having eaten pizza in Pisa and drunk cappuccino in Cappuccino, Ben is delighted to be heading for a town called Bar. I remind him that two years ago we also drank cognac in Cognac. We pass the roadworkers, who have also made a headstart on their day. I wave and walk on into the chilly morning, the views ahead spectacularly blue; green fingers of land reaching intermittently into the sea.

My mind is a-clutter with apprehension and disturbance. I am not sure about Albania, about walking blindly into this particular unpainted canvas. As I walk I do my best to separate fear from intuition, blind paranoia from lifesaving 'don't go there' instinct. As my mind begins to run with alternatives, 'intuition' comes unstuck: I could fly to visit friends in Spain – *the plane will crash*; I could catch the train to Greece and meet Ben there – *the train will crash*; I could catch a ferry back to Italy and hang out in Venice – *the boat will sink*; etc. This is how I know I am suffering a simple bout of 'absence of a known world', a minor crisis of confidence. This is fear, not intuition. As we walk over the top of a mountain and down the other side, I let my mind run with all the terrible things that might happen to me in Albania, wherever that is and whomever might be there. I touch base with my Steadying Hand and, shoulder to shoulder, we walk awhile. By the time we make it to midmorning breakfast, where Ben is in barnyard heaven with eggs and fat fresh bacon, my mind is clear and my spirit ready to walk head high into Albania and meet her, face to face – not because I've talked myself into it, but because it is the right and only thing for me to do today.

We wander around the stunning sunny coastline to Bar, through an industrial area nudging what will soon be, if local property developers have recovered their post-war commercial senses, a tourism jewel. Montenegro's southern coastline is 1970s Noosa Heads-at-Christmastime beautiful. I'm pleased we're enjoying it now. We pass a small grove of pines overhanging a pebbly beach and stop, lying back on our packs in the shade, listening to the waves rock the pebbles on the shore. I call to council my Steadying Hand and my Guiding Light and together we sit quietly in this beautiful peace of Earth. The flames of my natural fears were whipped to wildfire yesterday by an email sent to Ben from a couch-surfer in Albania. She told Ben Shkodra had just been removed from the US embassy's most dangerous cities list. She told him she and her friend had visited the week before and had a gun held at their heads. She hosed down her dramatic offerings with Western-too-confident dismissal. I imagine her to be big and rude. And I am annoyed with her for rocking my already quavering world. The truth is my walk is not a death wish. The truth is I do not want to be seen as reckless by those who love me. The truth is I feel bogged-in racked-up resistance coursing through my blood and knowing this resistance is only fear of death doesn't still the anxious tide. Fear of death. It is not intuition. It is fear also of another kind of death. If I die, let it be said I died trying! For this is the best I can do. I am walking the darker shore. I have no choice if I am to claim my life. I do fear Serbia. I do fear Albania. I am walking lands whose people have suffered and so too the land itself.

The rain these past days in Montenegro has matched my own spirits. I am learning to camp sweetly on the darker shore. I would like people to see me. I expect them to see me – yet am I willing to show them who I am? Do I have this kind of courage? By Istanbul, I would like to be able to show my face to my son, unprotected, undefended. Life is cheap in these countries. Or so I'm told. I wonder how much I value my own life? I am wary, not unlike the inhabitants of the darker shore. In truth I too am cautious, resentful, hostile and insecure, curious and incurious both – *just like them.*

I think about Yugoslav men. I am walking a land that is the Yugoslavia of my imagination – here I am among all that I abhor and mistrust about the masculine. His harshness. His ruthlessness. His humourlessness. His cruelty. His righteousness. His violence. As for my husband, he is off the radar. I have not spoken to him for at least two weeks. If he has rung, I have not answered the phone. I remind myself I can always take the bus and then wonder if I will. I am projecting… *the mountains … Albania … Macedonia … strangers … fear … lives on the line.*

The too-loud couch-surfer who emailed Ben with her intrusive, unwelcome, idiotic comments also said we should stick to the highway in Albania, which is flat and straight and safer than the mountains. She said that if we avoid the mountains, however, we may miss out on an 'adventure', because 'Albanian hospitality in the northern highlands is unmatched'. She said that according to the *Kanun*, the ancient northern Albanian code of customs and ethics, a guest in one's home takes the form of God and that people would treat us like royalty. Those who break the custom of hospitality would be killed, she added. Ben likes the idea of being treated like God. My mind is full of it … *the mountains … Albania … Macedonia … strangers … fear … lives on the line.*

I realise it is the projection that's creating the fear and anxiety. If I bring my awareness to my feet, to all I can see and feel right here, just here, only here, I am safe. My eyes and senses are open. Right now I am safe and content, I am all I can be, I am doing the best I can.

I wonder about my need to be on the edge of my life: is it false bravado? I think about Tracey, one of Tim Darwin's 'social climbers', the merry band of larrikins who climbed high and interesting places for dinner parties, starting with the Sydney Harbour Bridge and ending with the K2 summit. I have never forgotten his story of Tracey, at least the story as I heard it, the story I tell: Tracey was a climber of mountains and she decided to marry. In so doing she was giving up the mountains she loved. On her last mountain before the wedding, taking a photograph, she slipped on the edge of a crevice and slipped away.

The friend climbing with her told of the look in Tracey's eyes when they made eye contact, the moment before Tracey fell. I have always had the sense Tracey had struck a deal she was unwilling to keep. She would 'do the right thing' and marry but she would not surrender the mountains; Tracey would rather die than trade her spirit for marriage.

There is another whose death lives also in my heart. His name is Michio Hoshino and I met him in Lynn Schooler's memoir 'The Blue Bear'. Michio was a photographer who roamed Alaska's wildlands. He wrote a children's story, which included the following poem:

> *We are each an expression of the earth.*
> *When you pray for my life,*
> *you become Nanook,*
> *and Nanook becomes man.*
> *Someday we shall meet in this world of ice.*
> *When that happens, it does not matter*
> *whether it is I who dies or you.*

As it turns out it was Michio who died at the paws of the great bear, Nanook.

I have long been captured by the poignancy of these deaths.

They are not the same tale.

Lazing in the sunshine on the shores of a pebbly beach in an alien land, I caution myself about trading my life *and in so doing trade my life*. The truth is I have no choice but to surrender to a journey that will deliver to me all I know myself to be. This journey is choiceless. I wonder at the fragility and robustness of us humans, being. My spirits rise as we load up our packs. My confidence is true. My path is clear.

Bar is great! In just two places in Montenegro have we seen women on the street, relaxed and comfortable: Budva and Bar. Bar is filled with weird cement architecture and modern coffee shops. It's a strange place in a strange place, way down here in a distant corner of a new nation. We rest awhile in a Melbourne-modern coffee shop; we find a map; we eventually find internet. We walk out of town by the railway tracks in the midafternoon sunshine, seeking a country road and finding only the main drag. It's okay.

It's just a few kilometres before we wind straight up into the mountains to Dobro Voda (Good Water). We pitch camp in a stony paddock sandwiched between new cement ice-cream cake houses overlooking Adriatica, not minding the neighbours. We eat dinner in the darkness – bread, chocolate, cheese and mandarins – accompanied by a sweet cat, two cows and a pair of happy dogs. I lie in bed in the early darkness and imagine what the world would be like if more men had laughing eyes.

We wake to a feast of a day for pilgrims. We start early, packing tents wet with dew as we look out over the ocean from the dry and stony paddock that served us well as a bed for the night. We walk a country lane all day, even when we hit the main road; an autumn country lane, all the way to Albania. We meet strangers who wave us on our journey with smiles and pomegranates, old ones living the old ways. Daughter of a new world, *I cannot presume to know who they are and what they know.* Indeed, I am done with stories. For they are not mine. And they are not real.

We accept an invitation to sit awhile from a Narnia-esque picnic table, stone and circular beneath a bare-branched tree at a crossroads. We take this to mean 'time for backgammon'. With the mountains blue in the distance, the entire scene is an otherworld temptation. And there's nothing like stopping still for five minutes for life to come to us. In moments we are keeping company with cows drinking from an old fountain, an old man riding a donkey, an old woman herding goats.

We eat lunch in a village called Vladimir, where roadside hawkers sit beside rows of big yellow river fish on the patchy bitumen, the fish so fresh they're still gulping for air. And there, in a café that might easily have seated five hundred, we meet Mun Sung Do, a Korean vet with a magnificent smile who is motorcycling to Morocco. All day, animals and humans going about their business. And there in the distance, another unpainted canvas, a misty grey wash we know to be Albania.

Soon after leaving Dobro Voda this morning, we noticed a green and white rocket that I presumed was a kids' playground and Ben, laughingly, proclaimed a Soviet rocket. Seriously, we thought the green and white rocket was probably a grain silo. A couple of kilometres on we saw another. And then another. It wasn't until we passed a graveyard with a model rocket on a tombstone, surrounded by headstones engraved with five-pointed stars and sickle moons, that we realised our green and white rockets were mosques! Oh how we laughed at our ignorance. No doubt about it, the East has come for us.

The road signs are now bilingual, we presume Albanian and *Crna Goran*. More women wear loose white headscarves. Hay carts loaded to the sky roll on by. Come to think of it, it's been quite a few days since we last heard a church bell. According to my map, Albania to its own is *Shqiperia*. Imagine that – *Hrvatska, Crna Gora, Shqiperia*: Croatia, Montenegro, Albania. An old woman with a headscarf brings life to the lines on her face when she meets my eyes, a most wonderful greeting that lights my heart as I pass. Old men shake our hands. The closer we get to the border, the more pleased people are to see us. '*Albanija?*' they call. '*Albanija!*' We nod and smile, *Yes we are going to Albania*. They are *delighted*. We realise these are the people our newspapers might describe as 'ethnic Albanians', the ones whose lives are drawn on the other side of the line in the sand. Just before the border crossing, a small child runs to the gate when he sees us, his scarf-bound mother and grandmother laughing shyly from the verandah, urging him to greet the turtleback strangers. This touches me so deeply I begin to cry.

This morning, the politics of our times sheltered my heart from theirs, the shrouded ones for whom I will make a stand in my own country, but among whom, face to face on their own territory, the politics of fear unsettles me nonetheless … *a young man with a dark beard and jagged features drives by in a rattly old red car and the reality of where I am startles the blood in my veins … my eyes meet those of a robed woman raking leaves and I wonder, who does she see?*

There was a time I might have visited this country and the women and I may have found each other curious and interesting. Now we meet with mistrust. Once again, in the great circling wheel we call history, we must learn to meet beyond politics. Before long I understand – not just academically, but right through to my bones – the terrible, terrible injustice world leaders commit when they use fear to fortify their world view and justify the unjustifiable. And even if I lose my life doing this, it doesn't make world leaders right. This pilgrimage is a journey of reckoning for me, reconciling the unnamed tensions I hold in my bones with the staged and somewhat noble realities I hold to be true in my mind … who I am, rather than who I want people to see … who I am, rather than who people want me to be. By allowing 'unacceptable' fears to surface, the ones I have put on a brave and compassionate face to conceal, I am able to release the hold others have on my life, socially and politically. And so I allow deeper truths to bypass my mind and sink into my bones. It's not a matter of what *he* is or who *she* is, but that collectively the reality is they are not. We are not. That.

We. Are. Not. That.

We are the old men with laughing eyes.

We are the old women with smiling hearts.

We are the children who run to greet the strangers.

By midafternoon we reach the Albanian border. It has taken us just five days to walk the length of Montenegro. The guards at the crossing are so captivated by our cameras that one invites Ben to film inside the office. This causes considerable distress to the guard inside, to the amusement of the others. We wonder if Ben's going to lose his camera. By the time they check the film and are satisfied they cannot be identified, Ben realises his digital camera is missing. And no-one has bothered with our passports. We offer them up. The guard outside passes them to the guard inside who hands them back out the window without looking at them. Ben asks about his camera. Everyone looks confused. And then the camera reappears in the hands of another guard. After a round of photographs of guards and pilgrims, the camera is returned. We get the feeling they don't get many visitors in these parts.

We walk on through the golden fields of Albania with the sense we have entered a sideworld. The children run to greet us. Every few hundred metres someone stops to offer us a ride, occasionally in a car, more often in a horse-drawn buggy. Old Soviet bunkers, round and grey and overgrown with brambles, like little alien spaceships long abandoned, confound our sense of time. The sun is low on the horizon, the evening is extremely cold and we have yet to pass anything that looks like a bed with a roof or a decent camping spot. Shkodra is fourteen kilometres away and we're in agreement that it's too far this night.

We pass an empty concrete shell, a new house on the rise, and agree that in the absence of anything better it will do just fine for shelter.

We come to a *kaffe* bar and stop to assess our options over a bottle of wine and a few rounds of backgammon. The bar does not sell food. Nowhere sells food. Just like there is nowhere to stay. I look at Ben and tell him I am not going anywhere. And I know this to be true. I am not leaving this bar tonight.

We roll the dice quietly in the corner. We sip our wine. It is dark. It is cold outside. I repeat my resolve. *I'm not going anywhere.* We roll the dice. I am thinking when we get to Shkodra I will take the train to Tirana, Albania's capital. Deep in my bones I know I need to rest. And this will give Ben a chance to roll on into the night as he pleases, walking to his own steady rhythm as the night cold closes around him. We discuss our needs and possibilities. My need to rest wins out over my need to walk. We are in easy agreement.

And then a miracle. The bar closes. Everyone stands to leave. Except me. Without resistance, I stay right where I am. The barman comes over and speaks to Ben. It has been this way for weeks now, the further into the old world we go the less attention men pay to me. The men speak only to Ben. The women do not speak. Therefore I do not exist. I am learning to like it. I am learning not to mind not being seen. I am learning to appreciate being talked over. I am learning that this is the way of men in a man's world and, at best, they mean respect, no harm; at worst, they are signalling Ben they have no intentions towards 'his' woman, whether she is his mother, sister or wife.

The barman offers us the floor of the bar for the night. It is clean. It is warm. It is offered with goodwill and, in the absence of any request from us, without emotion. As he turns out the lights and locks the door, leaving us with the keys on the inside, Ben and I look at each other and grin: we love Albania.

We wake early, surprised how well we've slept on the cement floor. Although I don't know it yet, today is to be my last as a pilgrim on the road. We are woken not by the returning bar owner, as expected, but by praises to Allah booming into the pitch dark from the loud speakers in a distant paddock. We giggle. It is our first Islamic wake-up call. I in turn sing praises to my little blow-up mat, which has kept me warm and comfortable on the hard floor. We're on the road by six, walking into the coming daylight for an hour or so before the sun rises crimson-gold across the paddocks. Yesterday, about twenty kilometres shy of the border when we were still in Montenegro, the mountains and hills that have kept us steady company for the entire length of the eastern European coastline started to open out. By the time we crossed into Albania our world was a broad expanse of flatlands, wide and still.

It is a wonderful sight, watching morning come to new places, the light slowly revealing an unknown world and people rising to meet their day. We walk beneath dark clouds lit electric blue by the morning sun, past fields, green and brown; past a church a hundred metres up the road from a startlingly lime green mosque; past fields of rubble and rubbish; through villages with new *kaffe* bars hamming it up alongside wasted grocery shops where women too young to look that old stand behind counters heavy with scales that belong in a museum. Men riding donkey carts clip-clop by, a clutch of silver milk cans rattling in the back. Men on time-warp bicycles sail by. And everybody waves. The women shyly. The men with a great g'day-mate roar. And there are chickens everywhere. We are in a world neither of us knew existed in current time and space, not in 21st-century Europe.

I have walked through Europe many times over the past ten years. Peasant cultures co-exist with the modern world from one end to the other. Albania is different. For a start, their peasant culture is exceedingly friendly. Wonderful, innocent, everything people said about Thai and Balinese people forty years ago, before we put them to work and exhausted their domestic and sexual goodwill. The rural Albanians are welcoming and wonderful, no two ways about it. As we get closer to Shkodra, however, the poverty is relentless. I have seen such places on television and I've driven through them on buses once, perhaps twice, in my life. Never have I walked the dust and shaken the hands and met the smiles of those who live in the dirt. Until now. To my limited, first-impression eyes, the other difference between Albania's peasant culture and the rest of Europe is that here it is the rural dwellers who have the best of it. It is they who have decent housing, their new ice-cream cake palaces popping up over the landscape. Here it is the city folk and the urban fringe dwellers who seem to be doing it tough, who are the ones left behind.

By walking, we often enter new worlds through the back door. As we draw closer to Shkodra, the poverty concertinas, tumbling in on itself. We are extremely thankful we are walking the city's outskirts in the bright light of a Monday morning, rather than weekend darkness. It's not for nothing Shkodra has only just been released from the American embassy's list of dangerous cities. We come to a long and rattly wooden bridge that ought to have surrendered its legs to the filthy water below long ago. Instead it is a discordant dusty channel for humanity on the go, funnelling Shkodrans to and from the city centre. I stop to look over the edge of the bridge into the river, surprised to hear the horns behind me honking louder. *Fancy that, I am holding up the traffic.*

As we enter the city we see a sign that is a blast to our pilgrim hearts – Istambul 1,109 km. I stare at the 'm'. *Istambul*, how curious. We walk for a good hour along a dirty street, past mounds of rubbish and lines of dusty young men lurking in shadows. There is something about Shkodra that doesn't make sense to our artless eyes. The rubble, the rubbish, the holes in the walls. Shkodra looks like a city recently bombed. Yet clearly this is not the case. We are confused. So what is the case?

It is time for me to take the train. We beeline for a hotel called the Grand Europa, lured by its billboard promise of Western familiarity. We figure it'll be a good place to get our bearings. The hotel is on the edge of the city's main 'square', which is a startle of confused geometry ringed by a large mosque, a park, a small merry-go-round and a run of blaring honking traffic and pedestrians. The hotel lobby is scattered with men in business suits and the staff, though suspicious of us, are confused by our confidence.

With Western goodwill and self-assurance, we ignore their hostility and take our seats, ordering chamomile teas with all the charm of those who do this every day. We plug our computers and cameras into wall sockets to recharge. We go upstairs to the restaurant for lunch and are overwhelmed by the heartful welcome and quality of service offered us by the maitre d' and floored by the extraordinary feast he and the chef lay out for us, replete with complimentary champagne and dessert. We raise our glasses: we love Albania. I want to take the lift to the hotel rooftop and holler back up the valleys to the people of Herzegovina – 'IT'S OKAY DOWN HERE! THEY'RE REALLY VERY FRIENDLY!'

There is a small tourism agency in the hotel lobby. I ask the woman behind the desk about the train. She tells us it is three kilometres away. We take a taxi. The taxi takes us to an abandoned wasteland of barbed wire and rubbish with a building boasting holes in the windows and metal grates over the doors. We start to laugh. We tell the taxi driver in our best Albanian to take us back to the hotel. Clearly, I do not have my son's talent for asking questions of non-native English speakers. My question for the woman in the tourism agency ought to have been: *'Are there trains running?'* I call by reception and ask about a bus. It is across the road. I ask how much it is to spend the night at the Europa and she tells me fifty euros. This augers well for Tirana and I'm clap-hands delighted. And can she recommend a hotel in Tirana? She shrugs and says, 'Rogner.'

We find the bus station and grin at each other through the wide glass window of the purring coach. We'll see each other in Tirana in two or three days' time.

I sit beside a sad woman my own age. Although I do not understand her, I learn that she is a teacher. She has three sons. They all live in England and Tony Blair won't let her into the country. I look into her eyes to find the timeless sadness of a woman defeated. The bus pulls into the nation's capital on dark. I ask the driver for 'Rogner?'

A woman takes my arm and leads me to another bus. I surrender to the moment. We sit together among the peak-hour commuters. I presume she is showing me where the hotel is. Another woman gets on. She practises her English. After I agree that Albania is very beautiful, she tells me it was a Christian country dominated by 'bad Turks' for 500 years. She tells me she is Muslim and adds 'modern Muslim'. She hijacks me from my guiding angel, who happily relinquishes her charge, and we leap off the bus into the darkness.

She grips my arm and walks me straight across six lanes of traffic, holding up her spare hand and raising her voice to the cars: *'You must stop, we have far away traveller visiting, she is our guest, you must stop.'* They don't, but they do slow down enough for us to pass.

I farewell my guardian and head into the night, down a city block and up the stairs into the lobby of the Rogner Hotel. It is gorgeous.

It is divine. It is my resting place. I smile at the young woman in reception and ask for a room. She raises her eyebrows, takes in my road-weary face, my backpack, my clothes.

'Do you know how much it costs to stay here?' she asks in perfect primary school English, grazing the length of my body as she speaks.

I raise my eyebrows in return and breathe deeply.

'No,' I say. 'Would you like to inform me?'

'Three hundred euros a night is our cheapest room.'

I am gobsmacked – 300 euros a night! Has she any idea where we are?

Gobsmacked I may be, but I'm not going anywhere. Not tonight.

'Does it have a bath?' I ask.

'No,' she says.

'Three hundred euros and you don't have a bath?' I say evenly. I am attempting to claim the high ground. I take out my credit card. My husband will have a heart attack. Then again, given the circumstances and the alternatives, I am confident he would support me this night. I hand over my credit card.

'There is not enough money on your card,' she announces triumphantly to everyone in the lobby.

I snatch it back, biting my tongue about basketcase countries and their tenuous relationship with Western banks. This is the third time my credit card has frozen since I left Rome. I have learned the hard way that banks freeze cards whenever they appear in odd places, meaning outside 'the West'. This can be incredibly frustrating when the same 'odd' places are usually bereft of the kind of infrastructure one needs to restore financial liquidity. I stare at her rudeness and hand over another card.

I seek only rest. A bed. Warm white sheets. I take the lift. It is a king bed. It is a small, happy-enough room. I am in bubbleland heaven.

I sleep soundly, waking to delicious stillness and silence, stretching between the clean white sheets, sinking into the comfort of knowing I don't have to go anywhere. It's an illusion, I know. The price of this room is a once-in-a-pilgrimage event and today's mission is to find another motel, so that I might rest with the darkening moon, at least until Ben turns up. Much as I love the material comfort and beauty of the Rogner, I am annoyed by the unwelcome I received from the staff. How ironic that in fabulously hospitable Albania I must pay so much to be treated so rudely by children with impeccable English and a horizon as wide as a ten-leke coin. It shouldn't annoy me, but it does. I re-live the moment I blew in with the cold, seeking comfort, finding instead a receptionist with a sharp inhale. If I'd been quicker I would have given her that fabulous Dolly Parton line: *'Hey, it costs a lot of money to look this trashy!'*

I head into Tirana's morning to find another hotel. I ask people on the street for directions. They shrug. I ask a woman in a travel agency. She shrugs and asks 'which hotel?' I say any hotel is fine. She says she doesn't know. I wander around the cold grey streets seeking sunshine among damp shadows, eventually heading up the main drag towards the light. I have read online about the friendliness of the people of Tirana. All I can say is that compared to the warm hearts out there in the fields and the mountains, Tirana is just another busy grubby city going around in frantic circles, filled with expressionless no-help-at-all people and an awful lot of men standing around, like pigeons in Trafalgar Square.

It is here, just behind the man-pigeons, that I find the much more affordable, though still ridiculously expensive for where we are, Miniri Hotel, which is just across the road from a giant mosaic depicting armed peasants in revolt, which in turn is across the road from the Tirana International Hotel. I spend the next few days in the Tirana International drinking mineral water in the lobby and accessing wireless, sleeping at the Miniri by night. Interestingly, the women of Tirana do not wear headscarves.

Ben rings in the afternoon. He is walking along a dirt road running parallel with the railway tracks. I envy him his afternoon sunshine and wide blue sky, knowing all the while that this time of rest is right for me.

Evening comes and with it my exhaustion. I lie on a hard and narrow bed in a room that smells of old tobacco smoke, thinking of Albania and the conversation I had with Ben in Shkodra yesterday. *How on Earth did this country get left so far behind?* Way behind. Croatia, Montenegro, Bosnia, Herzegovina, all in various stages of recovery from war. We have the feeling war is irrelevant to present-day

Albania. There is certainly more rubble than usual, but the poverty? The poverty in this country is undatable and beyond reason.

I wake and greet the day, feeling as if I've been breathing tobacco smoke all night. I head back to the Rogner for breakfast and wonder how it is they charge so much money for a room in Tirana, capital of Albania – and six euros for a thimbleful of fresh orange juice. I look around at the diners. They are mostly men. They are men in suits. They are not tourists. And then it occurs to me. They could be representatives of other-governments, perhaps the European Union, perhaps the United Nations, bureaucrats and dignitaries charged with the resolution of Albania's 'problems', whatever they might be. The Rogner is set in parkland in the middle of this filthy, chaotic city and it's certainly a beautiful place for respite from the extremes of poverty knocking so boldly at the door. I don't blame anyone for choosing such luxury over the pit outside. That the Rogner exists, however, in this context, catering to this particular client base is perverse, even unconscionable. I recognise systemic problems cannot be fixed with money alone, yet I can also imagine the outcomes for community organisations around here if those travel allowances were funnelled onto the street, instead of feeding the elite; and the increase in bureaucratic will to create real solutions if those charged with solving the problems were to settle for the still relative luxury of the Miniri and the delicious, traditional pastries selling for pittance on the streets. It occurs to me that Albania is not unlike Thailand after the Boxing Day tsunami, yet for Thailand and Indonesia our Western hearts leaped to action – we knew we had to help. Not here. More than this, can you imagine our response if aid workers stayed in the Rogner and used precious disaster funds to eat so lavishly while those we have sent them to help starve in the gutter? I would suggest a little solicitude in return for meeting the eyes of those you claim to assist is not unreasonable.

Perhaps they get away with it because we-the-West are not watching.

By midmorning, I'm glad I took the bus. Back in my odorous tobacco room, flat on my back in bed, everything aches. My bones and joints are incredibly painful, my gums and skin sore to touch.

I'm cold to the quick and feeling incredibly sick. I take a painkiller. I stay put for the day, rising for a quick fish soup across the road at the Tirana International, vulnerable and defenceless against the looks from the waiters generally and a particularly well-heeled young woman in particular.

'You are dining *alone!*' she spits.

'Actually,' I say, 'I am dining.'

It is not easy being sick in a strange city. I return to my grim little room for the worst night's sleep of the pilgrimage, if not my life. I toss and turn on that hard little bed, my hips a riot of agony, waking every five minutes to peer out the windows, scouring the sky for morning, longing for reprieve from the piped tobacco in the air conditioning. I stare at the dark ceiling and wonder why I am fighting my husband. I wonder if any man would be enough to hijack me from the ordinariness of my own reality. I would like my husband to be on my side, yet clearly I am not on his. Albania is my 'been through the worst of it', my winter solstice, my return-to-the-light turning point, knowing all the while the worst of the winter is yet to come. In my husband I see my contemptibly idle, afraid-to-honour-my-creativity self. How did Albania get left so far behind? How did I get left so far behind? I smile with the realisation that my husband would be happy that I paid for the room at the Rogner, but appalled that I paid six euros for the orange juice. I won't mention what I paid for the water.

I make a note of what I know about my husband, and realise I do not know him at all; have not taken the time to know him. Nor he me, for that matter, but that is not my business here. That, in fact, is a game called marital ping pong, and it is a game with which I am thoroughly bored to tears. Feelings of invalidation course through me, mirrored beautifully by Tirana. Whether I'm on the street or in the big hotels, the voices in my head struggle to belong in either place. I feel obvious, judged, different, not enough. The strange stranger. Belonging nowhere. I wonder if the pain laying me low is cyclical, for was it not on the dark moon last that I was also gripped with the agony of something between constipation and flu? I wonder if this pain is in lieu of my bleeding? I thank my own god I had the foresight to catch the bus. I feel as if I'm attempting to sleep in an ashtray; the smell of the room has colonised my mouth. I fantasise about sunshine. I long for the companionship of my husband, for the comfort of home. Everything hurts. My kidneys are tight and I feel utterly nauseous. I long to cry but I don't know if there's anything left to cry. I have walked self-pity from my bones. And that leaves agony and silence and waiting for this too to pass.

Morning comes as morning does and I spend the day taking it easy, still not feeling great, hankering for sunshine to warm the cold in my bones. I'm sitting alone on a bench along a tree-lined pathway in Tirana's central park, surrounded by traffic and old men in the only aesthetically pleasing corner of the city I can find at short range, when Ben rings to say he is just fifteen kilometres away. I take photos as I sit, surprised to discover that photographically, the city transcends its own ugliness. I'm annoyed by Tirana. I don't like it. I don't like its lack of purpose. I don't like its absence of anything interesting. I don't like the unhelpfulness of its people and their standard disinterested shrug that sends their eyes rolling slowly to the ceiling. As with the woman in the travel agency when I asked about hotels, so too the receptionist at the Miniri where I am staying, when I ask her where I might find a chemist so that I might stock up on blister protection before heading into the mountains. She shrugs. Her eyes roll. She doesn't know. *You don't know?* So too the woman in the bookshop when I ask for a map. She shrugs. She rolls her eyes. She doesn't know. The people of Tirana are expressionless. I let the sound of the water rushing in the fountain soothe me; the trees rest with me; the sunshine filtering through the branches warm me. I am looking forward to the mountains, to air that is free from smog and fumes and cigarette smoke. I look through the cheerlessness around seeking expressions of love and immediately become aware that my body hurts, that I am sore and tender.

My attention shifts to the riot that has been my life: *what, exactly, have I been fighting for?* I have never been less attached to anyone with whom I am in relationship than I am to my husband, the one I married. Is this maturity? Suddenly I am enlivened by an insight: my refusal to feel good about what Ben writes about me on his blog is my own reluctance to speak the best of others. I am dazed by the paradox, because I do speak the best of others. And yet I do not.

And then, just as suddenly, I have had enough of the journey into self. I am tired of the exploration, tired of taking responsibility for all that I am and all that I see, tired of doing my best. I lay it all down, right there beneath the grand old trees in Tirana's central park, and wander up to the Tirana International for lunch, putting myself through another round of rudeness and greasy pasta while I wait for Ben, who rings to say he's fifteen kilometres away. Good maps, like help, are hard to find these days.

The hotel is throbbing with the 2007 Balkans Health Systems Conference. As I eat I watch the participants, bureaucrats and health care professionals, each and every one of them out on the verandah of the restaurant puffing away like 19th-century chimneys, the women clomping about in 12-inch heels. It occurs to me they're going to need a decent health system. I'm surprised they have to smoke outside. Fascinatingly, here in Tirana I have found the only two smoke-free zones in all of eastern Europe: the Tirana International and the Rogner. Smoking, I must say, doesn't usually bother me. Now I realise this is because I live in a smoke-free world, where smoking tobacco is so taboo even middle-aged adults shuffle red-faced outside in their attempts to hide their habit from each other, a situation I find alarming.

I move out again into the grey day, zipping across the traffic chaos to sit in the middle of a great roundabout in the centre of the city, lorded over by a bronzed national hero on a high horse, waiting for the precious sun to shine through. I am confused by humanity and lost among it today. I realise that if I were feeling more alive, Tirana would probably appear to be more alive. I resolve to be more helpful in my own world to people who appear to be not feeling well.

Ben rings and we arrange to meet in the lobby of the Tirana International. It's great to see him. We take a seat, we order orange juices. He's grinning wide with a wonderful time on the road.

'The first night? The first night was great. I met a guy who invited me to stay. His name was Kole and he spoke perfect English. He pulled up on a motorbike and tried to get me to jump on the back of his bike to go to his house – there was no way I could get him to understand that I was walking and couldn't accept a ride. His house was in Guri I Zi, about eight kilometres away, just off the main road, so I told him if I saw him when I got there I'd stay – an hour-and-a-half later, he was waiting for me on the edge of town.'

We laughed.

'I wonder how long he'd been waiting,' I said.

'Yeah, I wondered that too,' smiled Ben.

'His wife and daughter cooked up a huge pork roast, he pulled out a bottle of homemade wine and his son pulled out a 550-watt speaker and blasted us with music. The neighbours were lucky he only hooked up one – he had four of them!

'In the morning Kole asked me if I wanted English or Albanian breakfast. I wasn't sure if he was joking or not, but I figured that since I didn't know what an Albanian breakfast was it was worth a try. Lucky I didn't drink too much the night before, because the Albanian breakfast was a shot of espresso followed by a shot of homemade rocket fuel. Funnily enough, I felt great! Then Kole gave me a lift back to the main road on his bike. On the way he stopped at the bar for a second round of breakfast. The bar was packed. Another espresso and two shots of cognac later and I was on the road.

'I planned to head down to the river then along the railway tracks to Lezhe. The locals told me there were only two trains a day, one in the morning and one in the afternoon, so I figured the railway line was pretty safe for walking. Within minutes I had to jump off the tracks. Lucky it wasn't coming from behind me, although the speed it was going I reckon I would have outrun it anyway.

'I had a great walk through the fields, chatting to the kids along the way. I spent the night in Lezhe, figuring I'd keep it simple from there by following the railway tracks to Tirana. Simple as it seemed, thanks to my map I couldn't find the railway line and spent the day on the highway dodging cars.'

He looked at me quietly.

'The good news is the people,' he said.

'I hadn't walked for an hour before I was invited in for a drink. It's so strange that the poorer the country, the more giving the people. When I think of all the warnings we had to be careful. Strange how in a rich country people fear strangers and in dangerous countries they don't.

'My map was useless. The main highway wasn't marked and the railway tracks that are marked don't exist. I camped in a paddock, not bothering to ask permission from the neighbours. So this morning sure enough I could hear footsteps and voices approaching. I was already awake but it was so cold! I was savouring the warmth of my sleeping bag, wondering if they'd let me be. They said something in abrupt voices and when I didn't answer they got quite agitated – I thought I'd better stick my head out. When they saw I was a foreigner there were smiles all round. And then it was back to the boring, boring highway, stopping at every *kaffe* I passed looking for breakfast.

'And then I found this great little place run by kids! I asked if they had food.

'"Yes! Manjare, manjare!" they said.

'I asked if I could see the menu.

'"No," they said.

'So I asked them, Well ... what do you have?

'"What do you want?" they said.

'I decided to keep it simple, so I asked if they had spaghetti or pizza.

'They said no.

'So I asked them again, Well ... what do you have?

'"What do you want?" they said.

'I laughed, and said, *Just get me anything.*

'The younger one, who's about nine, runs into the kitchen and I hear cooking noises start up. All these thoughts are running through my mind, along the lines of, *Surely he's not making my breakfast ...*

'He was, and my apprehensions were completely unfounded. What appeared was a wonderful plate of rice and fried meat, cooked to perfection! I was impressed! It was even funnier when their mother came along, looked at me, looked at my meal, then directed a quizzical glance at the kids – she was as surprised as I was. That was my entertainment for the day.

'All day, when I asked how far it was to Tirana, no matter who I asked they would tell me anywhere between fifteen and thirty kilometres. All day, no matter how far I walked, there was still somewhere between fifteen and thirty kilometres to go.'

Ben rings the couch-surfer, the woman who'd advised him to go to the mountains so that he might be treated like God. She tells us she will meet us in the lobby of the Tirana International. Charis is beautiful in every way and I fall in love with her on sight. She is all that I bow to in American culture – intelligent and alive with goodness, humble and helpful, and she reads ancient Greek. She is a long way from the horrible Westerner of my imagination who rattled my nerves in an ill-considered email on the road to Albania.

We load up our packs and follow Charis into the Tirana night, crossing parks and busy roads, up an alley and up some stairs into a roomy apartment that is almost immediately plunged into darkness. Charis informs us this happens every night, though you can never be sure what time you will lose the lights. The entire city is blacked out for an hour or two each night, to save power. I've been too sick to notice. In minutes the candles are lit and the lounge room is filled with a gorgeous pocket of young Americans, no less than the entire contingent of Fulbright Scholars to Albania, all of whom are in love with a country that everyone else on Earth seems to have forgotten. There's nothing like a bit of 'local' input to change the face of a city. With the metaphorical flip of a coin, Tirana comes to life for me.

We eat with Charis and her friends at their favourite Indian restaurant. *Imagine that, an Indian restaurant in Tirana.* The food is vibrant and delicious and the owner loves us. Suddenly I am feeling much better. Charis and her friend Shaina give us a short tutorial on Albania's recent history – about its self-imposed ideology of isolation under a merciless Communist dictatorship, about the murder of intellectuals, the torture of poets, the abolition of religion, the burning of books and the reconstruction of the language – the beginnings of an explanation for the poverty that is beyond European reason ... and last weekend's delight amongst the villagers that we have taken the time to visit. Albania, they tell us, was governed for forty years by the tyrannical Enver Hoxha, who pulled a veil so tight around the tiny nation that the rest of us forgot she existed. They tell us he did this because he believed the Soviet and Yugoslav regimes were 'too lenient'. I am astonished, once again, at the power of one man to shape an entire world. I find it truly extraordinary that one man can summon the support he needs to murder all that threatens him throughout an entire nation. We cannot ignore this propensity in human beings. And we cannot continue to insist that 'he' is not 'me'. Or we can, of course. Just don't expect anything to change. And don't bore me with your surprise and bitter judgement that such a man should emerge. Again.

It is freezing cold on the streets. I wonder about the mountains of Macedonia, about the wisdom of heading into unknown territory that may well be snowbound. I haven't been one for looking at maps or sussing out temperatures. Nonetheless, there is a growing uneasiness in my heart about heading blindly into the mountains. Charis's friend Michael puts it to rest. He tells us it will be cold in the mountains, that there will be snow. He says there will be very little shelter and there will be basic food supplies. Most importantly, he tells us, 'What you are doing is not reckless and it's not dangerous.

'It's out there,' he says, 'but it's not reckless.'

This is all I need to know. While Ben and the Americans beeline for Tirana's night life, I make my way home and sink into Charis's bathtub. Imagine that! A bath! Not even the Rogner Hotel had a bath.

We wake late and take it easy, deciding to lay over in Tirana for another day so Ben can do his washing. This makes four days for me without walking. I wonder how my feet and shoulders will go tomorrow. Ben tells me that last night, high in the Sky Bar overlooking Tirana, a Canadian woman told him that Australians and Canadians need visas for Macedonia, the only two nationalities on Earth who do. He goes online to discover it's true, and that it takes five days to get a visa and no visas will be issued at the border – all because Australia, like Canada, insists on calling Macedonia 'The Former Yugoslav Republic of Macedonia'. Why? The best we can figure is that the Greeks claim the word Macedon – not the land, the *word*. We also figure that Australia, having the biggest Greek community outside Greece, has a lot to do with this diplomatic idiocy. That said, I'm pleased about the diplomatic stand-off, for it means we must skirt Macedonia and walk the lower hill country of Albania to Greece, where there are many more towns for shelter and not nearly so much snow. This route is green on the map, not white. For truth be told, when I look at our map and tune in, that sheer patch of whiteness over Macedonia freezes the blood in my veins.

My son, however, is not one for obstacles. I'm nearly fifty. I have little or no energy left for tackling bureaucracies. Not so Ben.

I watch my younger self leap to action. Ben wants to know if and where there is a Macedonian embassy. My heart sinks. Resistance kicks in. I want him to fail. I want him to go with the flow. I want him to recognise that we are not equipped for the mountains. I know that even when he discovers the phone to the Macedonian Embassy is not connected, he will pursue his visa to the end. I tell him I'm not here for extreme sport. He says he knows. I wonder if my son can be still. I wonder if he has a need for confusion and obstacles to overcome, to fill time and to keep him from facing his life. As he and Charis head off in a taxi to find the embassy, I look online for the weather forecast for Macedonia. Big black cartoon clouds drip water onto the cyber map. Thunderstorms are predicted for the first three days we plan to be in the mountains. The temperatures are below zero at night. They are single digit by day. I don't mind getting wet by day, but I have no desire to sleep wet in a tent on dirt that is primed to sap my warmth. And there are almost no towns through the mountain passes. I pray for the visas to fall through. Of course they do not. Even though the embassy was closed, who should come to greet my persistent son at the gate but none other than the ambassador himself, who, charmed by my son and his mission, stamps our passports then and there.

Ben and Charis return triumphant. I am proud of him. But I also think, *What for?* He wants to go to Macedonia and then to Kosovo. He is seeking the edge of danger. I wonder if he does this to prove to himself he is safe. I struggle to find, and be true to, my own journey, the one that runs parallel to his. My journey could have been undertaken anywhere, because I am simply seeking the unknown to reflect what I don't know. Perhaps it is no different for him. Perhaps he is seeking an outer manifestation of his own unexploded violence … perhaps I am too. He is not reckless, my son, but he has a habit of riding the edge. Or perhaps this is my way of explaining unexpressed anxiety about following him to my own edge.

And my husband? I am at peace with him off the radar. He is a concept, a 'husband', a man I do not know yet to whom I have bound my life.

While Ben does his washing I fill time reading his blogs. My heart sinks further. He talks about me as a stereotype, in a 'you know what mothers are like' way, as if the whole world is in agreement with his reality, as if he is dragooning their loyalty, dividing the world into teams, everyone versus me. I have still not resolved my sense that he is using me as blog sport. He writes about tension between us, without recognising that he is talking about my tears of vulnerability because he blogs me. Mostly, I am terrified my family will read his blog and reinforce their own judgements about me, their oldest sister, the selfish one, the greedy one. Families are attached to stories, old stories, war stories. I long for my son to tell it differently, to reframe my world for me, to show them the best of me. I long for him to show the world that he is with me, not against me. I long for him to rewrite the family stories. It hurts. I don't yet recognise that the voice might be only in my head. *Although it may indeed be in their heads too, but that is not my concern.* It is the power I give the voice in my own head that interests me – because, when all is said and done, the stories that live in me are no-one else's but mine.

I also remain apprehensive about the mountains. I am cold here in Tirana, sitting inside a sleeping bag, rigged up in my thermals in a house with the heater on full. I tell myself I can always bus it out, but the next voice down knows there are unlikely to be many buses on mountain roads whose narrow paths and steep inclines would, in any event, terrify me witless. The bus is not an option and besides, it is the least of it. I do not feel Ben and I are communicating. He is holding on to *something* and I am struggling with blindly following a young man with an active need for passport stamps into snowbound thunderstruck mountains on the edge of winter. When my thoughts quieten and I allow myself to be still, I am confident the right thing to do will come. I sit in the lounge room fingering Charis's small stash of books. In 'Empires of the Word' I am captured by the ideas of Nicholas Ostler, who outlines the case for not presuming English will always be the world's language of choice – because for all the reasons we might argue his point, English has staked territory that was not only unforeseeable, but, through these lenses, not hers to claim. And I am introduced to the famous Albanian writer Ismail Kadare, who leads me into the mountains, where for two hours I am one with the life of a young man named Gjorg, who has just avenged his brother's death under the ancient mountain code of *Kanuni i Leke*

Dukagjinit, the same code that would have Ben treated as God. And I meet Charis's favourite poet, the Albanian Visar Zhiti:

> *Time*
> *And how it slips through my fingers*
> *Without putting its ring on them,*
>
> *And I remain simply its lover.*

In the introduction to Zhiti's English translation, an American called Janice Mathie-Heck tells how Zhiti was betrayed by his fellow artists, who in order to protect themselves from the brutality of Hoxha's regime turned their backs on the poet when he was imprisoned and tortured. I am annoyed by her simplistic judgement about the 'unspeakably insidious and cowardly' actions of the artists, written from the sanctimonious certainty of another time and place. I wonder, faced with certain death, imprisonment, torture or all of the above, how Mathie-Heck can be so sure she would defend the right of her comrades to express themselves freely? Because such an action almost certainly requires one to stand alone. And even then no-one can or will be free, because those who turn their backs will break their own hearts. Hence, in part, the broken spirits of the Albanians all around us.

Charis makes soup for the Fulbright scholars. She is the heart-centre of their home-less lives. She is the one who cares for them, mothering without becoming mother.

Later in the evening we all go out for dinner. Rain is pouring from the sky, as if God has opened up all those great big holes in the road and let the water barrel through. Ben rocks up soon after we arrive at the restaurant, arm in arm with the incredibly vibrant Elira. They take their seats at the circular table. The Fulbrights are dazzled or shocked, I'm not sure which; either way, they are silenced. Elira has big round eyes and an aura that oozes healthy sexuality. I have never before experienced eyes that undress. It is exciting. As well as bright eyes, Elira has blonde hair. The Fulbrights are stunned to learn she is Albanian. Albanians are dark people. They are not blonde.

Elira has Ben and me in stitches as she recites for us the history of her people. The Fulbrights are bemused. Albania, she tells us, repeating for eternity one of the many celebrated stories that ensure the Balkans remain troublesome for some time, is the centre of Europe. Geographically, the Fulbrights tell us, she is correct. But she is speaking of more than geography. She tells us Albanians were – are – Europe's first people. Because they are – were – descended from the Illyrians. This, she assures us with her dancing eyes and genetic certainty, validates Albania's claim to all surrounding lands, including Macedonia, Greece and Kosovo. Charis, on my right, whispers to me that the link to the Illyrians is possible, but unproven. Lindy, a non-Fulbright American on my left, whispers that history and geography books in Albanian schools include a map of 'Greater Albania'. She tells me there is an alarming number of fanatics in Albania who believe the country's rightful geographical borders will one day be restored. She tells me all the Balkan states tell similar versions of the same story and all of them believe the others kicked them out of lands that are rightfully theirs. Between Elira and the Americans I begin to understand why the brightest minds on the planet cannot, and perhaps may never, 'solve the Balkans'. Ben and I roar with laughter at each new claim. Stories, myths. We have now heard their contradictory variations echoing over the hills from one Balkan state to another. Humanity. What we know. What we don't. And, most importantly, what we 'want'. Son and daughter of a new world, we can afford to laugh. What do we know about what matters?

It's been wonderful accessing Tirana through Charis's eyes, like borrowing a pair of glasses to help me see. Today, while Charis and Ben were chasing Macedonian diplomats, I ventured into the street to find Charis a set of drinking glasses. I returned home unreasonably pleased with myself for having found a kitchenware shop in a city that has few street names and no numbering and where crossing the street is known as the Tirana Shuffle – a slow dance in which one steps into chaotic traffic and shuffles across the road through small spaces between moving, incessantly honking cars. The honking drives Charis crazy. She doesn't believe me when I tell her they honk at least all the way back to the middle of Montenegro.

During my excursion I passed old men sitting on makeshift stools on the filthy footpath, concentrating hard on a game of square lines marked on a scrap of cardboard, moving rocks as counters. I sank deeper into myself in relation to the city, this city, this city of ... of what? Funny, isn't it, how stories generate compassion. *Why not compassion anyway?* I tried to imagine a people stripped of their language and traditions, religious or otherwise, for fifty years. Not so long in the scheme of things; a lifetime if it's your generation. I began to think of Albanians as 'the awakeners'. The ones returning to life. I wondered why, if Communism's grip was eased seventeen years ago, it is taking Albania so very, very long to recover? I wondered if the suits in the Rogner have anything to do with this? I wondered if, as with the Croatians, the fresh air brings with it freedoms they might never have known if not for the annihilation of all that was? Then again, the former Yugoslavs have not suffered like the Albanians. Not collectively. It is incredible to me, the difference in spirit between Elira's generation and anybody at all in Albania older than thirty. In Tirana, in Albania, there are only the old and the young – the young and everybody else.

On my way home with the shopping, I glanced into a great big hole in the road filled with rubbish and dirty water, a hole so big you could drive a car into it, and I wondered, *Is anyone in there?* I thought of death, of the infinite souls who have died in human history. Every one, dead. Time and place irrelevant. I wondered about those with whom I share a modern world, the ones whose outrage is a crescendo of blame whenever somebody under the age of eighty dies. As if we shouldn't die. As if death is someone's fault. We are temporary life forms. Every one of us will die. This is our story. And it doesn't mean anything. Imagine that. *Nothing means anything.* Not even the bath that warms my bones. Imagine that, a bath two nights running.

Ben heads into the rainy night to party with Elira and the Fulbrights chatter upstairs by candlelight. I forget that other people cannot see themselves in action, that they do not know how beautiful they are. These young Americans have a skittishness about them. They're charged, like colts in a corral. I wonder if this lack of confidence is born of a paradoxical insecurity about being American in a hostile world – they know they are good people, yet they know also that they are judged by the sins of their foreign policy. Americans are renowned for their confidence. Strangely, the Americans who least deserve it – the youth who leave the homeshore for the wounded unknown, bringing with them all the great gifts of their time and culture and education, offering what they can to a needy world – how sadly ironic they are the ones least able to look that same world in the eye. Perhaps that's why these particular Fulbrights chose Albania. Albanians, like Kosovans, *love* America, in part because Bill Clinton sent the US Air Force to save them from the Serbs in the recent Balkan war and, going back aways, because Woodrow Wilson insisted on preserving Albania when the big shots at Versailles were carving up Europe after the Second World War. Perhaps it is only among their fellow Westerners that young Americans feel the need to drop their eyes, ashamed to be *American*. They are so beautiful, so committed, my heart aches for them.

I unfold the lounge into the bed Ben and I share and tuck into my sleeping bag. I lie there tormented by my need to speak to Ben. Once again I am overpowered by the masculine's unwillingness to communicate, by his failure to acknowledge the need to share his thoughts and feelings with those most affected by them. It is so rigid and intransigent from the outside, especially when one is relying on their good judgement. I can rely on him or I can rebel – where is the truer path? I feel hogtied by the absence of alternatives. I could bus to Thessoloniki – but by then I will have been off the road for several weeks and it wouldn't be worth the agony of revving up my feet and shoulders all over again. Yet my pilgrimage with my son is not done either, for I am tearful at the thought of finding my own way and claiming what is true *without distress*. Meanwhile, I'm just lying here picking at sores. In a distant way I wish I had a husband to talk to. Or be with. In a distant way.

And then I understand the 'something' Ben seems to be withholding: it is open discussion. He's sticking to his path, across the mountains to Macedonia, as if I have no say in where we go. And perhaps I don't. His mind is set and while he considers me, he does not consult me. He is here for his journey, not the journey shared. I have allowed him to set the path from the beginning and I honour him for this and, in truth, I've been extremely grateful for his leadership. It is not danger I fear in the mountains, it is *severe* hardship. I have no need for severity. This pilgrimage doesn't require me to walk a road any more difficult than walking the road already is. I am sad that journeying together doesn't seem to be a priority for Ben. *How confronting is this for my marriage?* I lie in the candlelight navigating my feelings. It is not unlike doing the Tirana Shuffle.

I have the strongest sense my pilgrimage is over. I do not want it to be so. Yet, in truth, my body has known all evening that the walk is done. As the rain bucketed down today through those big black clouds a voice in my heart said, *It is done, you are not prepared for those mountains*. And now, no matter which way I turn the dial, the information is the same. My tent pegs have no capacity for hard ground. I can barely keep out the cold here in Tirana. We are too late to cross the alps. And, yes, earlier this evening in the bath I peeled off all my blister protections, so as not to make a ritual of it. More than this, it is time to go to Istanbul. The old city calls. The history of the world calls. Something ... else, calls. *It is time to go to Istanbul.* I will go to Istanbul and find the backgammon board I have long promised myself, should I ever go to Istanbul. I will miss Ben's ease with strangers and his ability to navigate non-English speaking worlds. I will miss the road. I will miss the company of my son. I will bid Ben farewell. For I am not one to fool with big mountains, not when destiny – my own, rather than my son's – is not calling me there.

I wake and watch my son sleeping, leaning on my elbow waiting for him to wake.

'I'm not coming,' I say when he opens his eyes. 'The walk is over for me.'

He blinks. I long for him to tell me that he is happy to take the low road around Macedonia, so that we might continue walking together. It is his call. He knows this is my preferred route. He asks me if I am sure. I tell him yes. I tell him I do not have the warm gear I need to walk in the mountains. I tell him I will fly to Istanbul and take the train to Thessoloniki to meet him there when he arrives. We are sad. I cry. I cry because he too is sad. The decision makes its way through my body. All of me wants to forget I spoke and go into the mountains, and yet in my deepest heart I know there is nothing to do but fly. This is the choiceless path. We figure it will take him two weeks to make it to Thessoloniki, unless he turns up in Istanbul.

And then we laugh, knowing it's a real possibility that the snow may yet drive him back to Tirana.

Ben packs alone and I walk with him into the city. The mountains looming large are dark, the clouds around their tips near-black. Now and then the chill wind blows the clouds clear and we gasp in awe at the blanket of snow on the high ground. I know I have made the right decision. We call by the Tirana International for another greasy pasta and a final round of backgammon and finally there is nothing else to do but walk due east to the mountains. I walk with him to the muddy edge of town. We are both shell-shocked, unprepared for such a sudden change in our easygoing roll across the eastern European landscape. We hug. I wave him on. In my mind I am walking him to the foot of the mountains.

I turn on my heels and return to the hotel lobby for bearings and warmth. My pilgrimage is done. There is not a cell in my body that's undecided, uncertain or unclear about this decision. Indeed, it is not a decision – to walk with him would have been a decision. Yet, and yet, already I miss being outside in the wilderness, the beauty of the mountains, the warmth of the sunshine, our steady companionship and, yes, even the rain. The romance of pilgrimage has already begun to play with my heart. I sit in the lobby with a fresh orange juice. The pilgrimage was never supposed to end this way. Neither of us is prepared for our journey to finish here, no finale. And now ... now my journey shifts to facing my own idleness, my resistance to connection with others, my inability to show up in my own life – all these Important Things that give me the shits about my husband. I raise my glass to Ben and make a silent toast: *Love every moment we have with our people, because this too will pass.*

And I did love every moment. And we loved every moment. This was pilgrim's purpose and we did our best.

I return to Charis's house and let myself in. I turn up the heater and sit quietly, somewhat disorientedly, on the lounge. Already I miss living in a parallel zone. Here in Tirana I have washed my hair for the second time in two months. I miss the oils on my skin. I miss my feet on the earth. I miss Ben. And yet I feel alive with the wisdom of taking this path, for this is the path of heart, of care, of love. My son is doing what he is born to do. My son is doing what I raised him to do. I wish him beauty and sunshine, all the way.

I sleep long and wake to a new round of sadness, overwhelming and tearful. I claw at my centredness, proclaiming, *It's not so cold*. I check again online. It's not so cold! Perhaps I should have just asked for more time. Perhaps I simply didn't have courage enough to face that wall of rock and plough through it into the sunshine. Into ease. Into the love of walking the wheel. I am not ready for an inside life. I am not ready for a world that gives me what I want, when I want, for everything I need to be provided, for polite conversation. My spirit is not ready to live within walls! Ben rings. I burst into tears. He offers to wait. I love him for this. And still I wonder why does he not offer to take the low road. Why can I not ask him to take the low road? Because I already have. Because this is my comfort zone. Because it is not about this. It is about a wall of cold that I am not willing to enter. I wonder what the inner parallel might be. Why the terror for the chill in my bones? Why the agony of bitter cold? My river is running elsewhere and I want it to run *that* way. I want to be with Ben playing backgammon overlooking Adriatica, eating bread, cheese, chocolate and mandarins in the sunshine and wind, setting our spirits free in the mountains. My soul cries out for love of the journey. Forty-nine days. One for every year of my life. And then it dawns on me: I weep for 'more', rather than what is – and what *is* is that I am going to Istanbul.

Istanbul

I joined the mainstream. Tirana airport, shiny and new and pothole-free, was surprisingly un-Albanian. And the laugh was on me. Because it took me an entire day to figure out Tirana had an airport. It didn't occur to me to ask anyone how to get in and out of Albania – I just presumed I'd have to catch a bus. No buses. Or a train? No trains. Ferry? No ferries. But planes there are aplenty. At the airport I was at the front of the queue because with pilgrim patience I had waited for several hours to check in; and then, suddenly, I was at the end of the same queue, because everyone else was in such a hurry. I was self-conscious about an orange juice stain I discovered on my shirt, about the earth-stains on my pack. From the airport lounge I could see the mountains outside through the great glass-panelled window. The dark mass of cloud moved on, leaving them bright and beckoning to my spirit. Sitting in the lounge, waiting for the flight to be called, I was surprised by a voice in my heart, clear as the now-blue day, saying, *I am going home.*

I flew over the mountains, scouring the Earth below for Ben. There was snow, but not too much. *The lake will be beautiful when he gets there.*

Preparing to land in Istanbul the voice came again, this time filling my eyes with tears: *I am home.*

I took a taxi from the airport to the motel, which I had the pre-science to book online. As we raced towards the old city I was dazzled. *Look at the pretty gutters! Where is the rubbish?* The taxi circled a most magnificent building, an edifice that thumped the beating heart in my chest and expanded my sense of self beyond reason, taking me far beyond my own borders. I peered through the taxi window into the night as a large white bird circled the dome of the building, as if in slow motion, then alighted on the top.

The hotel was around the corner. When the valet left the room and closed the door, I fell onto the bed and cried and cried and cried. My journey was for this. The very, very longest journey. All of my life, for this.

I am home.

The tears flowed, sobs released my body. Never had I arrived in a city and felt so relaxed. Everywhere I looked I saw the familiar. The vibration loosened me, sang to me. I experienced a deep and abiding contentment, a no-beginning no-end stillness, as if all of me was tuned to the pulse of the city. I felt loved. I felt honoured. I felt as if the whole hallelujah chorus of me had arrived, at one with time and place; as if lifetimes of struggle and darkness had come to this pinpoint recognition of golden light. Me and the dawn of all time.

> *I am queen and slave, conqueror and king,*
> *I am the great stone pillars connecting earth and sky,*
> *I am the wind and the sea and the wide flat plain.*

I wept with love and sorrow and exhaustion and an overwhelming sense of gratitude. *I did it! Oh my God I did it!* I am one with my own life.

And I am in love with Istanbul.

For two weeks I stayed in Sultanahmet, burrowing into the city's ancient heart, exploring her living past through labyrinthine cobbled streets and finishing what I started with the inner war on my marriage. Much as I loved that first night at the Pierre Loti Hotel, where my backpack and pilgrim's purpose were welcomed with open smiles and a bright orange cocktail, the following afternoon I moved to a sunnier, less expensive, fabulously blue room at the Side (pronounced see-day) Hotel, a stone's throw from my beloved *Ayasofya*, known in the West as the Hagia Sophia, the magnificent building with the circling bird, the creature who circled just for me.

I flowed through the city like an easy summer breeze, expanding my world in ever widening circles from the hotel, heart lit wide with wonder by the city that bridges two continents. *It's amazing how many Australians don't know this; just as we don't know green and black olives come from the same tree.* I came to know Sultanahmet like one immersed in the soft body of a lover whose destiny is at one with her own.

On the third day I entered *Ayasofya*, a Byzantine monument to grandeur whose tiny golden-tiled mosaics were plastered over by Muslim invaders 800 years later and which is now a monument to secularism, thanks to a visionary Turk whose accomplishments I would come to greatly respect in the coming weeks. I wandered through 1,800 years of magnificence, circling her great inner chamber on the heels of one whom I imagined to be a Jordanian prince, mesmerised by the dignity of his long black robes and the courtly grace of the woven cloth on his head, and mindful of his bodyguards. At the entrance to the great chamber, like thousands – perhaps millions – before me, I placed my foot on a dip in the stone worn by the ages. That dip is the point where, quite naturally, I and much of humanity merged to take the same step. I wondered, daughter of a new world, *in whose footsteps am I treading?*

There were many people in the stone chamber, though it wasn't crowded. And even if it was, I cannot imagine, with her great height, that Sophia could be crowded – unless, perhaps, by a coronation crowd or a certain riot and ensuing massacre. *A crowd in another age, certainly not ours. For ours are the crowds of the observers, not the witnesses; tourists peering into time rather than those belonging to their time and, lucky them, place.* I felt the emptiness of grandeur, the disconnection of the building from her purpose. I wondered if there were those in current time whose vision included reclaiming her for this or that religion, the obvious ones for whom she was created, and stolen: first the Christians, then the Muslims, and the invisible ones we cannot remember, the ones for whom the land itself was temple enough.

I filled my days exploring the bazaars, chewing hunks of pomegranate sweets in the Egyptian Spice Bazaar and disappearing into the corridors of the Grand Bazaar, looking for the backgammon board I promised myself should I ever come to Istanbul. My nonchalance confused the carpet hawkers who never, ever let a woman pass without a 'lady-lady hello lady how are you today lady'.

'*Merhaba,*' I would answer with a smile and a nod as I walked on by, rolling the exotic hello around my tongue.

I met a beautiful English poet called Grace, whose husband Richard was a dashing cut-out of the American writer in Istanbul, standing head high above the crowds in his long black jacket and Humphrey Bogart hat. Grace and Richard introduced me to mosque etiquette, the politics of scarves and shoes and timing and courage. We were joined by an old school friend of Richard's, and, as we wandered past the cemetery, Peter explained that the turbans on the headstones were shaped according to the rank of the deceased. While the men's tombs were crested with hats, he said, the women's were carved with flowers according to the number of children they'd had.

'At least here women are equal,' he said.

I turned slowly to face him.

'How, exactly, are they equal?' I asked.

Grace beat him to the punchline.

'They're dead,' she said.

Peter's wife Lamai joined us, a gorgeous Thai woman whose physique was unusually tall and strong for her people. Our merry band wandered past a shop selling hookahs and Peter was smitten by the blue glass and its magic pipes. Lamai grumbled about his smoking habit.

'I told you,' he said, 'when you lose weight and look like the woman I married, I will stop smoking.'

'But she's beautiful!' I wanted to cry. 'She is a woman! She's strong and she's healthy. How can she come to your bed if you don't think her beautiful? And besides, how is it possible for the girl you married not to grow into a woman – and why would you want it otherwise?'

And I gave thanks for my husband, who never, ever questioned or criticised the wobbles and bumps of the middle-aged woman he had chosen for his wife. More than this, he worshipped her, saw only the beauty of the flesh-and-blood woman who shared his bed. There are some things about my husband that all of mankind might take a lesson from and this is one of them.

I sat in the wide open spaces between the *Ayasofya* and the *Sultan Ahmet Camii*, known the world over as the Blue Mosque, one built to outshine the other. And I took a deep breath and immersed myself in the steam of *Cagaloglu Hamami*, the Turkish baths made famous by Indiana Jones, forking out forty euro for the privilege of having my head slapped around and my body scrubbed as if I were a wicked child. Surrounded by pink women, scrubbed clean and shiny as the marble walls around us, I closed my eyes and lay back against the warm wet stone of the steamroom, rain splashing my face through the star-shaped holes in the dome above. The voices of the women swirled around the chamber, like a great wheel spinning so fast it was impossible to focus on any one point. They rose and spilled into the cavern of the ceiling dome above us. If those voices were a picture they would be a meringue.

The baths were filled with blonde women: Americans, Germans and me. Tourist baths. Which was fine. As at the Hagia Sophia, we were all watchers. I tried to imagine the baths in their own time and place. It was easier at Sophia. At the baths it was like dancing with a beautiful woman and treading on her toes. She's tired. We keep demanding that she dance when she seeks only to sit down and read a good book. So too the palace, Topkapi Palace with its famed harem and treasury. I am Australian, daughter of a new world. Even though I knew these worlds existed, I didn't *know* they existed.

The first thing I spied in the palace, in the stillness behind dusty-dark glass walls, were Cinderella carriages. *Cinderella carriages!* I thought the pumpkin pictures in fairy tales were *illustrations* in fairy tales. It was the same sensation I experienced in Dubrovnik, among fairytale castles with pointed peaks and long pointy flags.

In the Topkapi Palace treasury I saw 'Open Sesame' treasures, replete with jewelled daggers and giant ruby pendants. I giggled to myself as the Sultan and his lissome guards sprang to life. Wandering around the empty tiled rooms I did my best to birth images of this apparently wondrous world as it was. In truth, I was a little embarrassed, because it was tired and tacky and I was surprised at the smallness of the rooms. The harem contained its own little hum, perhaps because of the raised level of interest among the watchers – which in turn lent it to an additional entry fee. I wondered what it is about an enclave of captive women in knife-edge luxury that excites us. *Phew*, I thought sardonically, *lucky that doesn't happen any more*.

Eventually my wanderings took me on the *tramvay* across the Bosphorous, the mysterious ancient waterway where Jason ambushed his golden fleece, to a great cement avenue of shops and embassies and mosques and churches and shoppers and cops driving erratically on the footpath. From the pretty round tower halfway up the hill, I looked back across the water at the old city in the night. The *Ayasofya*, the Blue Mosque, many mosques – they were surreal, as if they had just arrived from another world, hovering low to the ground unsure about whether or not to land. A turn of the kaleidoscopic lens in my mind and they were octopuses sitting squat on the Earth raising their tentacles high to the sky.

Five times a day the call to Allah rode the wind over the city, shooting arrow-straight from loudspeakers on the minarets. Sometimes the chanting was beautiful. I became witness to the ancient city's every mood, lit by the first light of dawn, backlit by sunsets pink and gold, awash with the rain and aglow in sunshine. And how I loved my blue room around the corner from the *Ayasofya*, its blue-clean walls and white ceiling trimmed blue-too, its wispy white curtains blowing in the breeze and the classical music wandering in through the window each evening from a restaurant on the street below.

Istanbul the Magnificent. I had the sense that from humanity's perspective, Istanbul is our whole. All other empires, no matter how full and rich and contained in themselves, are pieces of our puzzle. Istanbul is the picture complete, the point where we make sense of ourselves in relation to each other.

Istanbul is the mystery proclaimed.

Amid the wonder I got sick. Very sick. For three days I curled up in bed with aching joints and a sore throat, suffering excruciating bursts of pain in my anus and feeling as if my entire uterine system was about to evacuate whenever I went to the toilet. I could not sit. I had a headache. I was nauseous. I became disconnected from time and place. I tossed and turned through the nights, now hot now cold. I drank sage tea in the mornings and chamomile tea in the evenings. The sickness wiped out all I confidently thought I knew about my pilgrimage and this I welcomed, lest I fall pretty to telling new stories. I was nothing but pain, awash with pain, my whole identity pain.

In my lucid moments I read 'The Voyages of Sindbad' and was left wondering, from the end of the first chapter to the last, what it was Sindbad did with his hundred pieces of gold times seven, which I had presumed would be the point of the story. Which only goes to show, *nothing means anything.* And in the spaces between lucidity and pain my mind sought purpose from the city surrounding me, looked for meaning in Istanbul, *from* her: because I cannot walk forever.

On the third day of infirmity I woke bed-bound and exhausted, though not so sick and sore. I startled now and then with the old voices in my head rising to claim their place at the steering wheel of my life. It was so easy to see them when I was walking, on pilgrimage. And then I understood – *this was why Sindbad continually took to the high seas.*

That night, like a piece in a board game, my husband flew to Amsterdam, taking a significant geographical step towards me. He rang to let me know. We were respectful, a little awed now by the one we call 'husband' or 'wife', both of us anticipating the next move on the board: my flight from Istanbul to Amsterdam. *Dear husband,* I thought, *let us forget what we think we know about sex and money and start anew.*

I googled my symptoms and with the wisdom of mass self-diagnosis discovered I was suffering menopause. Menopause! It had never occurred to me that can't-sit-down was a primary symptom of menopause. And I was surprised to discover I was ashamed to be menopausal – that I, blessed with the genetic good fortune of perpetual youth, was on the downhill run. I haven't minded getting old, but I was terrified of looking old. Besides, menopause is an ugly word, a conjuror's meddle for pruned and rejected women.

When I was strong enough to leave the room, tender and still vulnerable, I ventured down to the bazaar for a small plate of eggplant couscous and a pomegranate juice. I sat in the sunshine and watched the street cats idle on the cushions of the hawkers. And I made an appointment with a gynaecologist at the American Hospital. As daunting as this was, the last thing I needed was a major health crisis in an exotic land. The gynaecologist was everything the Women's Liberation Movement challenged about the medical system, however he was kind enough in his professional distance. After probing around with his ultrasound, he declared my ovaries egg-free.

As I was leaving, I said matter-of-factly: 'So all this pain is a result of menopause.'

'Oh no,' he said, 'it's got nothing to do with menopause.'

I was thumped speechless. Not menopause?

'It will be one of your organs,' he said, and showed me the door.

I shook my head and laughed, figuring I'd place my bets on the collective experience of women and if my liver or bowels or kidneys were about to pack it in, then they could do so when I got home.

Menopause. Transition. Transformation. How utterly extraordinary, how uncannily symbolic, that I should undertake the journey from Rome at this time. I have walked my way through one of the most important gateways in a human life. I walked my menopause. When I returned to the hotel, the first thing I did was throw the few just-in-case sanitary napkins I'd been carrying in the bin. That part of my life was done. I had thought I would miss my bleeding. I did not. Do not. I have done my time as a fertile woman. I am free to no longer please.

Once again I took to the streets and alleyways of the city, on mission for my backgammon board. The narrow cobbled roads around the hotel were lined with tourist shops selling rugs, ceramics and food; so too the wide streets of the main thoroughfares. A man stood outside every shop, every single shop. Sometimes the men visited each other, a little gang of friendly competitors. I rolled from one verbal barrage to the next: 'Hello lady, hello lady, you want rug lady? Excuse me lady, sorry lady, let me help you spend your money lady.' *Let me help you spend your money lady?* Without hesitation I walked on by, a woman teaching herself to be unchained by the demands of men, freeing herself from a timeless and invisible contract to please, struggling nonetheless with silent accusations of rudeness in my heart. I watched as other women became entangled by the social demands of this invisible contract, the hawkers banking on their cultural confusion.

I turned away from the Arasta Bazaar and detoured into the great courtyard of the Blue Mosque, sitting against a pillar of cold stone in the sunshine, the wind whipping around me, feeling at peace with my world. The phone in my pocket started to sing. I smiled, happy enough to have a conversation with my husband. We were warm and pleasant, when ... whack! He announced that he might come to Istanbul. Strangely, the phone cut out at that moment. My heart was gashed. My day imploded. The world lost its shine.

I am not ready for my husband. He will want sex. I am not strong enough to be wanted from. Not now. Not yet. I try to make sense of my reaction. *How is it I have married a man I do not want to see?*

The floodgates of obligation let loose into my world all that is unresolved in me. And then I become annoyed with the stories men tell, my husband no different to other men I have known. My husband, who believes my need for lingering touch robs him of his masculinity. A former lover, who believed that if my nipples were erect I must be turned on – and if I am turned on then I must want sex. The lover before that, who believed that I would ejaculate like his former lover if only I would relax. And the one before that who swore to God that a woman's anus had ninety-seven nerve endings and was therefore primed for pleasure. All my lovers have been good men. And all of them have told themselves stories about women's bodies, stories that have nothing at all to do with the woman beside them and everything to do with what they want; stories I can only presume they learned not from women, but from other men.

I wandered up to the Grand Bazaar, a stained-glass and stone warren of archways and alleyways, booth after booth filled with the same stuff; like every tourist market on Earth, some of it was lovely, most of it not. I dipped my head into the booths selling backgammon boards; occasionally, if there was breathing space, I asked the price. Eventually I wandered into a treasure trove with no-one home.

I took advantage of the emptiness to have a hassle-free look at the boards, brushing my hands over the beautiful wooden boxes and boards inlaid with mother-of-pearl mosaic. The owner of the booth rocked up, balancing steaming cups of sweet apple tea on a silver tray. He offered me one. He spoke good English. He began to tell me about the boards, about the artful beauty of the mosaic designs I had admired. He showed me a walnut board, a simple board, praising its craftsmanship. Yes indeed, the board was beautiful, but it had a flaw. The hawker argued with me, commanding and patronising, telling me I imagined the fault before my eyes. Impatient and exhausted already by the demanding process required from me for the simple purchase of a backgammon board, I snapped at the hawker.

'You Turkish men have a lot to learn about Western women,' I said.

His surprised face jerked up at me.

'Like what?' he asked, genuinely interested.

'Don't argue with us,' I said sternly, 'and quit doing the "lady-lady" thing.'

'You don't like being called lady?'

No, I thought, *we don't*. But I wasn't up to a conversation about the politics of language, class and gender.

'I don't mind you calling me lady,' I said, 'but in my country talking to me in this way would be considered rude. It is okay here because you are using our language differently.

'The problem,' I said, 'is harassing us. Give us space! Give us room! You Turkish men are high pressure. You just want want, want, from us. You do not see me as a woman, as a person. Give me room to breathe!'

To my extraordinary surprise and delight, the hawker was grateful. Ironically, in turn I was thankful for his belligerent commands and would have liked to inform him he was excellent training for coping with the demands of a husband.

'Let us start again,' he said.

I smiled and pointed out the flaw in the board.

'I see,' he said.

We laughed.

'See?' he asked. 'I am learning.'

We bargained good-naturedly over the walnut board and even though I paid half what he originally asked, I was aware I had probably paid too much. I wandered past the tourist shops to my favourite restaurant, where I dined on pomegranate pasta by an open fire. A song that had long caused my heart to melt played gently in the speakers above ... *tell me have you ever really, really really ever loved a woman* ... Have I ever really loved a man? Yes, a long time ago. It occurred to me that it doesn't matter whom we love, it matters only that we do.

Into my nostalgia popped an old photograph of my sister and me, side by side as we faced the camera, smiling and sweet in our matching mohair jumpers with their fluffy berets my mother had knitted for her little daughters, pink for me and apricot for my sister. I wondered, with a jolt, if my mother knew of the love I held for such memories. And the quick answer was, *No, she does not,* for this was not our meeting place.

My mother's soft and fragile heart. She is terrified, or so it seems to me, of her eldest daughter's penchant for peering through the looking glass of time at the wounds of the female ancestral line, so she might heal the present and release herself from the bondage of rebellion and resistance; her angry daughter, too much to bear ... or perhaps the daughter is terrified of her mother's soft and fragile heart.

On the way home in the chill dark, past the street peddlers laying out their scarves on the dirty pavement, I caught the smiling eyes of a fortune teller. He was a young man with black curly hair and two white rabbits snuffling on the tray of a small black booth in front of him. 'Let the rabbit tell your fortune,' he called. We looked at each other and laughed. I couldn't resist. The fortune teller asked my name. He waved a sheet of folded papers past the rabbit's nose. 'Come on bunny,' he said, 'tell Stephanie's fortune.' Bunny eventually obliged and nibbled off a snap of paper.

The fortune teller opened it and read: *The world is like a mirror. If you smile, it smiles back at you. If you frown, it frowns back. Frowning is your big mistake.* The law of reflection from the mouth of a rabbit. The fortune teller bowed low and, as I turned to leave, I saw my backgammon board behind him in a shop window for four times the asking price of the hawker in the bazaar. I smiled, a little more content with my beautiful board.

Back at the hotel I checked up on Ben's blog and was gladdened to find a message from one of the good fathers we'd met in Međugorje, Father Ruairi. Around 600 people a week from all over the world were following our journey, their identities unknown to us, a cyber mystery. With the exception of my daughter and one of my friends, none of our co-journeyers in the blogosphere were friends or family. And just one declared his identity, Nicu of Romania, who had been with Ben all the way. How Nicu found him in the first place, we do not know. Yet Nicu's quiet, steady support was warming, and in the absence of interest from those who know and love us he was not unlike having God watch over us. Nicu believed in the journey's higher purpose and we loved him for this. Who the other watchers were, we had no idea, and I often wondered if such relationships were voyeuristic, which only begged the question: *who is the voyeur, us or them?*

Father Ruairi had me laughing out loud:

Dear Ben,

Greetings from one of the Irish priests you met in Međugorje. I have been following your progress since. When I read your last blog account and heard of all the rain you encountered, I thought to myself – the fool! He's taken a wrong turn and ended up in Ireland. Then when you met all the drunks in the bar who couldn't speak English I thought you must definitely be in Ireland. But finally I knew you couldn't be here when you wrote that the owner kicked the children out of the bar. We'd never do that here. How are the children meant to learn? ☺ I hope your progress continues well and that the winter doesn't do to you what it did to Hannibal and Napoleon before you. I still haven't forgiven you for not starting your walk in Ireland, by the way. So Godspeed, keep safe and know that you and your good lady mother are in my prayers.

Fr Ruairi

Ben rolled into Istanbul on the train ten days later. He'd spent three days of misery in the mountains of Macedonia, phoning me to say the agony was fun when it was shared, but was just plain vanilla misery alone. The wind and driving rain had blown him onto a bus bound for Kosovo, where, curious enough about the forthcoming elections to check out the vexed politics of independence versus autonomy for himself, he was greeted as a minor celebrity. No, he wasn't NATO. No, he wasn't a journalist. The Kosovans took some convincing that he had no motive; he simply wanted to visit them.

Ben was hungry for Syria, where he planned to spend the winter studying Arabic. He would resume his journey in the spring, taking up where he left off in Macedonia. I was hungry for Turkey. His money was running low and the cost of living in Istanbul, even though cheaper than Europe, was seriously first world. I offered to hire us a car so we could drive to the Syrian border. Ben loves to drive. It was an offer too good to refuse. And so began what we billed as the Whirlwind Iconic Turkey Tour.

On the following Saturday morning we checked out of the hotel and for the first time since arriving in Rome in September, not counting the taxi from the airport in Istanbul, we travelled by car. It freaked me out. Eighty kilometres an hour were seventy-seven too many. As we beetled down the highway towards Gallipoli, an imperative for any self-respecting Australian in Turkey, my neck was swivelling like a weathervane in the wind, unable to make sense of a world without connection. I felt *extremely* unsafe. I would see a tree up ahead and whoosh-whip-h it was gone. When I was walking I'd have seen that same tree and walked towards it for an hour, until I met it, perhaps rested awhile in its shade, and then I would have walked on, filled and enriched and connected to the world around me. I didn't know it at the time, but when I was walking I built relationships with *everything*. In the car there was no such time. No such connection. I could have wept. Something important was lost.

We raced the rain to Gallipoli, which took us quite some time to find on the map because the Turks call it *Gelibolu*, and pulled into the small, busy and not so well-to-do town late in the afternoon. Ben sat in the car with the engine running while I raced into hotels with iconic ANZAC names, like Anzac. No-one spoke English. Nor did they understand the word 'Anzac'. I suggested we try the internet. We realised neither of us had paid attention at school or on Anzac Day, because we didn't know what we were looking for. We googled. We found Anzac Cove – that's it! We googled again. It was on the other side of the peninsula. With luck we'd make it by sundown. We found the road and shot out of town, racing the dying light to the opposite shore, arriving on the beach just as the red sun dropped mercurially onto the horizon. We stood on the shore. We were alone. Two Aussies and an iconic memorial to death and courage and the ghosts of tens of thousands of young men from all over the world who died in ten thousand moments on these sands.

> *They shall not grow old, as we that are left grow old*
> *Age shall not weary them, nor the years condemn*
> *At the going down of the sun and in the morning*
> *We will remember them.*

I had recited this poem at school assembly one Anzac morning forty years ago. Australian children have been reciting it for nearly a century, adults too at dawn services held all over the country every April 25. And I recited it now on the shores of *Gelibolu*.

Ben and I could not believe our luck that we had Gallipoli to ourselves. We ran up the road in the dying light and wept before a memorial whose words split our hearts:

> *Those heroes that shed their blood and lost their lives …*
> *You are now living in the soil of a friendly country.*
> *Therefore rest in peace.*
> *There is no difference between the Johnnies*
> *And the Mehmets to us where they lie side by side*
> *Here in this country of ours …*
> *You, the mothers,*
> *Who sent their sons from faraway countries*
> *Wipe away your tears;*
> *Your sons are now lying in our bosom*
> *And are in peace.*
> *After having lost their lives on this land they have*
> *Become our sons as well.*

At that moment I fell in love with Mustafa Kemal Ataturk, a soldier who dedicated these words on a lonesome peninsula as a shrine to his 'enemy' and who, in the days and years to come, birthed a secular nation called Turkey from the ashes of the Ottoman empire. I'm sure he had his faults, but in the six weeks I spent in Turkey I came to appreciate the purpose of the man they called Ataturk, father of the nation, a visionary who banned headscarves in schools and plucked *Ayasofya* from the religious zealots of all persuasions and elevated her to the status of one who belongs to everyone.

As darkness fell on the sandy peninsula we spotted a small sign to Lone Pine. As with fairytale castles and Cinderella carriages, a-moment-ago words were transformed into the here-now of three-dimensional reality. Lone Pine? We knew it was important but we had no idea why. We followed a dirt track up a steep and sandy hill that was a rainstorm away from being four-wheel-drive country. At the top we found a cemetery. The graves. One memorial to the Aussies and another to the New Zealanders. And a lone pine. Scraggly and old and, unlike the pines in my own country, round and bent. A lollipop pine, right in the middle of the cemetery. We stood on top of the hill in the descending darkness, looking over the barely visible valley to the east. We paid our respects – and hightailed it out of there, hungry and hankering for the first decent bed we could find. The car might be too fast and disconnected, but its assistance was a pleasure when it came to finding beds in the cold.

We found that bed in Eceabat on what we in the West call the Dardanelles, a strait that connects the Sea of Marmara to the Aegean Sea and which, thanks to the 'elles', I had always presumed was in France. The Turks call it *Canakkale Bogazi*. A Turkish tour guide with a passion for the Anzac story was smitten when he realised we were Australian. He told us about a big red memorial on a hill that we must watch for, near where we would catch the ferry to the city of Canakkale. He translated the memorial's words for us, scrawling them across our tourist map:

> DUR YOLCU!
> *Traveller halt!*
> *The soil you heedlessly tread!*
> *Once witnessed the end of an era.*

We woke to a Sunday morning filled with the noises of Eceabat, an engine revving and a rooster crowing, and hit the road eyes peeled for the memorial. We didn't find it, but we did discover a magnificent castle, seven centuries old. It turned out to be a fortress, Kilitbahir, key of the sea, built by Sultan Mehmet II to defend Constantinople from the Venetians. We ran around the battlements into a black-dark stairwell, where Ben almost went the way of the Venetians by not looking where he was going just as the stairwell opened out into a high black hole. And from the beautiful curved battlement wall I found the Anzac guide's memorial, painted large on a nearby hillside for all the world to see. *DUR YOLCU!* Traveller halt! A white-painted soldier. A burning torch. A poetic command to *remember this*.

We caught the ferry across the strait to Canakkele and decided to take the coast road to Izmir, where Ben had lined up a couch-surfer for the night. On the way I saw a sign that startled the blood in my veins: *Troia*.

'Ben!' I yelled, 'it's Troy!'

The Whirlwind Iconic Turkey Tour took a sudden turn onto a long dirt road that led to Troy, of all places. We photographed each other inside a tall wooden horse and ran around the white stone pathways of an iconic archaeological dig. Once again, we had the place to ourselves. We sat on benches and marvelled at the old mud bricks; we watched a new generation of cats smuggle mice over grassy mounds; and we stood on a small rise where the Trojans might have stood, looking out over flat yellow farmland to the sea, marvelling that they pulled a wooden horse laden with soldiers so far. Of course, back then the city probably ran down to the sea. Daughter of a new world, it was impossible for me to imagine an ancient settlement so crowded. I decided to call Turkey by the old name, *Anatolia*, because this made much more sense to me. Not that I knew any more about *Anatolia* than I did about Turkey, but *Anatolia* rang in my bones like the hum of a tuning fork.

In Izmir we met Erdam, the couch-surfer who welcomed us into his lounge room and whose newly made bed I mistook for my own – probably because, unbeknownst to me until morning, he slept on a foldout in the lounge room of his tiny flat. Lucky for me, he didn't have the heart to kick me out when he and Ben returned from nightclubbing in the early hours of the morning. Erdam told us two things that stuck like paintball to our minds: Izmir had a huge Kurdish population (*fancy that, we were surrounded by Kurds*) and headscarves were banned in Turkish schools (praise Ataturk).

In the night I dreamed of walking through an apartment building, peering into the open doorways. In each room was a woman sitting on a chair, her neck taut and exposed, a man with a knife at her throat. There was no emotion, just the tension of an abstract reality accepted by everyone: *I am murderer and murdered, both*.

At the crack of dawn we left Erdam to his hangover, his third in three days, and beelined down the highway to the ruins of Ephesus, an ancient Greek city that boasts the augured Temple of Artemis, one of the seven wonders of the ancient world. We followed the signs to Selcuk and from there to Ephesus, which the Turks call *Efes*, where yet again we had an iconic sacred site to ourselves. We wandered through an avenue of old trees, the grass belittered with white stone pieces of stuff, columns and bits of columns, walls and bits of walls. We found the amphitheatre and scampered up and down its old stone steps, until Ben took the high ground and filmed me being dramatic on the stage. We explored tunnels and streets lined with archways and temple doorways and tombs; we wandered through what was left of an old city 600 years abandoned, looking for a temple to a huntress that was supposedly still intact. We found the library and marvelled at its likeness to our own imaginings of Ancient Greece. We photographed each other on pedestals and clambered over sun-striped geometry; we bowed in wonder at the names carved in stone. But, as far as we know, we did not find Artemis's temple.

Heading back to Selcuk we saw a sign we couldn't resist: it said '*Meryem Ana Evi*', the Virgin Mary's House. We laughed so hard we could barely keep to the narrow road. Imagine that, the Virgin Mary's house. The entry fee was twenty-two Turkish lira – which was close to fifty Aussie dollars for both of us, and they wanted an extra dollop of cash for the car. Knowing the Virgin Mary still had a house here on Earth was enough; we figured we'd give it a miss. We headed back to Selcuk for lunch, where we moved a table from the restaurant into the sunshine on the other side of the road to play backgammon while we waited for our pasta. The waiter was delighted that I could play well enough to beat a man. Three times, no less.

Before we headed inland to the famed hot springs of Pamukkale on the road to Konya, home of the celebrated mystic poet Jalal ad-Din al-Rumi, known in the West simply as Rumi, we stuck our heads inside the 800-year-old Isabey Mosque, which was undergoing a second round of renovation since its partial collapse during the earthquake that rocked the middle of the 17th century. Isabey, apparently, according to the onyx hawker across the road, means Jesus.

We turned our backs on the coast and beelined due east to Denizli, through a landscape of distant mountains, plains and sawn-off hillsides, passing trucks piled high with hay and concrete settlements red and grey, a dusty haze bleaching colour from the land. We circled Denizli twice before finding the road to Pamukkale, where we pulled up at the foot of a white limestone hill late in the afternoon. We pulled on our jackets against the chill of the dying light and started to walk up the wide white track. Within metres a man in a kiosk wanted money. Five Turkish lira. Ben flatly refused. I didn't blame him. It was late, it was too cold to swim and even if we wanted to swim we had to pay extra and we were tired of the Turks wanting money for every overturned rock. Which is seriously not true, except for this particular day. We agreed I'd fork out the money, just because we were there, and Ben would drive up and meet me at the top.

The white track wound around the edge of a watery white world, surreal and slippery. The hill looked like a snow field at the end of a busy day, dirty tracks carved into the hillside and mud seeping through the snow-melt. At the top a hundred tourists stood barefoot in small grooved channels, humanity's attempt to make sense of a white world shaped by earthquakes, hot springs and an abundance of calcium. I shrugged and walked on, happy enough that I had value for my five Turkish lira and confident Ben hadn't missed much.

I clambered onto the path at the top of the hill, where my lower jaw bounced on the meandering stone pathway. Atop the white hill were the rambling ruins of an ancient city *alive* to its own memory. I wandered along the path, salted cliffs to my left tumbling white to the dusty valley floor, hemmed by a ruffle of snow-tipped mountains. To my right were the ruins of who-knows-what city or civilisation meandering into small green hills reminiscent of the spotted hills of Croatia. This was the sight-so-far of the Whirlwind Iconic Turkey Tour. I rang Ben.

'You have to see this place,' I said. 'It is much, much more than you could imagine.'

The pseudo-snowy world flattened out and there before me, in the middle of a chalky terrace, was a beautifully set stone shelter, small and safe from the shifting sands of its quaky world. In one mind it might have been a small barn in an Arctic field, in another a miniature Japanese temple in a midwinter garden. In the world I was in it made no sense at all. Except that its beauty ripped through me along with the last of the afternoon light.

I turned from the white world and ran through the ruins of the stone one, through avenues and archways, eager to soak up this fantastical ancient world before nightfall took it from me. I stopped still on the white cliff edge to watch the sun slide behind the snow-capped mountain cradling the valley. The sunshine backlit the smog, so that the world of factories and farms below, and the otherworld where I stood above, were, for a moment, blasted with a sheen that crystalised all of time into a living, panoramic whole.

I turned from the dying light and ran through the square-cut boulders, either piled high on top of each other or burrowed deep into the grassy earth, the high points struck pink and the low grown dark with shadows. Darkness was falling too quickly. Ben and I played phone tag, our need to find each other in direct competition with our immersion in this undreamed world. The moment we met, from the corner of my eye, I spied a tall column standing alone on the city's distant edge. It beckoned me. But Ben wanted to see the red rocks in the amphitheatre. There wasn't time for both.

I bow to the authority of the masculine, distressed and wondering how it came to be this way – me, of all people. I am tired of arguing with 'him', the collective him, tired so very tired of his disapproval and the urgency of his need to tell me what to do. We walk towards the red rocks. The column calls me. Red rocks. Column. I tell Ben I have to go, I will meet him at the gate. Ignoring the pathways, for there is no time for polity, I step over the ruins in the cold green grass and walk quickly towards the column. As it draws near I slow down; I begin to sing:

> *This is holy ground*
> *I'm standing on holy ground*
> *And she is here*
> *And where she is is holy.*

At the foot of the crumbling stone steps leading up to the column I begin to cry. I climb the stairs and stand beside the column, looking out over the vast valley into the faint red ring of dusk now circling the mountains.

I recite:

> *At the going down of the sun*
> *And in the morning*
> *We will*
> *Remember her.*

I kiss the cold grey-white stone of the column; I feel the peace. I celebrate in my heart what was, the women of the temple who might have stood as I stand now, looking out over a bustling city and a snow-white mountain, and I release myself into the present. A current of peace circles time, enthusiasm for life floods my spirit. I had thought that I must release myself from the old ways of the past in order to be free in current time and place, free to conform. Standing on the steps of an ancient tide I understand that I need not turn my back on one to live happily in the other, that I can simply allow the old ways to inform the modern woman. The moment is exhilarating.

That night, Ben and I were the last to leave the ruins of what we now know to be Hieropolis, cold and alive to the wonder of life on Earth. We decided we'd earned a good night's rest in a hotel with hot springs and drove into nearby Kirmizi Su, famed for its red waters and, to us, for its bizarre central fountain – a misshapen glob of red salt in the middle of a muddy street, with an iron rooster perched on the top.

Floating in the red water baths at the hotel, I released from my body the violence that had collected there for what seemed like millennia – myriad lifetimes or generational inheritance, stories either way, whatever your preference for telling them. As I lay alone in the dark that night, bones warmed by the red waters, I thought about declarations of love, as when a man and a woman declare 'love', each for the other. This feeling they've named 'love', I thought, is like a child at the beach filling a bucket with water and declaring to those around her, 'Look, I have the sea.' She has a bucket of water. She is experiencing a bucket of water. She has not the sea.

I realised, *I do not know love.*

The following day, the fourth of the Whirlwind Iconic Turkey Tour, we took the back road to Konya, through grassy golden plains that might have been endless if not for the snow-capped mountains in the distance. A pale blue sky prettied up the day; steel giants carrying power lines marched side by side with the railway line across the plain. Buildings were in various states of returning to the earth. Rocks looked like ruins, mosques lost their spires and no longer did we hear the call to prayer.

'Maybe the locals around here don't believe in harassing people with prayers,' said Ben.

'Is that the only reason for a minaret?' I asked.

'What else is it for?' he said.

'Maybe to remind everyone of the god above – or maybe they think it's rude to point.'

We laughed. And we drove in silence. We turned away from the pretty blue sky and headed for mountains shrouded in the grey of distant snowfall, winding our way through a small mountain pass where red dirt hills opened onto a fenceless plain with barely a tree. It was easy to picture the nomads who might once have wandered through such unbounded space. And the herds that roamed before them.

We spent an hour or so driving around the edge of a crystalline lake filled with islands of floating birds, the nesting mountains now a translucent pale blue. We passed an eagle perched high on a branch in a small grove of trees; the only other vehicles on the road were a tractor and, an hour later, a horse and cart.

We stopped high on the red rock cliffs above Konya, the city blanketed below; we saw a tower piercing the cloud cover below us, then two towers, then three. And then we realised the cloud cover was smog. Konya was, to quote Ben, a 'basin of filth'. We drove down the red rock face into the city, the bleak landscape giving way to the delight of original architecture and trees carved into Sufi swirls, their foliage shaped like the proverbial whirling dervish.

Konya was everything I thought Turkey would be – and nothing at all like I imagined for Konya. For the first time since leaving Istanbul we were outside the concrete bunker monoculture of urban design that is Turkey's southern coastline.

We stayed with Konya's couch-surfing king, Yhsan, a young man with an eye on his future who lived alone with his mother in the sweet ground-floor unit they had shared since his father died, fifteen years before. On hearing that this night's couch-surfer was travelling with his mother, Yhsan's mother had bought new linen for her bed, a welcome gesture for the strangers. Yhsan's generosity flowed in equal measure to his overbearing nature, increasing the intensity of the headache that pounded my temples, a tension amped up by the email I'd received from my husband who clearly thought I was in Syria. *Why does it bother me so much that my husband does not listen to me?*

Yhsan took us to the city's new auditorium to see the famous Whirling Dervishes, a Sufi order founded by the poet Rumi and a vibrant expression of Islam's mystical heart. He introduced us to his girlfriend, the first Kurd I had ever met, a sassy-mouthed beauty who chewed gum, spoke no English and worked for the local television station. Yhsan confessed, after the event, that he'd never seen the dervishes before. We laughed: *like living in Sydney and never visiting the Opera House*. We had no time to immerse ourselves in the treasure chest of the most famous Sufi of all, the great Mevlana, the poet Rumi. I vowed to return on the train after Syria.

At daybreak, Ben and I were on the road to Cappadocia, the final leg of the Whirlwind Iconic Turkey Tour. The car raced through the wide, flat landscape. I wished I was walking the endless plain. *They must have seen the invaders coming forever.* The dark and cloudy sky was as vast as the landscape we traversed. It was impossible to tell clouds from mountains. This was a commonwealth of dust and I longed to let the big wind outside the car blow right through my condensed heart.

The highway out of Konya was busy with trucks, modern-day traders riding the plains. We had our eyes peeled for signs to Catalhoyuk, thought to be, at 10,000 years, the oldest city in the world. It had taken some talking to convince Ben it was worth the stop. Today he was a man whose single track mind led to Syria, preferably yesterday.

Neither of us had any idea what to expect from Catalhoyuk, although a bigger road sign might have headlined the list. We swerved off the highway onto a web of dusty roads etched into the endless plain. We drove and we drove, racing the wind alongside cement aquaducts channelling water to the turnip fields, past rickety wooden carts piled high with turnips clodded with fresh earth. The labyrinthine roads led through an entire township built from dirt. Silver satellite dishes gave clues to which century it inhabited. A dog crouched low on the edge of a field of white grass that looked like a crop of soft fluffy wool. Without us noticing, the season had turned from autumn to winter; the only life left in the bleached grasses were the seeds waiting to be scattered by the bitter wind.

Beyond the shelter of the car, the lonely plains tested me. I laughed at the bullet I would once have imagined hurtling through space to get me, hatred destined just for me. There was now space where the survival stories once broiled. The murderer within was leaving. I grinned at the plains. I felt safe. I could see clearly. I was free, for the first time in my life, of the wasted energy of dreadful imaginings. The world outside the window was one waiting for snow. My husband rang. He wanted to know if I'd received his email, the one where he thought I was in Syria. 'No,' I lied, tired of being the only person on Earth who tells the truth as best she knows it, and pissed off that the only thing he had to tell me was he hadn't received the mail that was supposed to have been forwarded to him from our postal address. As if there was anything I could do about that from an endless plain in the middle of *Anatolia*.

The signs to Catalhoyuk grew smaller and smaller still, the further we drifted from civilisation as we knew it. Eventually the road petered out to a bumpy trail that stopped abruptly near a house. A big sign told us only accredited tours were welcome. No bus, no visit. We ignored it, struggling with our jackets against a cold so harsh our lips turned blue in the wind. We ran up a dirt road into the empty plain. We had no idea where we were. A man shouted at us from the house. We were too cold to argue. We ran towards him and he pointed away from the house in another direction, content to let the crazy foreigners loose on the plain.

We ran over a rise, blown low by the wind, our scarves flailing and our noses running. There in a field was a huge steel barn and, inside the barn, a small excavation site, dusty and neat. Once again, we had an iconic sacred site to ourselves and we laughed from behind a small rope as we frisked the bricks for signs of life and told stories through the masks of our ignorance. We marvelled at the archeologists, the ones who can tell civilisation from dust, and we wondered about the ancients, the ones who settled for life on a cold and windy golden plain.

There was one stop left on the Whirlwind Iconic Turkey Tour before we traded the car for the train to Damascus – *imagine that! the train to Damascus!* – and that was Cappadocia. As with everything else on the tour, with the exception of Gallipoli, we had never previously heard of Cappadocia and we had no idea what to expect; we knew only that it was a must-see on the traveller's grapevine. We raced across the cold and windy golden plain, sudden bursts of wind buffeting the car, looking for Cappadocia, which wasn't on the map and elicited only strange shrugs from the locals we asked along the way. Eventually we realised that whatever Cappadocia was, it was not a town. And then, without warning, we beheld one of the strangest sights on this good Earth, a world so unimaginably bizarre that even Ben, my travelling son who has visited more than fifty countries in the past decade, was eyes-wide stumped by the spectacle before him.

Cappadocia, 'land of beautiful horses', was a cityscape of tall rocks rising up from the land, some red, some white – fairytale spirals forged by the millennial activity of volcanoes and erosion. That's the geographical story. It is the human relationship with the landscape that had us dizzy with wonder. The skyscraper rocks had been burrowed out from the inside, creating entire communities of mushroom homes with windows and doors and stairways, and little hats that seemed to greet the day. We scampered through the dust, careful not to slide into oblivion through a sudden doorway. We drove through a settlement of hotels and caves and houses all carved from rocks, *a modern town living in rocks*. As evening shadows slid down the white sandcastles of the plain, we looked at each other and grinned.

'This is the most fantastical place I've ever seen,' announced Ben.

'Best trip of my life,' I answered.

We spent the night in Nigde, planning to rise with the sun for the two-hour drive to Adana, where we'd drop off the car and catch the train. Ben was skip-in-his-step excited about Syria-tomorrow. We woke to a rainy day, the mountains around us grey and white, the sky frowning above. Over breakfast we watched the news on a television mounted high on the wall, images of excited young men going to war, raising their rifles and shouting *Allah!* And for the first time in my life I understood the *idiocy* of 'fighting for God'. I turned to Ben:

'Imagine fighting for God?' I said

'Shhhh,' he hissed.

My heart hissed in turn with unspoken thoughts, like a pin-point pressure valve releasing steam: *fighting for God places us firmly outside of conversation; for whomever is fighting for God is not available for anything else: not ideas, not connection, not love. More than this, fighting for God is to presume to know what God wants you – very special no-one-else-but-you – to do.*

'By all means fight for the imposition of your culture or values,' I whispered across the table, 'but please don't tell me you're fighting for God.'

Within the hour we were on the road. The golden plain was now black and stony. The day was low to the ground. The hills along the roadside were dusted with snow and old cabbages lolled in the fields. A big wind shook the car; black rain in the distance linked earth and sky. Half an hour later we were crawling through snowdrift, small flecks of white floating around the car. I am a daughter of the driest continent on Earth; snow is a minor miracle to me. Fifteen minutes later we were wedged stock still between trucks and vans on a winding mountain pass. And so began one of the most beautiful days of my life. My first blizzard.

The traffic piled up. The snow blew sideways. We stripped the gloves from our frozen fingers to put snow chains on the wheels. The traffic crawled. Three hours and thirty kilometres later we stopped for lunch, a fireside feast of lentil soup, salad, *pide* warm from the oven and roasted vegetables. We rolled out the backgammon board and laughed at the uncanny ability we share to call the dice. *What does this tell us about how we live?* We hit the road again and within five minutes four lanes of traffic were at a standstill, the world around us a mystical white, a colourless land of light and shadow. We sat in the car, sandwiched between dozens of trucks, occasionally moving a few metres down the road before rolling to a steady halt. The heater howled and dried our skin. The landscape slowly changed: a river, a bridge, a small town, trees, a stack of firewood. All frozen white.

Now and then I'd take a hike through the slush and diesel fumes, sharing biscuits and smiles with good-natured men with better things to do. Including my son. While I marvelled at the day, Ben slowly stewed. Those twelve hours ought to have put him in Syria, but instead they dumped him stock-still in a snowstorm.

'You could do worse than be trapped in a Christmas card,' I laughed.

And then I remembered – there's nothing worse than your mother trying to cheer you up.

I thought about my reaction to the hitchhiker Ben had plucked from the rain just out of Nigde, earlier in the day. 'It's my fucking car,' I had hissed at his presumptuousness, as the dark stranger hopped into the back seat. I'd long had a no-hitchhiker policy, one born from the security of never having to decide who was 'safe' and who was not. My son had just tipped my unchallenged world on its head. I had peered around at the stranger and relaxed when I saw he was old, very, very old. Five kilometres down the road we set him down. As we said goodbye I looked into his face and was startled to find he was about thirty. *Stories. I had seen what I needed to see.*

Night fell on the blizzard-bound, bringing to the world around us a relentless beauty. The minaret of a small mosque rose streetlamp yellow from the dark-light world, illuminating the falling snowflakes. Car tracks in snowy nearby streets marked the travellers' journeys home. In the past four hours we had travelled ten kilometres. A man in a silver car wound down his window and yelled, 'Follow me! Go!' Ben was in no mood for hesitation and a little local knowledge was about to take us a long way, relatively speaking. Ben threw the car into gear and we followed the guiding angel down the road, gliding through the slush between the trucks and weaving along the outside edge of the road, until he pulled over into a service station. We followed him in, figuring we may as well fill up too, and there I looked into the face of my Enlightened self, a man who reflected *the wonder of me*.

While my heart embraced his easy smile and humble manner, he and Ben introduced themselves and discussed our blizzard options. He was an officer from the nearby air force base; he was confident in his knowing and I watched the flame in his heart flicker and burn on his face.

The officer turned off the main road while we edged our way back into the immobile traffic, inch by inch. Enlivened by his example, Ben, eyes on the rearview mirror, was enthralled by an official cavalcade of sleek black vehicles crawling towards us along the snowy verge. As they passed us by, he threw the car into gear and pulled in behind them. Whoever they were and wherever they were going, we were going too. As we cleared the front of the halted traffic, the cavalcade moved onto the other side of the road, the 'wrong' side. Police officers tried to stop the parade, with no luck. With us hot on their heels, the cavalcade picked up speed and suddenly there was mayhem – not only were they on the wrong side of the highway, the road was now a freeway with a huge concrete barrier down the middle. If cars came towards us … well, we've all seen enough television to imagine the outcome.

Ben cut back to the 'right' side of the road, where the good officers of the law stopped us at the front of the idling, long distance traffic jam. And there we sat, staring into a tunnel of night empty freeway, surrounded by whiteness and the beauty of a moonlit forest. Inquisitively, we watched the unfolding battle between security services, as the cavalcade got the better of the situation and raced away. I looked through the window at the car beside me to find a family staring straight back at me – a teenaged boy gazing awestruck into my soul, a halo of wondrous light around his face as if he were staring at the Great Goddess herself; his mother in the front seat excited and curious. The father unwound his window.

'Turkey good?' he shouted.

I smiled and laughed. 'Turkey wonderful,' I called back, thumbs up. 'Turkey best!'

The train to Damascus took us through the Taurus Mountains, or *Toros Daglari*. We rattled our way through the winter landscape, past cement bunker homes with birdcage verandahs set amongst rubble and mud and puddles, through a landscape spotted with winter-ready fields, soggy soccer pitches and plastic greenhouses. Turkish men hung out the train windows, blowing smoke into the morning. I stared at the star and sickle moon transfers on the train windows, amazed that I was: a) in a Muslim country, and b) loving every minute of it. I sat back in my seat, soaking up the atmosphere in my body leftover from last night's dream.

I dreamed of Karol, a man I know, former Yugoslav, now Slovenian, 25 years Australian, a man with whom I have never had a relationship but who represents for me something whole and strong about the masculine, and the divinity of love between two human beings. In my dream we were together, not being tested but tested nonetheless. And he walked away from me. He turned his back in sadness and walked away. And I too was sad, although accepting. He preferred to walk away rather than burn in our fire. For he could not open his heart. And there was an angel, almost a woman, who visited me in recognition that he had walked away. I was fine until she wrapped her arms around me, pulling me close to her chest, holding me with such love that I wept with dismay and confusion and sadness that he would not continue with our journey. The sadness I experienced as she held me was beautiful; full and true.

I looked out the window at wide open fields and potted settlements of poverty, at misty mountains and petrol stations with names like O-pet, A-pet, B-pet, Star-pet, Sun-pet, Moil, Soil, as if every town had its own oil company. A white bird flew with the train. An old woman with a stick walked at right angles to the ground. The aura of the dream filled me, first with the wonder that another human being could evoke such feelings, then with surprise that I had forgotten what it was to feel such 'love', and then with sadness that my husband and I had never experienced such a connection.

Turkish gardeners smiled up through the train windows, grinning white teeth on brown skin. I waved. I liked the Turks, by which I mean

I liked Turkish men. Men in restaurants, men behind counters, men on streets. Women were 'around', but it was the men who engaged.

The fields got bigger and tall skinny trees clung to yellowed leaves; the houses were now a two-tone geometry of paintwork, some shades of the same colour, blue on blue or green on green, others a riot of purple and yellow or red and green. As Ben slept on the seat opposite I bathed in the dream. My thoughts wandered to my husband and I decided to experiment with lying, given that my husband lied all the time; for it was my ill-conceived belief that if he were braver he would be more truthful; everything would not be 'oh fine' and other smokescreens that keep him from the unnamed and unexpressed truths of his life. I would free myself to not-speak the truth as best I knew it. No justification. No explanation. I would 'just be', exactly as he claims to want it.

The train pulled into Fevzipasa and we threw our bags onto the tiny station platform to change trains for Syria. Despite all our attempts in the past twenty-four hours to understand how to get to Syria, and despite Ben's brilliance at pidgin languages, we had no idea what to do when we left the train at Fevzipasa. We asked a group of Turkish men standing around and I was reminded of the old joke about how many feminists it takes to change a lightbulb. There on the platform at Fevzipasa a thousand all-at-once answers about the train to Syria blew at us like a helpful wind, before the bedraggled collective threw us into a mini bus and ordered the driver to take us to another station, Islahiye. As we left, I saw a young man greet an older man, bowing to kiss his hand, bringing the hand to his forehead and then kiss-kissing each side of the old man's face. The first time I had seen this I thought the young man had tripped. I marvelled at such public displays of respect.

We learned from the mini bus driver the train was due to leave at 9 am. It was now 10.30 am. We laughed when we saw the train was still at the station in Islahiye and laughed harder when we realised it was a goods train ten miles long – with one small passenger carriage 300 metres up the line. We scrambled along the rocky tracks and clambered aboard without the assistance of a platform, finding our seats among a handful of Syrians sitting on a huge pile of cheap new blankets. The carriage was filthy. And cold. So cold we blew mist with every breath. And there was no food. We looked at each other and laughed. We had just paid the equivalent of ten dollars to travel a thousand kilometres. What were we expecting?

The train pulled out of the station and we crossed more plains, now green and filled with cropped vineyards planing red and yellow to the mountains, near and far. The sky hung low, the Syrians smoked, raindrops snaked through the dust on the windows. I unpacked my sleeping bag and snuggled down for the long, long ride to Damascus. Twenty minutes later the train stopped. The Syrians got out. Ben and I looked at each other. We sat and we sat. We figured it must be a passport check. We pulled our gear together and jumped off the train. One of the soldiers inside the station spoke a little English. It took about twenty minutes for us to understand that the train was not going to Damascus. No train was going to Damascus. No bus either. Not just today; not any day. I sat down and let Ben deal with it. An hour later the soldier returned with an offer. His friend from the muddy town behind us would drive us to Aleppo and in Aleppo we would find a train to Damascus.

Ben and the soldier haggled over a price. We threw our packs onto the tray of a small truck, unprotected from the rain, and crowded into the cab, Ben in the middle and me on the outside. Ben was high on adventure. I was riddled with confusion, my life suddenly outside my control. We drove through small hills grown old with olive groves. Our driver was a Kurd and all around us, he said, were Kurds.

The hills opened out again onto another broad plain, the Syria of my imagination. Lightning flashed the horizon. The driving on the road through the middle of the plain was madness, worse than Montenegro, cars and trucks hurtling flat out down the middle of the narrow bitumen honking and shrieking. When a truck stopped suddenly in front of us, nano-seconds from oblivion I found my confidence. Ben thought we were cooked. I came to life, no longer at the mercy of the overbearing masculine. *I may not be in the driver's seat, but I still have a beating heart* – and a modicum of understanding about the transfer of energy.

Our driver, fearful of being busted by the constabulary for having passengers, kindly dropped us on the edge of Aleppo. We looked around for the train station and Ben beelined for the buses. I was furious. I have a terror of travelling in buses. I'd rather walk. The bus station was crowded with fumes and smoke and hyperbolic men. We pushed our way through the crowds milling about us, haggling with us for our fare. While Ben bargained I put my pack down on the filthy asphalt. A Syrian dived on it, ready to throw it into the undercarriage of a nearby bus.

'Drop it,' I commanded, surprising myself, as well as the men surrounding us.

I was livid with the pushing, shoving throng of men telling, telling, telling me what to do with no intention of listening to me. I commanded them to give me a wide berth. And they did. Ben chose a bus and I took my seat. I was angrier than I'd felt for many, many years. I drank the anger, for it was the pure anger of a moment, a woman's anger unburdened by baggage, either collective or personal. I was intoxicated with the power of *woman* ... and then the fury of the ages set in. I sat in that bus seat and my heart raged about my son the fucking misogynist, my son the Arab. And then I understood there was a reason I was in Syria and that reason was to find my pleasant nature in the presence of the contempt I held for men. For there in the bus station I discovered rage beyond fear. I was on a bus with no food and no toilet; five hours as the only woman among a pack of men. *My son in this moment is an arrogant sanctimonious prick.*

Whether or not this was true, it felt good to feel it. To let it live. To breathe my story. No longer pleasing. It was only a moment, after all. As I sat on the bus alone, I hoped the bus would leave without him. The bus driver wanted me to change seats. I ignored him. He could go fuck himself too. I sat with my contempt. With the sickness of spirit I felt for the women outside the window, the ones I could not see with their faces covered in black. I felt the bile and the fire and the fury that my son could not communicate with me, that he would *presume* to make my decisions for me, that there was only his need to get to Damascus. Amid the barking, shrieking, smoking men I lay back in the arms of the ogre from the movie 'Bridge To Terabithia', in the arms of the timeless one; I lay back and wept for my voice, for recognition in my world. Eventually I obliged the driver and changed seats, sitting without speaking beside my son. Arab music floated through the bus speakers. *Their music looks like their writing sounds.* I hum with fury. *No man will push me around again.* It was fascinating being around Muslim men in this space. I held no fear. Once the rage passed, there was only the fullness of my own being.

Halfway to Damascus the bus stopped for dinner. The restaurant was crowded with men. And me. Blonde me. Female me. I was assertive and powerful, snatching back my money from the toilet attendant when he would overcharge me, asking the group of men Ben was speaking to for change, making no apologies for my boldness. A man selling kebabs offered me a salad for free, nodding with welcome-to-Syria kindness. I celebrated my freedom. This was not the stand of a rebel. This was fullness for fullness's sake. I felt the difference radiating from me. *I will not smile because you command it from me and neither will I close my heart to you.*

We pulled into Damascus and the bus dumped us in a dark and empty carpark miles from the city centre. The small group of men Ben befriended in the crowded restaurant picked up his bags and carried them for him, leading him to a crowded busted-up minivan. I was left to trail along with my own bags, cursing the Arab in my son's heart.

The following morning I bowled onto the dirty streets of Damascus, alive to the Arabs and their flowing robes and turbans and muumuus, all the colours and styles and manners of headwear and dress concocted by our magnificent world. I *loved* being on the streets among Arab men, the hostile, the gawking and the welcoming, but I could have wept for the absence of women, for the missing vibration of love and life in our world. I was still angry with Ben. One moment 'we' are journeying, the next I am journeying on my own. No discussion. No sharing. Just a decision based on the power dynamic of 'consent' and invisibility. In truth, I was grateful for his Arab behaviour – *because of course it was not the behaviour of Arabs but the behaviour of men*. In the West, not so long ago, we had a revolution because of this, remember?

I was confident among the men, but to my ignorant face the women in black on the streets of Damascus were denied social engagement. I could not meet my sister. *Don't tell me women choose this! To convince ourselves she 'chooses' this is to abdicate our responsibility for each other as human beings. The question is this: is she free not to choose it? Only then can we know if such a life is her choice.* I looked around me. Yes, I could accept this world. Yet in my heart I could not accept its values.

Over the next three days Ben and I explored Damascus, him looking for a school to teach him Arabic, me exploring a world which was as alien to me as I was to it. We took to breakfasting on fresh-squeezed grapefruit juices and pastries at a small café up the road from the hotel. Sitting on the footpath in the sunshine one wintry morning, feasting on our breakfasts, Ben stood to get a serviette from the counter. I called out, asking him to bring one for me. Every man on the street within cooee turned and stared at me. In that moment I realised that women's voices could not be heard on the streets of Damascus. I hadn't noticed. And so I was pleased to have raised a woman's voice.

When it was cold I wore a beanie on my head. When it was not I took it off, my shorn blonde locks waving in the wind for all to see. I would accept this world for what it was. In return, I would be accepted for who I am. And I am woman. And I will not bow to the dis-grace of men, here or anywhere. The beauty of all this was that I experienced life free from defiance. There was simply and only the truth of me. The comfort of a woman at peace. And that peace bought me a freedom that would have torn me up had I been raging a rebel war on their streets. Among the men of Damascus I found my Self as a woman. Among the Arabs with their straight spines and flowing robes, I felt the safety of being among men whose energy was contained within the energetic boundaries of themselves. These were men of extraordinary power. And they allowed me the same. To my eternal gratitude and delight, on the streets of Damascus I found my liberation, as a woman.

For three days we sat among the Arabs, drinking tea and playing backgammon. A small boy with his shoe-shine kit followed me for five city blocks, begging to shine my shoes; after three blocks I turned away from his 'lady-lady come on lady' and left him to his manipulative pouting and belly rubbing, unmoved and obligation-free. Christmas was two weeks away and we revelled in a world mercifully oblivious to the commercial assault of Christmas. The exceptions were the restaurants in the city's Christian quarter, where trees were decorated with tinsel and a sense of noble purpose – and a crowded, distinctively non-Christian restaurant that blasted carols from its speakers: ... *man will live forever more, because of Christmas Day.*

We laughed. There is the West – and the rest. We loved Damascus. And as we rolled the dice, happy now to be in Syria, I understood that just as Ben's was not the speed of ease, but hurriedness born of frustration and quiet aggression, mine was not the politeness of grace, but rather a politeness born of desire for acceptance, recognition and approval. And this desire came with stories.

Grace, on the other hand, has no story. Grace is *what is*.

We walked through Damascus's old city, through a sea of Arabs, Syrians and Iranians and there we met Suleyman, an old Iraqi from Baghdad who spoke great English.

'I cannot be in Baghdad,' he said. 'It is very bad there, because of the war.'

I wanted to speak, to apologise for my government. For my countrymen were among those who had invaded his homeland. Yet I knew if I spoke I would weep with sorrow and shame.

We followed Suleyman through ever-decreasing alleyways to a big tiled café packed with men drinking coffee and smoking hookahs filled with the sweet tobacco favoured by Syrians and Turks. The wonder was my strength of heart and purpose. I decided who I would look in the eye and who I would let pass in a blur; I decided whether I would get out of a man's way or he would get out of mine. And these were decisions of the heart, decisions made with the grace and ease of each moment. I claimed my values and my life and allowed the Arabs to claim theirs. And I celebrated goodness in the places we met, accepting our bigotry as part of our shared humanness.

I dislike your insistence that the feminine have no public face. I will not condemn you, yet neither will I cover my face. See? Here I am. I am her. And where she is is holy. Here I am. And I raise my voice for her. Because I can. And because I am a woman. And I am free.

It took the three days that I was there to organise a train out, back to Turkey, mainly because, as is usual among us humans, everyone we asked thought they knew but in reality they knew nothing. The first three people I asked about trains gave me directions to three different 'train stations' in the city, none of which yielded so much as a track. The woman in the tourist information centre, who spoke great

English, said there were no trains to Turkey. No trains? No trains to Turkey? I found this startlingly implausible. I asked her where the train station was and she marked it on her toy map. That afternoon, Ben and I made it our mission to visit the station for ourselves. It was miles out on the edge of the city, which enabled us to visit the rest of Damascus through the bubble of our taxi window.

In Croatia I had marvelled at words packed with such letters as z, x and k, a Scrabble master's dream. I had been looking forward to Greece, whose alphabet was the realm of simple geometry. In Syria, I had not a chance in hell of pronouncing anything. The graceful writing of Arabia beamed at us from signposts and I could only smile at the beauty of a world that made no sense to me, no sense at all.

The station master was home. There was a train to Turkey the following night. The good news plunged our hearts with sadness – one train a week meant Ben and I would be parting ways sooner than we'd anticipated. Our journey together was done. From the station we ambled back to the city centre, past street hawkers surprised by our presence in their world, past fruitsellers whose baskets were piled high with fresh dates and figs and mandarins. I stocked up for the journey ahead. As I bargained with one fruitseller for a parcel of mandarins a crowd gathered, one man a little more hostile than curious. And out of the throng emerged an old man, another of the old ones whose English spoke of a previous age and a different relationship between East and West. He looked me right in the eye and asked if I was all right, ignoring his brothers yet somehow stilling their torment. The invisible language of men.

I am reminded of my surfing days, not so long ago when I took to the waves as a woman of middle age. I'm surprised that other people are surprised when I tell them surfers are hostile to women. And yet for every man who would exert his troublesome territorial testosterone over a woman on the water there was another who would make his presence known, quietly and with sudden certainty, looking me in the eye with an, 'It's all right sister, I see you, I love you, I will look out for you.' These men are God's great gift to women.

And so they were on the streets of Damascus. Every time there might have been trouble, there was an angel with his eye on the feminine stranger on the street.

While Ben waited for a sugar cane juice, I stood on a corner and listened to the story of the streets: the honking traffic whirling around the city, ignoring red lights until policemen on motorbikes dove into the fray, holding them back with a sideways glance; men old and young walking along with their heads bowed, sliding prayer beads through their fingers, sometimes with a burning cigarette in the same hand; the old arches, the weathered stone geometry, the genie caves of polished treasure, the hookahs, the brass pots, the food and the kaftans and the hole-in-the-wall ovens. The 'welkum, welkum' of the street hawkers in the covered bazaar was a welcome change from the 'lady-lady' commands of the Turks.

Damascus is an old city and she is not expected to perform for anyone. Here in this layered world the old is living young, it is current and without apology. Waiting for Ben, I looked around to find the pleading eyes of the shoe-shine boy staring into mine. There was no sign of his shoe-shine box, just an empty hand held out for money and a spirit full of harsh bravado. I leaned forward to see him up close. He was about ten. He made hungry gestures. I was looking for an honest encounter and, not finding it, shook my head. I wondered if I was asking too much. I glanced around again to see him standing against a street pole, vulnerable now, a child in a hostile adult world. I watched to see if an adult would appear for him. None did. He recovered his confidence and tried again, this time with a group of men sitting around on stools on the footpath. I wondered what the child's gift to me might be. And what might be my gift in return. I found my answer that night in a book I was reading by Lewis Hyde: *We are only alive to the degree that we can let ourselves be moved.*

In my pre-pilgrimage life, I had never thought of Syria as a Muslim country. Or Egypt. Or Turkey. Or even Palestine. Yet, I was correct in my ignorance – their expression of themselves, through art and dress and architecture, is cultural as much as religious. Surrounded by Arabs blowing in their lovely robes, I was reminded of the desert, hot and cold. In this context their covered heads made good sense. But to name this as a command from Allah and apply it to one gender is to attempt a crude marriage of culture and religious imposition. God does not ask a woman to hide her public face. Man does.

Perhaps man once did so to protect his daughters from the Sultan's raiders. Or Alexander's. Or perhaps there was a woman who so grieved the loss of her husband or son that she swore only to wear black forevermore, and so it was that others held up her actions as virtue and insisted their own women act accordingly and soon everyone forgot that what was one woman's honest expression became every woman's imprisoned oppression. Stories. Stories I tell to make sense of a world for which I could weep. At least some men have the grace to cover their own heads and, in some cases, their lips and faces. Why does it matter? Because it lives in me. *As without, so within.* It claws at my heart. And if I can free my heart, then I can free those for whom it weeps.

That night I lay on my bed in the hotel, exhausted. Not from this particular day. Not by Damascus or Syria. Not from the journey across Turkey or my time in Istanbul. Not even by the walk from Rome to Albania. I was exhausted by the whole. The inner journey and the outer journey; the physical and the spiritual. The day when I would be united with my husband was drawing near and I was still not ready to be demanded from, to be not listened to. This night, I was lonely. And the best I could offer myself was surrender. *There is no decision to be made about my marriage. Or my life for that matter. If I am making a decision then I am doing too much.* The wide empty expanse of my life opened up before me. I reached for the book I was reading, 'Rumi's Daughter' by Muriel Maufroy: *Love is an ocean without shores. You have to learn to bear it.*

I woke to the darkened room and lay curled up in my warm spot, softly witnessing the thoughts that wandered through my waking mind. They led one to the other and perched on the one about longing, the longing that my husband and I might spend time in each other's company, talking, sharing, sitting together, gradually moving into shared space. *Eventually, perhaps at the end of the second day, making love.* I felt the longing that we might create an invitation, each for the other, and then step into that loving place. I felt the breathless tension of the reality that he would be pawing at me, wanting, hungry, clumsy, too fast. And then I asked the question: who have I pressured in this way and how have I lived this dance over and over, playing both roles? And there in the warm spot I began to burn. I burrowed into the darkness beneath the blankets as first my heart and then the rest of me flamed. I burned. I burned it up. I burned it out. I reduced to ashes this dreadful dance of obligation and demand.

Pleasing born of obligation and demand is not consent – these are the troubled waters of sexual assault in the courtroom. This is the difference between how men and women view consent. Yes, she did – but what of the responsibility of the entangler? He who knew, if he'd listened to her, or at the very least listened to his own heart, that she did not want to. She too bears responsibility for this destructive age-old dynamic – and between them we arrive at the gateway of blame, the encoding of the feminine to please the masculine, to please him or else! That 'else' is the reason women appear to consent, when in fact what men call 'consent' is for us a matter of life or death, whether it's the roof over our heads or the knife at our throats; it's obligation, pure and simple.

Via the black shrouds favoured by the women of Damascus, my wandering thoughts took me to all those hidings I had received from my father for 'silent insubordination'. Many years later, after I'd left my father's house, I glimpsed my face in a mirror as I became embroiled in an altercation with 'authority'. *So that's it! That's why Dad was so angry with me.* My contempt for his irrational bullying must have been writ large all over my pretty teenaged face. *These women, the Syrians and Iranians around me, must enjoy enormous freedom of attitude beneath their robes.* Perhaps the veil is a blessing after all.

Later in the morning, as I was standing at the counter in a bookshop lined with magnificent Arabic books, one of the most beautiful women I have ever seen entered the store. She was wearing a long mantle of black lace that cascaded down her back like a waterfall, in the style of a medieval princess. She walked tall, her face a mask of beauty; her clothes immaculate, of the style worshipped by the cadre of Carrie Bradshaw. And in the manner of one accustomed to attention, her own attention was focused entirely on her mission. In the 1950s, the Americans might have called her a *first-class dame*. And then I saw him. In the far corner of the shop sat an elderly man with a ginger-grey beard curling around his unlined face. He was clad in a long olive green robe, his red velvet cap trimmed with a white cloth band; a fancy green sash circled his waist and a string of orange beads hung low from his neck. To me he was like the desert after rain.

He felt my gaze rest upon him and as he turned to look at me the room turned to light. We smiled at each other, the smile of hearts on fire. This was Love. A shared transmission with another human being. The kind of love that might travel and inform the rest of the world. Beyond man, beyond woman, yet a meeting of man and woman that was outside space, time and dimension. Eternity, in the eyes of an Arab.

I loved Syria. I loved Damascus. I loved the desert I had never seen, its camels and Bedouins riding through my heart. I loved the robes and the rugs and the dust and the finest of salutations that seemed to blow with the wind in an Arabian heart. *I am speaking of the men, of course.*

In the Balkans I obsessed about war, the physical and material expression of annihilation of that which we loathe and fear; in Arabia it was the inner plane, as represented by the veil, its varying shades complete with the sinister black shroud. In Istanbul I heard a Western man scoff about how happy such a woman was in a family he met – this is not the point. The American poet Maya Angelou knows why the caged bird sings. The women on the streets of Damascus ranged in their degrees of shroudedness. I did not hear their voices. Their public invisibility was complete in the silence. I remembered my mother telling me as a child not to draw attention to myself when I called out. Yes, not so long ago things weren't so different in the West.

I remember women putting scarves on their heads to go out in public. I remember nuns all cloaked in black with their black veils. I remember when women could sit only in the ladies' lounge at the pub. When a woman's value was measured by her ability to bear children. When a ringless finger beyond a certain age was cause for the family shame. When women who were married could not work. When women's pay was a fraction of men's for the same work. When a woman who was raped must have been 'asking for it' and no-one ever, ever spoke publicly about the sexual use – these days we call it abuse – of children. In truth, women in the West are only one step ahead. And it took a revolution to achieve that. And even then, have we not simply traded corsetry for the knife and modesty for promiscuity?

We might have 'equal rights', but we do not have ourselves, because the jailer is within.

One day I noticed that while the shrouded ones showed only their eyes to the world, I shaded mine with my sunglasses. How ironic for the men of Damascus, that they could deal with all of me *except my eyes*.

On my last evening in Damascus we caught a 'taxi' (young man with shonky car pleading for our fare) to the top of the highest hill overlooking the city, a hill that hasn't seen rain for centuries. Through plastic-sheeted windows in a café along the roadside we watched the sun go down over Damascus. Ben ordered a hookah and we rolled the dice for the last time as we sipped minted tea. Five games we played and five games straight I won. I wondered if I'd sat up there with my husband, would we have had anything to say?

We ate that night in our favourite restaurant, a feast of desert delights, and I stocked up for the train. By midnight I was alone in my sleeper carriage, no sign of my son, not this night, not tomorrow, not for some considerable time to come. Through our journey together, Ben and I had founded a cooperation based on the preservation of greatest need. Mostly unspoken, at 'need' junctions we had continually surrendered to, and given credence to, right action determined by the authenticity of the moment, right up until the fork in the road where our needs were equally great. I am pleased that I made no attempt at coercion when Ben chose the high road through the white-capped mountains of Macedonia, when I'd have preferred the low road through the villages of Albania. We had each honoured the other's choice, trusting that only he or she could know the most authentic path to travel.

Alone on the train, I was rattled by the absence of the journey shared. In twelve days' time I would be with my husband. A gap between men, the train a metaphor for my passage into the next life, letting go the safe passage of my son, surrendering sight of the shore and learning to bear it.

Six hours later I was one among a hundred travellers lolling around the station at Aleppo, changing trains for Turkey. Again I was undone by my own assumptions. I thought I'd simply turn up and buy a ticket to Konya. The ticket box was closed. A French-speaking porter told me the ticket box would open at 1 pm, which was fine and dandy except the train was leaving at 11 am. Before the morning was out I understood why foreigners ask locals the same question fifteen times. It's called 'making sure'. Over the next three hours I learned the ticket box was opening at 1 pm, 7 am, 8 am, 10 am and 9 am. Same when I asked which platform would take me to *Turkiye*. It's the reason Ben doesn't ask directions and never, ever shows them the map. Of course, all my wonderings led to a ticket in hand, one that was handwritten, stamped and carbon-copied in duplicate, triplicate and more.

I sat contentedly among the Syrians, admiring women of power, beauty and abundance lining the station walls and men who genuinely liked each other. More than this, Arab men are in love with each other. *This man is my brother ... unless he is not, in which case I might kill him.* They touch, a lot. They liked Ben too, would walk with him, talk to him, pat his back with a friendly touch and tell him they loved him. Such public affection is unknown in my own world.

Soon I was snug in the sleeper, warmed by the babble of Arab voices in the corridor outside. I unpacked my culinary treasures: seasoned spinach tartlets sprinkled with pomegranate seeds, trays of hummus, olives and halva, fresh dates and mandarins, and three different pastries filled with honey or soft white cheese. The little train – and it was a little train, just a sleeper carriage, two small freight carriages and an engine – stopped at the border and the guards leapt onboard to check our passports. Through the window I saw the guard who helped Ben and me get to Aleppo a few days before, *the one who told us there were no trains to Damascus – ever.* I hoped he would be the one to knock on my door, so we might smile and say hello, but he stayed on the platform among a sea of luggage and people and child-porters pushing wheelbarrows.

I left the world outside my window to life's grand parade, settling into the clean white sheets of the narrow bed, letting the train rock me to sweet surrender as it pulled out of the station: *I am at the Gateway of Lost. Pilgrimage lessons dictate that I surrender resistance to my marriage, totally give in to it, yet I fear getting lost. A creature inside me kicks and screams and fights for her life. She cannot breathe. She is furious. All her loathing for him rises in her throat. But the soul of* him, well she adores that one. Love and respect abound. It is its physical manifestation as 'man' that she cannot abide, as if by walking with this one she will become him.

I woke feeling better, although surprised to find I no longer knew what my husband looked like. I did not miss him. And then I was struck dumb with a question I answered immediately: *how is it that my gifts so freely offered to my husband became subject to 'demand' and 'right'?* Because we legalised them. We turned a gift into a legal contract, thus giving such gifts a measure of worth. We contracted them. *I throw open this door. I peer into the cold, empty darkness. My footsteps echo on the hard stone floor. The walls are damp. There is no fear. No apprehension. Just the surefooted certainty that sunshine must come to this place.*

The train was a very slow little train. Outside the window the ploughed fields were soft and green; distant mountains, grey and barely visible through the fog, curved around them. Lights went on in people's houses, warming their nights. The world outside was a wavy ridgeline, a celestial map shaded blue along the shoreline where earth meets sky. *Of course! We must un-marry. Liberation washed through me. Yes. Yes. Yes.*

That night I dreamed I made love to my husband, tender and sweet.

Yes, I must be free to offer my sexual and domestic gifts, for they are not his or anybody else's by 'right'. For even though nowhere in our vows was such a right encoded, our DNA is riddled with the expectations and experiences of our culture and our ancestors. We cannot *but* expect from each other, however unconsciously: me financial support, him domestic and sexual service. The irony, of course, is that neither of us had to expect anything *from* the other to create such an oppressive arrangement. Rather, based on our conditioning, *we have expected ourselves to give it.* Was it possible to free ourselves from these bonds of obligation? And what new ways might come in their place? I gave thanks again for the cocoon of the train, my own little cradle rocking me gently across Turkey on a journey I hoped would never end. But of course it did. At 4 am on a dark-cold platform in Konya.

I found a hotel and by midmorning I was walking along Konya's busy main street, or one of them, when a man stopped me short.

'You are a tourist,' he said.

I kept walking, an obligation-free woman. The masculine was demanding my attention and I owed him nothing. He persisted.

'You know how I know?'

I kept walking, for all the world my eyes and heart immersed in the noisy concrete world around me.

'You are wearing sunglasses.'

Inwardly I smiled. And kept walking.

'You know why Turkish people want to talk to you?'

I laughed.

'Because they want to sell me something?'

He laughed.

'The first reason,' he said, 'is because Turkish hospitality, we want to say hello.

'Second reason, I am nomad.'

Nomad, call of my childhood. This got him the attention he was looking for.

He pointed to his shop.

'Not now,' I said, as he steered me towards it. 'Not now.'

'Maybe later,' he said. It was not a question.

'Later,' I said.

'Do I have your promise?'

I nodded. *You may have my promise, but I am a woman learning to lie.* Besides, it was an escape route, not a promise. Duress is not grounds for a promise.

I was out of sorts all day. I longed for the company of friends, longed for anything at all to stand between me and the gaping hole of my last week before re-entering my marriage. I called Yhsan, the overbearing couch-surfer who Ben and I stayed with on our way through Konya on the Whirlwind Iconic Turkey Tour. We met for dinner. We wandered through Konya's busy night, chatting with the camaraderie of old friends. Yhsan told me he had no addictions.

Not religion. Not football. Not alcohol. Not his girlfriend. A Turkish man's order of priorities. He told me his friends and work colleagues think he is going to hell. And of course Yhsan was not overbearing, not any more – not to a woman who knows her own centre, a woman free from obligation. This was the Great Gift of Turkish men to me.

We wandered into a toy shop, to buy presents for the children of one of his friends. The woman behind the counter thought I was Yhsan's wife. Outside, as we wandered along in the dark, the plastic toys bulging from Yhsan's pockets, he asked me if I wanted to marry.

'I am married,' I said, pretty certain it was a generic question rather than a proposal.

'Nooooo,' he replied.

'Yes, I am,' I said, holding up my ring.

'Anyone can wear a ring,' he said.

I laughed. He told me he thought I looked no older than thirty-two. I threw back my head and laughed. To marry a Dutchman was one thing. A Turk was another league altogether. Yhsan was indignant. He was looking for protocol.

'Thank me!' he demanded.

I smiled, resting my case.

There was only one reason to be in Konya, and that was to visit the tomb of the great Mevlana, the poet Rumi, to be one among the 'seekers' and discover what, if anything, was there for me. I had expected, being a pilgrim who had not absorbed her lessons about expectations, Rumi's tomb to be a small grave beneath an old tree, perhaps fenced off by a rickety rusted iron fence, perhaps with a turbaned tombstone and a sign to mark the spot. And there I would sit alone and commune with the great teacher. I got the turban bit right. The tomb of the mystic poet was mausoleum and museum. And it was packed with seekers:

> *Come, come, whoever you are*
> *Wonderer, worshipper, lover of leaving.*
> *It doesn't matter.*
> *Ours is not a caravan of despair.*
> *Come, even if you have broken your vow*
> *A thousand times*
> *Come, yet again, come, come.*

And come they certainly had. Heads bound and heads unbound, bearded and not, young and old; women and men from all the worlds within our world they were there, heads bowed, many weeping. The tomb was at the back of the museum, past the weathered pages of the ancient Korans and Persian artefacts, on a raised pedestal behind a gilded cage. I wondered who had made the burnished cloth. I marvelled at the pointed finger of the turban that marked the poet's station. How wonderful, I thought, that the Turks reserved their most magnificent tomb for the one who was neither warrior nor king, but poet.

As I walked softly on the old carpets laid thick on the floor, obligatory blue plastic bags rustling on my feet to keep the carpets clean, I was reminded of Uluru, the big red rock that rises from the Australian desert, where they also come from all over the world. Not tourists, pilgrims.

I stopped beside a big bronze bowl, *Nisan Tasi*, the April Bowl, made for the Ilhanli king Ebu Said Bahadir Khan and donated to the Mevlana museum in 1333. An April Bowl to collect the rain in April, for in Turkish and Islamic tradition April water is held to be sacred.

I found a place on the floor and sat among the seekers, my mind not on the poet but my marriage. I sweated a subterranean fear: *If I am sweet with my husband I will drown. If I am alive to myself – and him – he will consume me again for his own unconscious needs.* And I pondered the paradox: *how do I surrender to my husband and stay true to myself? For presence, at least as I know it in relation to my husband, is separation. How does a woman be at once present and surrendered in holy union with another?*

A beautiful head-bound one fell to her knees before me, clasping her palms to her face. She encroached well into my space, as the Turks do. She drew her pink scarf around her face, shading herself as with an awning; her black trousers collected dust from the carpet as she rocked and wept her tenderness.

I can no longer offer myself in bondage to my husband, I thought. *Will he freely offer me his support or is it conditional? Or can I strike a bargain with my soul – sex as the price for never having to work again?*

The woman in the pink scarf moved her sorrow from her heart to her hands, a child's comfort before the master. I was hungry. I was out of sorts in the tomb of the poet. I did not, could not, feel any transmission at all from the shrine. I had come to Konya to pay tribute to the great Mevlana. Yet I had not the education nor the inspiration to truly receive him, not in this place. *I admire him; now and again, through his legacy, I meet him; I am not him.*

I spent the afternoon reading in the hotel lobby, sheltering from the rain, filling time before my train left for Istanbul. Eventually, tired of the poor light, I grabbed my umbrella and walked onto the street, surprised to find myself heading towards the tomb of Mevlana's teacher, a mystic called Shams who had held no interest for me whatsoever. Besides, like the body parts of Jesus' disciples, Shams of Tabriz was supposedly buried in at least three places across the old Persian empire.

I had ignored a faint call to Shams all day, telling myself I was there for Mevlana and had no interest in a two-bit mystic whose aggressive fire was so great he scorched a world. The barely smiling woman in the information centre told me Shams was behind a mosque 400 metres up the road. I walked in the rain and circled the big stone mosque, peering in to find no sign of Shams. I couldn't be bothered with mosque etiquette, so I gave up, wandering back down the street in the pouring rain, shortcutting through an arcade filled with dreadful dresses that only the tackiest Turkish princess might wear.

The call to Shams, which means 'sun' in Arabic, persisted. *Look again, look again.* I rolled my eyes at myself, and, as the rain fell harder, headed back towards the mosque. An old man putting on his shoes outside the mosque seemed to know what I was looking for and pointed his crooked finger down a distant tree-lined pathway. A small sign declared I had found what I was looking for: Sham Tabrezi Mosque.

I am still reluctant, still unwilling to bother with mosque etiquette. I make a vow: I will not bow my head to the sun. Nor will I allow the tight minds of strangers to dictate how I meet the sun. I stand outside, peering through the watery glass. 'Come, come,' says an old man behind me, the Imam. He opens the door. He tells me to take off my shoes.

He does not tell me to cover my head. I decide that I will stay as long as I am welcome on my own terms. Inside, men are praying. I walk to the bright green blanket draped over a coffin and stand, uncovered and unbowed, raising my eyes to meet the energy of this tomb. The air around me crackles. I feel my heart filling with love, radiating as it meets the sun. I am a woman of fire and as I stand before the light of Shams I meet the fire within me. All the anger I have carried in me as a woman drains from my legs into the floor, through the rugs and the stone into the Earth. I am released. The old Imam comes to me with rosewater to wash my hands and offers me a sugary sweet. I breathe into my heart, standing full and tall for the feminine in this holy place of worship as I receive the Imam's offering. I breathe the sun and release our imagined stories about what is required from us to be holy. And I stand for Aqsa Parvez, the young Canadian woman murdered yesterday by her father for refusing to wear the veil. I have no doubt the man Shams was of his time and culture, the one that brought women to task. Yet here he is receiving me, the universal holy energy receives me. I receive. We exchange. I am one with the infinite universe. I am wonder. I am free.

Shams of Tabriz was the true purpose for my visit to Konya, not the mystic poet Rumi. I left the tomb when I was ready, leaving the man they called the Sun to a handful of covered Westerners, their palms raised in silence.

I walked briskly through the rain, alive and empowered, ready now to make sense of Rumi's palace. Shams of Tabriz had delivered me to Mevlana. Now, instead of sitting in observation at the mausoleum, watching and witnessing the seekers, I was one among them. I no longer saw them, just as I no longer saw the maroon carpets, the hanging bowls and crystal chandeliers. I did not hear their voices or the rustle of the blue plastic bags on their feet. I was delivered. I had been confused about Shams's place in Rumi's world. The poet was a rich man from an established order, but why were he and his teacher not buried together? Now I understood – they are! They are buried together here in Konya, divided by class and status, although Shams too has a finger-pointing turban. At least that is the story I tell.

Rumi's tomb is gorgeous; love is poured into every stone and knot and seam and brushstroke – but it is not him. The ones who built it did so to the glory of themselves, reflected onto the canvas of a mystic poet; the tomb reflects their social class and artistic magnificence. Yet the man to whom it is dedicated, the great Mevlana, he is not here.

The reedy flute plays high in the ceiling, I smell the rosewater. This is a memorial to seeking hearts, to the ones who bow their heads and pay tribute. Yet something is missing ... Rumi ... Rumi is not here. Rumi is in the marketplace, the puddles and the trees. The poet himself is riding the wind on the golden plains outside the city, where the camels and caravans carry silks and stories and spices. The rigid celestial geometry of the rugs begins to blur, becoming stars and archaic signatures. The back of my heart, prickly at Shams's tomb, now aches and hurts to touch.

A well-dressed man with grey hair and sparkling eyes apologises for interrupting me and asks where I am from. In my best pidgin Turkish I tell him, 'Ow-strah-lia.' He smiles and tells me he is from Ankara, that he has just arrived today. He tells me it is a pity I do not speak German, because if I spoke German he could express himself more eloquently. 'Oh,' I say, 'your English is very good.' He smiles, his hands deep in the pockets of his long black coat. 'Ah,' he says, 'it is not perfect.' We smile. We return to our own lives.

As I left the mausoleum that afternoon, I looked back towards Mevlana's tomb, skilfully lit through the darkness and the rain, and finally I understood. I saw it for what it is and was: a dedication by the Mevlevi Order to their tradition and home to the Sufi Dervishes about whom I knew absolutely nothing – except that they are beautiful and their women are missing from the show. Mevlana's tomb is a shrine for the seekers, a rite of passage for swollen hearts. And these are just stories. In truth I know nothing at all.

That night I returned to Istanbul on the train, grateful for small mercies: the train was packed and there would be no sleeper for me, but at least the smokers in the crowded carriage were forced into the corridor. As the train rattled gently through the night, moonshine split the light on the wet road outside the window. I stared into the emptiness, drinking in the sizzling energy that still coursed through my body from Shams's tomb, the power of standing true, uncompromised and unbowed, being received wholeheartedly by the Imam. I thought about the Canadian girl murdered by her father. *If I were Muslim I'd be really pissed off at suggestions that religion was the motive for her murder.* Perfectly good Muslims don't wear a veil. And perfectly good Muslims do and don't murder their unveiled daughters. Let us not confuse religion with culture. Or religion with violence. This was an insane act of control. A young woman who refused to submit to the will of the father. And the price she paid, and she paid it in the West, will be a warning to others. *Let us not be blinded by correct thinking that says women wear the veil by choice.* It is a choice only if she is free to choose otherwise.

I woke to the grey light of a cloudy day, pleased the night was done. A river ran beside the train, flat and wide and stumbling over grey stones; trees stark and yellow stood knee-deep in muddy water; neighbourhoods slept in the early light; paddocks rested. The bare vineyards looked like winter fields of wooden crosses; a bird flapped hard in the wind to keep pace with the train, racing us through the wild grasses. Turkish flags flew high on the hills, others rested dormant on the inside of windowpanes. The Turks love their flag. I loved its red. We crossed the muddy river. Snow lit white the mountains. Soldiers with machine guns stood at ease outside bright pink stations. The river became a lake and the lake became the sea. Two days previously my husband had sent me a Christmas card that had made me laugh. It was an e-card in which elves with our faces danced merrily together. A rush of possibility had lifted my spirits: not only was the card light and funny, the elves were *dancing*. I called him from the train. He said he wished he could stay longer with his father in Holland. I told him that if he wanted more time then he must take it. He scoffed at my 'new age ideas about time'. I closed myself to his closeness and wondered if we would ever enjoy ease of conversation.

My husband wants what he does not have. There was nothing to stop him spending more time in Holland.

The train chugged slowly through the suburbs of Istanbul. I had seven days in this magnificent city to prepare myself to meet my husband, the one who wants what he does not have. I looked out the window, not seeing the city, absorbed in my thoughts. One thought in particular had been circling these past days and in that moment I caught it: *If I were independently wealthy would I be with this man?* The answer was, *No*.

The city blurred as I relinquished the resistance I held in my body, not to the answer but to the question. For the impossible allowance of the question was held deeply as tension in my legs, my tongue, my hands. As I released the question I stood at the gateway of chimerical truth. This was my obligation – that I was bound by money to a man with whom I shared a demanding existence and I was not willing to pay the price. Our courtship had wooed me not to him, but away from myself, away from responsibility for myself.

I returned to the blue room at the Side Hotel and took up the rhythm of the ancient city of Istanbul, my known world, my place of return. The old man in the Arasta Bazaar, who called me 'dear friend' and smiled at me with his heart, served me grapefruit and pomegranate juice, fresh-squeezed and overpriced, lentil soup and baklava fresh from the oven. He asked me where I had been.

'Syria,' I said.

He threw his head back and laughed. He turned to the cook and told him where I had been. They both shook their heads.

'*El-Suriye?*' he asked, to make sure.

I laughed, unsure of the joke.

'And Iraq? Did you also go to Iraq?' he asked.

They laughed louder. This was not the only conversation along these lines I had in coming days with Turkish men.

I sat in the sunshine eating my breakfast, watching the cats stretch lazily on the rugs in the bazaar. There was a new caller at the mosque, this one making long notes that wavered all over the city before cutting himself off short. I imagined him collapsed on the stone floor of his minaret, making ready to rise again for the next jagged cry.

That afternoon, I walked along the street munching on a cheese pastry when the air around me prickled. Absorbed in my thoughts I failed to pay attention. I jumped on the *tramvay* for a ride across the Golden Horn to Beyoglu to buy a book and a cherry *tiramisu*. The tram was standing room only, until two women left at the same time and I took the window seat. A man sat beside me. At first I took no notice and then, from the corner of my eye, I saw his striped shirt. This man had shadowed me when I was eating my pastry! I breathed deeply, gathering my thoughts. The ghost of the hunter I had been in the wild places of New Zealand possessed every cell in my being, every quiver in my senses. I became alive to my surrounds. I left the tram at Karakoy. He followed me. I stood looking at a map at the station, a test to see whether or not he would leave without me. He did not. He looked at another map. The station cleared.

And then I had what I can only describe as my Harry Potter moment. The world around me shimmered and stilled and in a flash I was on the other side of the tracks. A heartbeat later, the tram heading back to Sultanahmet pulled in. I sat where I was on the station platform, unmoving. Through the tram windows, in one side and out the other, I could see the stalker looking around, bewildered and foolish. Making sure he stayed on the other side of the tracks I boarded the tram, allowing it to ferry me to safety. How ironic, I thought, that I have freed myself from the murderer within only to meet a stalker!

Winded by the experience, over the next few days I stayed close to the hotel. I dressed differently. I followed my instincts. I carried my camera in my pocket, close at hand. I strategised about allowing him to follow me until I crossed paths with a policeman. And slowly the stalker vanished from my inner world and I exhaled, putting my faith in another tenet illuminated by Paulo Coelho: *Everything that happens once can never happen again. But everything that happens twice will surely happen a third time.*

And I gave serious thought to the role I had invited the stalker to play.

Slowly I stretched my wings into the city again, amazed by the familiarity I felt there. At the same time, I was pulling away from my own shore, preparing inwardly for my meeting with my husband. I grew explanations for why it was okay for him to support me, unconditionally. And I toyed with the idea that the giving and receiving of such support might be one of the most life-honouring dances we can enjoy on this Earth.

I woke to music most beautiful in the pre-dawn light, confused about where it was coming from. Could this be the wake-up call to Allah? It was indeed: a new call, soft and sweet. Clearly I wasn't the only one in the city who'd had enough of the new muezzin and his fervent cry.

Every day I strolled through the open space between the *Ayasofya* and the Blue Mosque, wandering down to the meeting place of the big waters that split the city: the Golden Horn, the Bosphorous and the Sea of Marmara. It was there the hum of the city through all time came together. I visited the Istiklal Caddesi, famous for its bookshops and desserts. One particular day I noticed Tracy Chevalier had a new book out. I was hungry enough for a good read to pardon Tracy for squashing a girl-child beneath a hearthstone a few books back, leaving only the beautiful blue thread of forbidden cloth as evidence for the mother to find her. That image has never left me and for that, at a deeply unsettled layer of my being, I had never forgiven Tracy; nor, for that matter, the austere rigidity of the French peasantry. As I reached for the new book it occurred to me that such sacrifice was only a clutch of generations away from the murdered Muslim girl in Canada. This was the same day the Saudis unleashed the wrath of the court on a young woman appealing her sentence of 90 lashings and six-months imprisonment for 'being in the company of a man who was not a relative'. The man had forced her into his car and raped her. On appeal, the court had upped her sentence to 200 lashings and six months, 'for attempting to aggravate and influence the judiciary through the media', the price of Western attention. For good measure, the court also revoked the licence of her lawyer. This was also the day that a young American woman named Jamie Lee Jones testified before Congress about the gang rape she had endured as an employee of Halliburton, the US corporation charged with rebuilding Iraq. Her attackers were her co-workers. As I paid for Tracy's new book, the lament of the Russian American revolutionary Emma Goldman struck an easy chord in my heart: *As a woman I have no country; as a woman, my country is the whole world.*

I sat in the cold watery sunshine of the garden in front of the *Ayasofya* and rang my husband, hanging up when I couldn't be bothered explaining for a second time what he hadn't listened to the first. I had only rung in a moment of boredom, which in any other circumstances might be sound reason to ring a loved one. Even from afar, he rattled my radar and colonised my senses, like the force of water holding me under so that I was unable to navigate my world. It was easier just to hang up and blame the poor signal. Later in the day my husband rang back. I was prickly, feeling like a little clump of mercury to his big fleshy forefinger pushing me around. It was as if our dynamic was a vortex I was unable to resist, sucking me round and round and throwing me out of centre so that I could see only the past. I made a list of three things and kept it in my pocket:

> *I do not have to struggle*
> *Nothing is as it seems*
> *I owe him nothing.*

I felt like a wild animal who'd been brought in from the cold, unsure of the price to be exacted from her in exchange for the warmth. I wanted to cry in the way I hadn't cried in months. If I paid attention to the deepest part of me, I would have to admit that I was petrified about leaving Istanbul on Saturday. In no way did I feel I had what I needed to go back in there, into marriage, to be petted and stroked and wanted from. It was a breathless place for me, a death chamber.

Yes, I must unmarry, so that I am free to choose. I am Karol, the man who turned his back on our love in my dream, only now it is me who is walking away because I do not have the courage to go further. I am Annie Proulx, the writer who chooses her horses and land over husbands and obligation. I am August from 'The Secret Life of Bees', the one who chooses honey and family over husbands and obligation. I am myself. And I am not the marrying kind.

For I cannot bear the namelessness, the facelessness and the directionlessness of marriage. If I stay married, I will only keep running, because that is all there is to do. I must start my life again. I will choose a home, a cat, a garden and a shelf to fill with books. I might be bored, but I will not be lonely.

Paradoxically, marriage had anchored me. I was a woman claimed and I was surprisingly content with this. I just had no capacity for living as a wife. Cruel or practical, I could not tell. My thoughts went round and around ... perhaps it was only this marriage ... maybe it would be different if we liked each other, listened to each other, were interested in each other ... maybe we have burned each other too badly ... or perhaps I'm terrified of letting him down, knowing in my bones that a wife like me will always be a disappointment to a husband like mine.

I wandered through the bazaars, becoming friendly with the carpet sellers I'd ignored for so long. One asked me where I was from.

'Ow-strah-lia,' I said.

'Oi, oi, oi,' he cried.

We laughed. I had this conversation at least three times a day.

'Where does this "oi, oi, oi" come from?' this one asked.

I shrugged.

'Beer?' I suggested.

He thought about this for a moment.

'Germans drink a lot of beer and they don't say "oi, oi, oi".'

I couldn't argue with that.

My husband sent me a text in the middle of the night telling me he had 'dressed the Christmas tree' at his father's house. 'Am I a good husband or what?' he wanted to know. *To your father?* I wondered. The sentiment was sweet, but nonetheless my husband's need for approval was exhausting. I wondered what a wife was for. *Now I come to think of it, what the bloody hell is a wife for? And what is a husband for? To bring in the wood? To protect me from stalkers? Good God, what is our marriage for?*

I realised my terror of re-entering the marriage had everything to do with trusting him. I did not trust my husband – and nor should I, for trust was, in both our cases, a transfer of responsibility for ourselves. *If not trust, then what?* Wide open presence, that's what. Because living with another is not a matter of trust but of being awake to ourselves. With presence trust becomes irrelevant. If I am present and accounted for in my own life, a whole self receiving my husband, then I am free to make no assumptions about who he is and what he wants. Trust is a concern between me and my own conscience.

Late one afternoon I sat among Sunday families spilling out of the gardens between the Blue Mosque and the *Ayasofya*, enjoying the last of the day's wintry sunshine. From a cold stone bench I watched a magnificent moon rise gold behind Sofya's great walls, now red in the afternoon light, white gulls circling her domes. I closed my eyes and imagined I was listening to all the languages of the world. Who, I wondered, had sat here before me? For even though the fountain was not so old, this was public space and it must have held all who travelled to and through this city for the past 3,000 years and more, the hearts and minds of all time.

I was surrounded by Turkish women, mostly scarved, many not, the scarved ones often arm in arm with those who were not. Praise Ataturk. At the end of my bench sat a young woman, head-bound and dressed in darks and gray, popping bubbles with her pink chewing gum and texting back and forth on her phone, a maths text splayed open on her lap filled with deceptively simple graphs.

A stately young woman clad in black walked by, only her eyes to catch the sunlight. She reminded me of a dream I'd had the previous night: crows! *A pair of crows alighting at my feet. They flew for me then settled on a winter-bare branch nearby.* Two little girls ran at the feet of the tall one dressed in black. Her children were ablaze with the colours of childhood. I wondered when, or if, they would be required to surrender colour, self-expression, choice.

In the far corner of the gardens an old man kneeled on the footpath holding out his cap, shielding his shamed face with his free hand. Another black one wandered by, a tight mesh her only window to the world. She walked with her husband, arm in arm, speaking to him in muffled tones.

At least her husband has an excuse for not listening to her, I thought.

My last day in Istanbul was so cold the air outside was wet without raining. My bum was always cold these days. Why is it that denim, such thick cotton, does not keep us warm? I caught the *tramvay* across the water for my last cherry *tiramisu*, my last day of white food. As a vegetarian in winter Turkey, my diet consisted of lentil soup, pasta, risotto, *pide* and pastries. White food. On my way up the wide cobbled street, busy with holiday shoppers – the 'holiday for cutting up meat', the man in the laundry told me – I saw the old gypsy woman who sold lavender seeds from a hessian bag and promised myself that five dollars would be my parting gift to her. Hopefully it would be enough to send her home, out of the rain and off the freezing cold street. After my beggar experience in Pescara I was selective about my giving, now reserving my donations for the elderly, the crippled and the hungry. The strong and well-fed may be no less needy, but they had options denied the others.

These days, when I found myself looking away, I made a point of turning to look properly at the one from whom I turned, for the helplessness or shame was mine, not theirs. I had found a way to give that was neither reckless nor blind to my own responsibilities, for I had learned in Pescara that reckless giving, the absence of responsibility, was the flipside of a judgemental call to rescue another human being. Now I sought only to help, or ease; and I was comfortable rather than distant; at peace rather than troubled by the destiny of soul that is each one's journey. Now I make a ceremony of giving, so that the action itself is each and every time an act of love. I pour my gift into the bowl of the beggar as if I am a teapot, thankful that I am able to give.

On this day, my last in Istanbul, I walked back down the street on my farewell stroll, swinging the plastic bag that held my new book and a celebratory cherry *tiramisu* in one hand, my umbrella in the other. The lavender gypsy came into view, huddled against the shopfront window. Tucking my umbrella under my arm I reached into my pocket for the farewell five. As I drew near, I looked up to see another old one, a wrinkled man hunched over a wooden crutch, holding out a palm filled with small packs of tissues. My giving struck a snag. What to do! I considered walking past him – the money was, after all, pledged to the old woman. I thought about sharing the money between them, but that decried the spirit of my salute and would give neither of them enough to call it quits for the day.

I walked into the scarf shop and traded a ten for two fives. I crossed the cobbled mall and traded the money for a packet of tissues and two packs of lavender. I felt the tears as I met each one, heart to heart. Here was Love. Their gratitude was expressed as light and the light was the connection and the connection, the seeing of another human being and the being seen, was the gift.

I walked back down the hill and across the bridge that spanned the timeless busy waterway, past the fishermen with their yoghurt buckets filled with saltwater to keep the prawn bait fresh, their fishing rods dangling into the cheerless water far below, hauling up herrings for sale between toasted rolls along the water's edge. I wandered into one of the tea shops in the Spice Bazaar.

'Finally,' said the street hawker, 'finally she comes into my shop.'

Evening came to the world outside my window. My pilgrimage was done. I could have wept. Not with sorrow. Or joy. Just with the satisfaction of a journey complete. And in the spaces there was anticipation, a cold of sorts in my bones, a quiver in my belly. Soon I must face the place from which I had fled. Did I fear my husband's willingness to accept me as a free woman? Or myself as a free woman, unbound, unchained? Would I choose a married life? Would I choose to be a wife? This was the threshold on which I stood.

I flew to Amsterdam to be with my husband in the village in which he grew up, an hour's drive south of Amsterdam. For three weeks we roamed time-worn tracks through the woods of his childhood, the midwinter trees stark and plantation straight. My husband had grown a beard and this pleased me, because the face I looked into was fresh and I could meet him anew. At first we were polite and cautious. My husband listened to me. He was attentive. He did not demand. We made love easily. My husband is an elegant man. I watched him dress. I experienced the wonder of him.

And then we reached a crossroads, the moment we had to decide what to do next. We thought we might go to Berlin together. My husband said he was not ready to decide. Instead, he waited for me to choose a path that did not include him, before claiming for himself the path we were to share.

I was thrown back to the verandah at Wilsons Creek, to a husband paralysed by his wife's enthusiasm. I lashed out, angry and confused. My husband let loose his own fury, raging at my son for allowing me to have my own way, telling me I was a spoiled princess who was always complaining. I found this intriguing. What's more, from the 254th floor of his tower, I could see how his tirade might even make sense. My rage dissipated. I looked attentively into his dear face. It occurred to me it was to my advantage that he held tight to this story.

He is parental. I am his project. He can deal with this perception of me as long as I don't fight him, as long as I allow him to have his way. My husband does not have to change for me.

I decided that as long as I did not spend too much time in his company, I could be married to an elegant man. My husband could override me and I would remain unaffected. I would continue to care for him and keep my innate enthusiasm bubbling along via the company of others. In this way I unwittingly found the key to what other women have known all along, the great secret that eluded me all of my life: silence.

I sealed my lips. My world went underground. My husband would think he was married to a pleasing woman, while in reality his wife was orbiting another sun. This was the world of the Honest Lie. It was like a spiritual practice. Every minute of every day I let him have his way. Sometimes I did so quietly; at others, I must confess, I snapped with the sharp edge of a woman in control. Most of the time I experienced a maturing peace, like a good cheese sweating the dark in a Basque cave.

I was able to do this because I created a world in which I saw my husband as an old man unbothered by the concerns of the energetic. I said 'yes' to him and was thus released from the bondage of pleasing him. I retreated to my silent world and, to my surprise, discovered legions of women occupying this land. We shared an existence of smiling pleasantly, listening vaguely to husbands rattling on, content to validate and nod, all the while becoming freer and freer to please ourselves. Here was the world of manipulation I had scorned for so long. Now I was again 'wife', it was a sanctuary. For it was a place he could not follow. A world where he had no control, no voice.

And even though I longed to meet a man who was willing, perhaps even longing, to engage with a woman, to *know* her, for now this journey was enough. Because I also realised, set free and faced with my husband's public likeness, I would fall for him again. Therefore I may as well do the best I could with the situation as it was. As long as I spent long periods of time away from my husband, I could be pleasant and engaging *for him* in his company. This would be my thanks for his support and my gratitude for our marriage.

For what is marriage but a threshold to transformation, a gateway into the mystery of human life, a testing, a weathering, a maturing. I was even delighted to make love to him from this place. It was the least I could do. The Honest Lie was a lifeline, a haven beyond the exhaustion of resistance to being told what to do, respite from ceaseless penetration, both physical and energetic, rest from the incessant call for attention. *Yes dear, whatever you say.* And I meant it. *Dear man, husband.* In this way I found peace. *We will do it your way because then I am released.* There was no room for me but, paradoxically, all the room in the world. Because instead of egoic chattering minds occupying my waking life, I was in contact with my own deepest well, a direct line to self. This was the honest part of the Honest Lie.

My husband asked if I had missed him.

'Yes,' I said, God's honest lie.

The only problem with the Honest Lie was that it quashed my life-force. There was no room for enthusiasm in the world I created with my husband, for an enthusiastic life-force is spontaneous and uncontrollable: you never know what will come of a situation fully embraced – and my husband likes, nay needs, to know what will become of situations. It is his lifeline.

I was surprised that this left me with little more than a lump in my throat and a breastbone sore to the touch. And a dream. *I dreamed I lay in the arms of a man I loved. We laughed. We shared conversation. It was beautiful to be held. The man was not my husband.*

My husband's face was a poem of itself. I decided to love the poem. By living the Honest Lie I learned that by pleasing my husband he would do anything at all to please me, and I played a new game which lent fast rewards, not least of which was peace.

And then we resumed our places on the sexual battlefield.

For my husband, sex was his signal that all was right in his world. I was terrified of the trade between silence and sex, between sex and financial support, between financial support and silence. It wasn't long before pain took permanent anchor in my chest. One morning I woke feeling like a bird who'd slammed into a glass window. As I lay in bed, burrowed deathly still in the silence underneath the sheets, an impossibly holy truth galvanised my spirits: extraordinary as it sounds and as difficult as it might be for a husband to accept, *you may be my husband, but I owe you nothing. You may be my husband but you have no dominion over me, my life or my body. You may be my husband but you have no 'rights' concerning me at all. And if your support for me is conditional, then state your conditions!*

The novelty of living the Honest Lie had worn off. My inner world had exposed me to a private war within. I was mercenary and soldier. I was a child lost in a forest with no crumbs to guide her home. I was paralysed, a big claw rent inside my heart. I returned to sleep and dreamed of a man ... *we smiled at each other and every thirst I ever had was quenched.* The man was not my husband.

There were three things I walked on my journey from Rome. I walked the geographical landscape, allowing myself to meet the world and her people, the earth and its forces: the sunshine, mountains, wind and ocean. I walked the inner world, as within so without, exploring how the world before me mirrored my thoughts, beliefs and prejudices. And I walked my marriage. As I embraced the Honest Lie, I began to understand that ours was not a great love story, an affair of the heart, but a marriage of practical purpose, not unlike the arranged marriages of previous times and other cultures. Accepting this enabled me to abandon the world of the Honest Lie, easily and without apology. I no longer sought shelter from my husband and, in so doing, no longer sought respite from my own life. This also meant I no longer sought death, through fear or favour. *Life is for the living. If death wants me, let death come for me.* I snagged the anchor chain dragging my heart. Mercifully, it snapped.

Looking back through the settling dust of our marriage, I realise my husband and I fell in love not with each other, but with the idea of each other. Our disappointments and furies were a direct reflection not of the one we call 'husband' or 'wife', but of our failure to impose our own limitations on another human being. The man I struggled with may have been 'my husband', yet, I must confess, not only have I no idea who he is, I made scant attempt to know him at all. For we failed, my husband and I, failed utterly to cherish the spirit of the unique soul who pledged to share our journey through life. Curiously, we also flatly refused to see our own majesty reflected in the eyes of another. Our Eugenia Street Prayer puppies were not only off the lead, they'd torn up the house.

My husband, of course, has his own version of this story. I do not recognise myself as the protagonist in his tale any more than he sees himself in mine. What is the truth? The truth is we wanted only the best for each other and ourselves. What stood between us was our inability to accept each other's stories, the inherently flawed reality of another human being. That, and laughter. We may not be skilled at allowing another to live freely, my husband and I, at honouring the truth of another, in freeing ourselves and others from the historical conjugal legacy of possession and imposition, but we know now what is required from us to do so, to live fully, to live freely. This is our gift and our glory.

Looking back through the settling dust of our marriage, I realise love is not mine to give or take. Love is all around us, a force we can receive or resist, an energy that is freely available in every moment, a wellspring of grace and beauty that is ours for the choosing. Love cannot be 'given' or 'taken' because that which can be given or taken is not love. More than this, love is not the tortured existence I shared with my husband; nor does love demand a tortured existence from us, from any of us.

Love is a universe, it is beyond story and, as such, free from the linguistic smokescreen of 'because …'.

We say 'because' when we need to tell a story, weave a legend, justify our fears, shore up our ignorance, explain our actions, impose our reality, bind ourselves to a conditional existence and mire others in our web of obligation. When we say 'because' we smother the myriad possibilities of explanation available to us and in so doing create a myth that is about to limit and shape the rest of our lives; and shrink that which we cannot understand to a kernel of misunderstanding that, once nurtured, renders to us the gilded cords of bondage, our own and everyone else's.

We say 'because' to engage reason in lieu of our sovereignty.

Looking back through the settling dust of our marriage, I ask myself a question my own sense of righteousness has obscured, an obvious question, a look-if-you-dare question: *if it was not love that underpinned my marriage, what was it?* The answer shakes me to the foundations of my known world: it is greed. I had been greedy – greedy for love, greedy for shelter, *greedy for what I do not have*. I was a survivor exhausted by the albatross of her own survival. In the end it was not my husband I was attached to, not my husband I feared letting go: it was his credit card. The reality, and the truth, if I dared to look at myself honestly, was that by this time I was in a subterranean state of alarm at the thought of having to fend for myself in a masculine world, again. The connection between survival and greed was new to me and it floodlit my universe, exposing an emotional triad of interdependence: survival, greed and trust. I have not trusted life. *I have not trusted myself.*

My husband and I broke no promises when we parted, for we did not promise forever on our wedding day; we vowed only to do our best and this we have done. As the dust of our marriage clears I can see, stark against the lightening sky, that I have been angry. So very angry. I have been at war. A very old war. And the war has been within me. I had projected onto my husband the face of the tyrant. Enraged and contemptuous of certain aspects of his masculinity, I had enlisted him to play for me the role of bully, murderer, suffocater of all that is good and right about the feminine.

In truth, I am the one who failed to find the words to communicate the longings I hold in the deep silence of my heart. It was me who yearned for my husband to commune with my soul, yet was without the means to meet him there.

And this is how I came to understand that the wounds of our parents are the legitimate inheritance of humans, being: *that this is the purpose of our time here on Earth*, and it is now my turn to meet the challenge of healing the ancestral wounds. My husband was the tail end of this journey home. He offered me so much and I bathed in the comfort of his offering – having someone to look after me, surrendering all responsibility for my own survival. It was wonderful, but of course it couldn't last. His was, and is, the offering of the benevolent parent, the patriarch in its purest form. To the not-well-fathered like myself it was a wonderful gift. But I am woman, not child. I adore my husband's public face, but I cannot remain the child in his company, the one who worships him and cedes to his authority. I do not think he requires this of other women – just his wife.

In the spaces left by my husband, a beautiful peace has flooded my being, a peace that can only be described as happiness. For the first time in years and years and years I am happy: weightless, timeless, without excitement or concern, beyond thought. And for the first time in my life, a most essential aspect of my being is released from her prison. She is my gentlest feminine self, the one who believed, for so long, there was no place in a masculine world for her.

I stand at the end of human time as far as we have come along our road, at the edge of my own narrative. It all starts again now. I have climbed a great mountain and from its peak I can see all that has gone before and all that is to come. Sunlight streams through me, through our collective clear blue day. I stand strong and true, certain that everything, all our stories, deeds and actions come down to this, to my life, my children's lives, my grandchildren's lives and their children's to come. Who am I to struggle with sex and money and power? These things are not personal. They are the currents that carry the human story — forwards, backwards, sideways, upwards, downwards, inwards, centre. They are the framework of our lives.

I have felt imposed upon by this conflict, the rebellion of my early years shading me from its ageless glare. Yet it has to be resolved, here, now, in this woman's heart.

I lay down my swords.

Jerusalem

In September 2008, almost a year to the day after setting out from Rome, I flew to meet Ben in Amman, Jordan, perhaps to walk the final few days with him into Jerusalem. My heart smiled as I flew low over a landscape of yellow-grey dust to land in a desert city, the same desert my son had spent the past three days crossing in the shadeless heat. In the weeks to come I would spend the night in the desert sands of Lawrence's Arabia, bow low to touch the silver star that marks the spot where Jesus was born, stare into the face of time in the Cairo museum, sleep soundly among the people of Palestine and float down a sacred river beneath a full moon.

My heart was brisk to the impulse of entering the Arab world once again. Flying into Amman, I could not tell road from sand drift. The brown earth below was streaked with gold, all of it unsheened despite the sun beating the earth, as if we must rub our eyes to see it clearly, as if the tide went out a long time ago and failed to return. My blonde hair blew in the desert wind as I drove in from the airport; I would tie it back in the city. The morning sun, not yet high in the sky, was a swirl of red and yellow dusted light burning through a hazy sky. I have seen this sun in paintings. I have wept for it in the words of poets. I did not yet know that my pilgrimage was not finished, that my journey with the son was incomplete.

It was wonderful to see Ben again, so close to his journey's end. We found a café and ordered fresh orange juices. We unfurled the backgammon board, for all the world as if I had simply taken a bus to rest for a few days, as if the journey had never been broken. All my apprehension about walking with him into Jerusalem – about blistered feet and overburdened shoulders – vanished. For I was a woman in love with the company of laughter and the warmth of a desert people.

Within hours of landing in Amman, spots of blood appeared on my underwear. I was shaken. Confused. I was, after all, officially egg-free. I had not bled at all in the past year. In the days ahead the spots became a tidal flow and a riddled knowing whispered in my heart: *you will stop bleeding when you get to Jerusalem*. And I knew with as much certainty as a human being can know, which is to say not much at all, that the bleeding was for the journey of the mother, a timeless and inexplicable occurrence that had everything to do with karmic release. Deep in my soul I understood it was a physical manifestation of a peculiar vibration, an inconvenience I had no choice but to accept.

A week later, Ben and I left Amman at the breakfast hour of Ramadan, the great ringroads that pool out from the city centre marking our progress through the darkness. Once again, we left without a map, confident in our bearings, certain that by day's end we would be resting in the fertile crescent made famous by the Holy Bible, beside the River Jordan. We knew the road we needed to take because we'd travelled it three days earlier, when we'd hired a car and lapped the tiny desert nation on the Whirlwind Iconic Jordan Tour. We knew the city itself was flat, that the road down the hill to the crescent was extremely steep, that the lush green valley below was level ground. The walk would exhaust me, this I knew, but it was flat and the journey would be relatively short and this was the least I could offer my son, who had come so far on his own.

By midmorning the sun was high and hot. By lunchtime we were rested beside a shady creek filled with rubbish. By early afternoon we were on a country road that wound around stony hills pockmarked with houses and groves, the lush green valley nowhere in sight, our bellies rumbling and our water bags empty. We stopped for shade beneath an orchard beside a grand house. A man came out to speak to Ben. He explained with his hands that he could not show us his usual hospitality because it was Ramadan, but he could bring us water. Ben nodded and the man returned with a jug and two glasses. As Ben and the man were speaking I observed a dynamic that had confused me but I had not previously brought to consciousness – Ben never introduced me as his mother. I was hot and exhausted, I was bleeding a river, I was at the end of my reserves. Instinctively I knew that if the stranger had known I was Ben's mother he would have invited us in, handed me over to the women, offered what comfort was available in his home.

We walked on, the spaces between settlements growing wider, the grand houses giving way to poverty. On dusk we reached the top of a long, long hill and looked out over ... nothing. And I burst into tears.

How did this happen?

We had walked sixteen hours, I had given my son all I had to give, we were supposed to be in a fertile valley and here we were on sundown with no food, no water and stony hills rolling bare as far as the eye could see. In a thousand ways, I was depleted. I sat on a rock. I cried and cried. *Once again we had set out for a fertile valley and once again we were in a barren land.* Ben asked me if I wanted to walk on or camp. I told him not to speak to me. He told me I needed to take more responsibility for myself. I told him it broke my heart to hear him say this, *because I had taught him this.*

A debilitating exhaustion broke in my chest. I sobbed and sobbed as the light dropped away and darkness took the land. *My son and I have been confusing independence and tolerance with a cruel sort of loneliness.* I looked around me, bewildered by the barren landscape, distraught that it was no accident we had ended up here this day. I sobbed for thwarted dreams, I sobbed for loneliness, I sobbed for the bleeding woman, I sobbed for the endless road.

Eventually my tears dried and I looked to the night sky. It was a brilliant night, the new moon on the slide, the star patterns unfamiliar to my southern eyes. I unfurled my sleeping bag and lay it on the rocky hillside. Ben, high on the unknown, lay down beside me. We didn't speak and I didn't sleep. I watched through the night as Orion, upside down, wheeled through the sky, split wide here and there by the hunters on nearby hills shooting in the dark.

At first light I packed, telling Ben I wanted to be in civilisation before the sun was high. We walked on, the endless road, the endless road. The damp heat between my legs chafed at everything I thought I knew, fleecing my spirits of any and all of the stories I might tell to decry my own reality. My heart was not finished with its breaking and I started to cry all over again. I cried for my son and his longing for the barren places and I cried for myself: *this is my legacy to him.*

Here is our loneliness. Here is our stark and ravenous beauty. Here is our inhospitable nature. Here is our disconnection, our absence of nourishment, our dry and stony interior. Here is our comfort, here is our freedom. Here is our spirit waiting for rain. *The tears of all time, projected onto the heart of the son.*

By the time we reached the highway, our bodies leached of water by the high heat, I was sane enough to conduct myself in civilisation. We stood on the roadside flagging me a lift. I wanted to return to Amman, to begin my journey to Jerusalem again. A taxi stopped. We bundled me in. I waved Ben goodbye, stuffing into his hands the gifts I had carried from his sister and father to honour the end of his journey. I could no longer carry them, could no longer carry his relationships with them, could no longer stand invisible as the mother before the adult son who failed to acknowledge the *relationship*.

Within half an hour I was back in the Toledo Hotel, flat on my back between clean white sheets, staring at the ceiling, making sense of the past twenty-four hours. *My son and I have been confusing independence and tolerance with a cruel sort of loneliness.* Heartbreakingly, I realised that for too long I had been supporting my son's separation. Fearful of what I perceived to be his contempt, I had allowed the arrogance he inherited from his father to reinforce the shields of protection he inherited from me, unchecked. *I have not served him well as a mother.* The longest night in the mountains was an initiation, a transformation; I tested my throat, free now of the awkward inability to speak to my son. The voice I found was confident and true. I stared at the ceiling of the Toledo Hotel and realised I had been guilty of showing myself to my children, the response of my generation to the brick walls of the generations before us: I had shown myself to them so they could see what they had inherited. *Here, my darlings, here is your story.*

Have they mistaken this for attempts at friendship?

The man I left by the roadside is my son: even though we share camaraderie, I am his mother; I am not his friend.

My son has called me by my first name since he was five years old. This has long caused me discomfort, an unsettling that this somehow absolved him from the relationship. I resolved to no longer answer when he called me by my first name; in this way he would speak our connection.

I wondered if Ben understood that so many of my tears this day were for him. I felt sad leaving him out on the highway, leaving him with the knowing that something important had changed. *Something important and unspoken, because true to the way of the broken masculine he had declined to speak our vulnerabilities.* I realised I'd been trying to give my son a soft cushion for the hard places ... and that now and forever I had no choice but to leave him to the hard road; I no longer needed to walk it with him and I could not walk it for him.

I have felt guilty around my son. Guilty for being alive. Guilty for the things I'd do differently. Guilty for wanting what he doesn't. *This is my pilgrimage to Jerusalem.*

In the mountains during the longest night I learned about leadership, about the paradox with which my son presented me when he spoke of 'taking responsibility for myself'. As I stared at the ceiling of the Toledo Hotel, I understood that the art of living is taking full responsibility for myself *and* not turning my back on the needs of others. *It is inclusive action, not exclusive.*

My son is a brilliant man. His journey has been heroic. His is the charmed life of the wanted man. He's the boy who needed a job and came home with five, so he could choose. He's the man who has walked alone for months at a time through unknown landscapes and summoned so much goodwill and assistance from strangers that he has been accepted over and again as one among them. He's the human being who does not ask for help and does not share his vulnerabilities and this, of course, is integral to his confidence and charm. My son the roamer, the loner, the world traveller, the one who sets out for the fertile valley and is happy to find himself on the mountain barren.

I resolve to live a different story.

The following morning I was up again for Ramadan breakfast, hightailing it out of the city on dark, this time in a taxi bound for the River Jordan, ready for the crossing into the Promised Land, known officially as Israel. I scooped up Ben from the side of the road where he'd spent the night and together we drove to the border, which he'd been turned away from the day before, informed that it would be open for just an hour this morning.

We wandered past a mile of idling cars and, too early, into a room filled with rows of seats and empty counters. The border guard invited us to wait in his office. He was a commander in the Jordanian army and had served with Australians in a peace-keeping force in East Timor. He wanted to know why Ben wasn't married.

'The love of a woman,' he said, 'that passes. It is the children who teach you about love. No matter what they do, you love them. Your children will haaaaate you and still you love them.'

Ben nodded, receiving the wisdom of the elder with the respect it deserved. I couldn't help feeling the commander was delivering a message, from God to me.

And then the commander said something that caused me to fall even more deeply in love with Arabia, because I love contradictions and I adore challenges to the known world:

'In Arabic we have a saying,' he said. 'If your first child is a daughter your life will be sweet.'

From Jordan, we had no choice but to bus it to Israel. Even though, in the spirit of pilgrimage, Ben had challenged border guards from Europe to the Middle East to allow him to walk through borders barred to pedestrians, he lay down his need to walk across the border for the soldiers of Israel, the youths in striped t-shirts and baggy shorts who looked for all the world like the easy-going teenagers in my own country *but for the black machine guns slung lazily over their shoulders.*

Israel.

Tears spring to my eyes as I write the word.

Israel.

From the Israeli border, Ben and I agreed to meet in the Palestinian city of Jericho, the settlement closest to the border. Done with walking, I would take the bus.

When Ben asked an Israeli man for directions to the road to Jericho, he snapped, 'What ya wanna go there for?'

Said Ben: 'For lunch.'

The bus was packed with Palestinians. And I grinned a heart full of merry laughter when I realised I was surrounded by *Philistines* – it is the name the people of Palestine call themselves. Three times in the next half-hour the bus was boarded by Israeli soldiers and checked for passports.

'I've never seen an Australian on this bus,' smiled one, as he handed back my passport.

In Jericho, finding my bearings in the small grassy park in the city centre, I closed my eyes to the stares of the men around me and breathed the warm wind of an ancient land.

I am in Palestine. I am a woman alone in Palestine. If my life ends this day, for no other reason than I am in Palestine, then my life has come to this and this is my gift to my world and to the grandchildren of the refugees of this unholy war, the ones who have lived for three generations and more in the lands of their neighbours, welcome or otherwise, the ones who still wear the keys to their grandparents' homes around their necks. For I am in Palestine and I am in love with her people, for all their faults and for all their anguish, and there is a message for me on the wind and in my heart I know it to be true. It is this: I am among people of peace.

And so I was. I found an internet café and the man behind the counter could not do enough to help me orient myself to this land. I bought a new SIM for my mobile and the man behind another counter would not receive my phone from my hand, instead gesturing for me to put it on the counter. I suspended every single one of my stories about why he would not risk touching a woman.

Before leaving Australia, the exhilarating promise of the desert wind whipping wild in my veins, I vowed two things: I would learn to see through Arab eyes and I would connect with the women of Arabia.

This past week, throughout the Iconic Whirlwind Jordan Tour, I was delighted to be returned to the Arab world, accepting the billowing black shrouds of the women without emotion, experiencing a magnetic pull to be one among them – not to *be* them, just to take my place as myself among them.

The deeper I went into Arabia, the more deeply I travelled into myself. A covered one sat next to me and I felt excited, as if I were a man, curious and shy. I relished the empowerment I felt as a woman in this world. A woman on her own terms: *here I am and this is me, my culture, my being, my way, my tiny world bordered by the great thrum of your world.*

And then, driving through Amman at the end of the whirlwind tour of Jordan, I wrapped the white scarf I had bought in the desert around my head and peered out at the world from my snowy white shroud. I felt safe. I felt protected. I felt beautiful. I felt a rush of liberation. I could be in the world and be spared the intensity of the energetic demands of the masculine, Western or Arab. *This is the liberation Muslim women speak of when they insist their shroud is a choice that gives them freedom ... it also places full responsibility for the hungers and ill-considered behaviours of men onto the hearts and shoulders of women. My liberation is short-lived. My heart sinks: we are free from prying eyes and merciless judgement, but we are not free.*

The Arabs we met from the desert to the Red Sea were warm and welcoming: exuberant with Ben, timid with me, as if they were the ones peering out from behind a veil. *I am speaking of the men, of course.*

'Welkum!' they would cry.

They patted Ben on the back, laughing and telling him they loved him. They stole glances at me. I am Australian, we say 'g'day' to everyone we meet as we walk by, this is our way. It was a hard habit to break and the Arab men were confused when I met their eyes with a gentle *'marhaba'* nod.

I danced with their ways and eventually understood that for all their bravado these young men were innocents. Denied access to their own women, they find women like me accessible, for no other reason than they can *see* us. We are an opportunity to engage with a woman without triggering an honour killing. How I handled these engagements was up to me and I weighed this with the integrity of each moment.

The reality is I am no more unsafe among the men of Arab nations than I am among my own.

I took off my sunglasses, thus allowing the men to meet me on their own terms. Surprisingly, this was also my passage to the women. I soon learned that if I held their eyes for seconds too long, counting one, two, three, almost without exception she would meet me with an explosive smile that brought tears to my eyes, because even though I couldn't see the smile on her lips her hello burst from her veil with all the gusto and love possible in a transmission from the human heart.

Because I was allowing myself to be seen.

It was my public engagement with the Arabs that had a voice, however.

'Welkum,' the men would bellow at Ben, jumping up from their seats to greet him. 'Welkum, welkum, where are you from?'

'Australia!' Ben would cry in return.

At this point, one of two things happened. If they understood 'Australia', their hearts and minds would gush with the light of effusive welcome. And there in the golden desert of Arabia I understood the debt of quiet gratitude us Aussies owe our soldiers, for how else could it be that from Turkey to Timor we are honoured and treasured as *Australian*, even when counted as one among the enemy? Alternatively, they misunderstood him, thinking he said 'Israel'. In this case, time and again, without exception, these fine men would gulp, take a slow breath, bow their heads slightly and whisper, 'Welkum.' I was awed by the humility of this action, humbled by the honour at stake and the chivalry in play. My love for this world was amplified by these actions and my respect for the Arabs sweetened.

I thought often about meeting Israelis in the days ahead, about what I would say to them, because I am one among an entire world outside the United States of America seriously unimpressed with their actions. I thought perhaps I would say: *I too live in a country claimed by my people, who tell themselves that it was empty land. I too live in a country that has no choice but to retell its story and make peace with its past.*

And I knew, with the wisdom of pilgrim's progress, that once I was in Israel her people would win me over, that my prejudices and stories about this loaded land would be cast to the winds of peaceful intent, that I would empathise with a people whose actions I found abhorrent and whose legitimacy I had long questioned.

It was not to be.

In Israel I met my hardest heart.

Our darling Lily flew from London to meet us in Jerusalem. In the days to come we were floored, each one of us, by the rudeness, resentment and hostility we encountered in the shops and on the streets of Jerusalem.

Ben finished his walk – 16 countries, 9 months, 7,000 kilometres and countless invitations from humanity – by ambling through iconic religious sites in the Holy City, with Lily and me in tow. For the Jews, he touched his forehead to the Wailing Wall; for the Christians, he knelt before the shrine to the martyred Jesus in the Church of the Holy Sepulchre; for the Muslims, he circled the Dome of the Rock. The Holy City may be filled with religious significance and the act of pilgrimage an ancient diversion, but my son finished his walk in 21st-century secular style: in an Irish pub in downtown Jerusalem.

At the pub, after a toast to the miracle of the journey complete, I met a UN soldier, an Australian, a Middle East peacekeeper. I decided to test on him my perceptions of Israel.

'The Palestinians seem to be gentle, friendly people,' I said.

He raised his eyebrows and nodded, just once.

'The Israelis are incredibly hostile,' I said.

He raised his eyebrows and nodded, just once.

'I cannot imagine negotiating a peace deal with these people,' I said.

He raised his eyebrows and nodded, just once.

Israel.

In Israel I met the timelessness of unsustainable rage. I met the broken hearts of humanity, denied. *I met my father's hands around my mother's neck, the family scattered to the winds of madness.* Struck dumb and tearful by the blowtorch of hostility and rage that is an Israeli heart, neither Ben nor I could get out of the country fast enough. Nowhere, in all my travels, did I feel as unsafe as I did within these misbegotten borders. Or as unwelcome.

Israel.

Israel shattered my illusions about what was possible in our world, because I had entrusted to her the fulfilment of my doubts about my own perceptions: *that Israel, in its current ideological state, has no right to exist.*

More than this, in the name of Israel I have no right to speak these words; and so I will say them again: *Israel has no right to exist.*

Not because of politics and not because of religious righteousness; not because of shades of right and wrong and not because one mob has behaved more badly than another; and not because people have memories too-long nor even because Israel has no right to exist.

The reality is that Israel cannot exist.

And her people know it.

Theirs is the fear of losing what we have, that takes root when we know that what we have belongs to someone else, regardless of the stories we tell to justify our grandparents' wars.

Theirs is the self-righteous paranoia of those who know their time is up.

Because, in their hearts, the Israelis know this land is not theirs by God-given right but is the birthright of all the people who call it home. *The land belongs to everyone by that same decree.*

Because in their hearts the Israelis know that to continue this war is to condemn all the children of Israel, the living and the unborn, to an eternity of vigilance and hostility.

Because the rest of the world cannot keep supporting Israel's foundation myth: that God 'chose' these people and 'promised' them this land.

It is too late to return the homes of the Palestinians to their grandchildren; the keys may not have rusted with time, but they no longer fit the lock.

There can only be one solution to the 'problem' of the Holy Land and that is 'one nation'. All the people of this land must have the same rights within her borders; in my country it is called 'equality' and we settle for nothing less. Because the democratic world and the non-democratic worlds alike cannot – and should not – support the status quo. Like the Berlin Wall, we will all wake up one morning and Israel as we know it will be gone. *As within, so without.*

After Israel, Ben and I rested on a big white boat floating down the River Nile. Early one morning, standing alone on the deck in the cool light of dawn, I raised my arms to the heat of the desert sky, the soaring sun rising red-gold over the river's eastern bank aloft on the palm of my raised left hand; the full moon setting silver, floating on the palm of my right.

My prayer for our world.

Returned to my own land, I have posted sentries outside my new home: two big white flags flapping my surrender to the war within. Peace on Earth has only one requisite and that is peace in our own hearts.

In truth, I can no longer remember my own stories about marriage or my journey with the son or even about my travels through alien lands. All I know is that the stories I tell belong to the moment of telling, and because they are my stories I can tell them any way I like. I can acknowledge the Jewish patriarch believes he is doing his best by all that is right in his world. I can recognise my humanity in my husband's heart. I can offer only love to the generational legacies that live on in my children and grandchildren and their children to come. I can forgive us all our cultural inheritance and our broken hearts. Because beauty and goodness are everywhere – all I have to do, all that is required from me, from all of us, is to see it: to see only that.

www.ingramcontent.com/pod-product-compliance
Lightning Source LLC
Chambersburg PA
CBHW051935290426
44110CB00015B/1988